Lahure Women

Two Centuries of Struggle, Service and Silent Fortitude

Lahure Women

Two Centuries of Struggle, Service and Silent Fortitude

David Seddon

ADROIT

Adroit Publishers

NEW DELHI • KATHMANDU

ISBN : 978-81-87393-67-2

2021

Published by
ADROIT PUBLISHERS 4675/21, Ganpati Bhawan, Ansari Road,
Daryaganj, New Delhi-110 002 Phone : 011-23266030
adroitpublishers@gmail.com

Typeset in Garamond Premier Pro by Arun, Akriti Graphic
Solution, Delhi-110081 E-mail: arun263923@gmail.com,
Ph: 9999414390

Contents

Preface

As we move deeper into the third decade of the 21ˢᵗ century, and reflect on the impact of the corona virus pandemic, it remains the case that the economy of Nepal, and the survival of many households across the country, depend heavily on the migration abroad of men and, to a lesser extent women, and on the remittances they send back home.

The most recent official data suggest that, in 2020, more than 3.2 million Nepali migrants were working abroad (Bhattarai & Magar 2021). The real (unofficial) number is likely to be far greater, possibly twice as many, most of those being in India. Despite the covid crisis, the net migration rate for Nepal in 2021 was estimated at 3.6 per 1,000 population, a 24.5 per cent increase from 2020. The net migration rate in 2020 was 2.9 per 1,000 population, a 32.5 per cent increase from 2019, and in 2019 was 2.2 per 1,000 population, a 48.25 per cent increase from 2018. Remittance inflows to Nepal had previously risen steadily each year through the last decade: by 2019, the annual total had doubled to more than $8 billion, compared with just over $4 billion in 2011. Whether this upward trend will be continued in 2021 and 2022 is not yet clear, given the effects of the covid pandemic in 2020-2021; but all the signs are that remittances held up (Seddon, Adhikari & Gurung 2021).

The general trend upwards in foreign labour migration and in the remittance economy of Nepal has been evident for three decades at least. But even before the 1990s, when the growing importance of the phenomenon of what some called 'the New Lahures' became evident – in part as a result of research by myself and two Nepali colleagues (Seddon, Adhikari & Gurung 2001) - men and women had travelled away from home to seek employment and other economic opportunities abroad. Indeed, the history of migration and of the Nepali diaspora goes back to the latter part of the 18ᵗʰ century.

* * * * * *

The majority of those leaving to seek livelihoods abroad in recent years have been men; but a significant and increasing minority – possibly as many as ten per cent[1] - have been women. In fact, a significant minority of women from what is now Nepal have, over two centuries at least, left their homes for a variety of reasons, whether to accompany their husbands or to seek employment and other economic opportunities for themselves; in some cases, their migration has not been voluntary but the result of trafficking.

But while we have a good deal of information about the migration of men over this long period, mainly through the many studies of the Gurkhas and their involvement with the British in India and overseas, little attention has been paid to the women who went abroad, and even less to those who remained at home while their menfolk were away, to their lives and their experiences – particularly in the earlier part of this period. Their story remains largely untold and unknown. As Aryal pointedly notes, 'hundreds of thousands of lives have been touched by Gurkhas soldiering. Many toasts have been drunk to and books written about the Johnny Gurkhas, but reference to their womenfolk has been scant' (1991: 18).

What Aryal does not mention, however, is that the Gurkhas themselves have rarely been able to express themselves and provide an account of their own experiences. Apart from the letters written home from the front-line while deployed abroad or overseas, which have been referred to and cited, by Pratyoush Onta among others (1994)), the interviews carried out by J. P. Cross and Buddhiman Gurung (2002) provide one of the rare opportunities to hear the voices of Gurkhas, and for them to tell their stories. But those 'stories' are usually about their experiences while serving abroad, although Cross and Gurung emphasise that, just as war is drab, full and dangerous, so 'life in hill villages is drab, dull and sometimes dangerous' (2002: 27). And that is where, for the most part, the women remained while their menfolk were off soldiering.

What we do know, from scattered references and from more recent sources, is that life for 'Gurkha wives' was always a life of struggle and of hard work, as indeed it has always been for Nepali women more generally (Acharya & Bennett 1983) - whether they remained at home to bear the burden and the responsibility of maintaining the well-being of their family and their household while their

1. The precise number of women migrating from Nepal for work abroad is unknown, as the majority go for work in India, where there are no border checks or controls, or else make informal arrangements to work overseas, often having gone first to India.

menfolk went off to seek employment or other economic opportunities abroad as soldiers or in other capacities, or they accompanied their menfolk, or, more rarely, they migrated abroad themselves to live and work. But it is true that relatively little attention has been paid to them, and their voices have not been heard; their stories have remained untold and their experiences have been largely unexplored.

As Nanda Shrestha and Dennis Conway have remarked, 'there is no shortage of migration studies. The literature on migration is replete with studies of its economic consequences, including remittance flows... Yet research on its domestic effects and emotional bearing on wives and children is virtually absent' (Shrestha & Conway 2001: 157). Their own essay on 'the shadow life of a migrant's wife' is a rare example of a detailed, personal account of one young woman's experiences as the wife of a man who had been working in India as a guard (*chowkidar*) for the previous eight years, often for two to three years at a time when they met her in 1979-80 (Shrestha & Conway 2001: 153-177).

So, at this difficult time, at the beginning of the third decade of the 21st century, when Nepal's continuing reliance on men and women migrating abroad and sending back remittances has been high-lighted once again in the midst of the covid-19 epidemic (see Seddon, Adhikari & Gurung 2021), this book puts together the little we know about the women who ventured abroad from the regions that include what is now Nepal, over a period of around two centuries, about the women who remained behind, and indeed about of all those women, whether Nepali or not, associated, like it or not, with the Gurkhas in their many campaigns in India and overseas and, more generally still, serving the British Empire in India and beyond.

This partly fulfils a promise made 20 years ago in *The New Lahures*, where the authors recognised that the book 'lacked historical depth' and hoped to develop 'a research programme which will eventually result, we hope, in the publication of three books – each able to stand on its own, but linked as a series', covering the periods: 1750 to 1950, 1950 to 1990, and 1990 to 2005 (2001: xix). A further initiative in this regard was undertaken in a book on *Nepali Women and Foreign Labour Migration* (UNIFEM & NIDS 2006), where I discussed the foreign migration of women from Nepal and their experiences while abroad, during the 19th and early 20th centuries (Seddon 2006a and b). That discussion provides the core of this present book.

To understand the historical context within which the foreign migration of women from Nepal and their experiences while abroad should be situated, it is important to consider the expansion of the petty state of Gorkha and the establishment of the Gorkhali state, which took place during the latter half of the 18th century, just at the same time as the expansion of the British East India Company.

❀ ❀ ❀

CHAPTER 1

The Making of the Gorkhali State

The expansion of the petty hill state of Gorkha, which began in the early 18th century, involved the deployment of armies across the whole of what is now Nepal and beyond. The Gorkhali armies were made up, not only of fighting men recruited from many different castes and ethnic groups - mainly, it seems involving Chhetris (Khas), Gurungs and Magars from the far western and western hills - but also of camp followers, which often included women and even children. There was it seems, a long tradition of women accompanying their men in war, and even of joining in the fighting – as we shall see.

By 1748, Sindhupalchowk and Kabre Palanchowk and other areas in the vicinity of Kathmandu had been subjugated, and the passes of Kuti and Kerung, which constituted the main routes through which flowed trade between the Kathmandu Valley and Tibet, subsequently also came under Gorkhali control. The key event, however, was the conquest of the kingdom of Makwanpur in September 1762. This gained the expanding Gorkhali state access to areas of the eastern *terai* through which the kingdoms of the Valley had historically maintained contact with India and from which they had benefited from the exploitation of natural resources.

The conquest of Kirtipur provided a crucial foothold in the Valley itself, despite the desperate defence of the city by its inhabitants. These included (the legend has it) a Newar woman, called Kirti Laxmi, who fought the invaders disguised as a man named Bhairav Singh. Armed with a bow and arrows, it is said, she kept fighting even after the Gorkhalis had taken the town. She was finally captured, however, and kept in captivity, where she took her own life. She is honoured today as the heroine of Kirtipur, and is often identified as an avatar of the Holy Goddess Ajimaa of the Newars[2]. But, despite the defiance of the men and women of Kirtipur, the city eventually fell to the Gorkhalis and in 1768, the kingdom of Kathmandu was overcome; a year later, Prithivi Narayan Shah also controlled Patan and Bhadgaon (Bakhtapur).

Once the Valley was secure, Prithivi Narayan Shah turned his attention to the *chaubise* states to the west and to the territories of the *kirati* peoples to the east. In 1771, Prithivi Narayan Shah instructed his generals to advance against the *chaubise* states on two fronts, but they were ignominiously defeated. This lack of success in the west led to a focus on the subjugation of the eastern hills. Between 1772 and 1774, the Gorkhalis were able to subdue *majh kirat* and to secure the surrender first of Chaudandi, and then of Bijayapur in the eastern *terai,* thereby securing control over a fertile region whose economic wealth far outweighed any benefit they might have gained from the conquest of the west. By 1774, the Gorkhali forces controlled the entire eastern hills and the eastern *terai* up to the Tista River bordering Sikkim.

By 1775, the expanded Gorkhali kingdom, with its capital now in Kathmandu, included the whole of the eastern *terai,* the eastern and central inner *terai,* and the eastern hills up to the Tista River, and a small part of the western hill region, including Jajarkot. 'In the western and far-eastern hill areas', as Regmi explains, 'Prithivi Narayan Shah generally followed the policy of subjugating principalities without actually annexing their territories' (Regmi 1999: 12). 'As a general rule, the territories of defeated *rajas* were... annexed only when they resisted the Gorkhali invaders to the last, or rebelled after once accepting their suzerainty' (Regmi 1999: 13). This form of indirect rule, enabled the local rulers to maintain their capacity to exploit their own peasantries and thus sustain their position as overlords, despite accepting a degree of political subordination. Jajarkot was the first principality to accept the status of a vassal under the Gorkhalis in this manner.

Circumstances, however, sometimes compelled the Gorkhali rulers to annex territories directly, as when they resisted or rebelled. For example, Kaski, which had initially been given vassal status, was later annexed when the *raja* rebelled – an example of elite politics, one might suggest. Some of the *rajas* displaced by the Gorkhali state were, however, later restored as vassals when this seemed

---

2. *Kirti Laxmi* (1997), a historical novel by Basu Pasa in Nepal Bhasa, based on 'the true story' of a woman named Kirti Laxmi who fought the Gorkhalis disguised as a man, was published from Kathmandu by Thaunkanhe Prakashan.

expedient to the Gorkhalis. The *raja* of Bajura, for example, was granted such status in 1791 in appreciation of the assistance rendered by him during Gorkha's wars with Achham, Doti and Jumla (Regmi 1999: 13).

Also, many of those who at first fought against the Gorkhali state, later joined as part of its armed forces against its enemies. For example, Bhakti Thapa, who was later killed while fighting in the Gorkhali army against the English in 1815, had originally been a commander in the army of the *raja* of Lamjung and had been taken prisoner by Gorkha in 1792. After the death of Prithivi Narayan Shah in January 1775, his successors carried on the process of the expansion and 'unification' of the Gorkhali state. To the west, successive defeats at the hands of the *chaubise* states through the late 1770s led to a policy of 'indirect rule' in this region. It was not until 1785 that the Gorkhali forces were able to defeat the Lamjung alliance and move further west to bring the *chaubise* under control and initiate an assault on Jumla.

In the far west, as Whelpton comments, 'Gorkha rule seems to have been felt as more of an alien imposition and particularly strong resistance was encountered in Jumla, which had previously enjoyed a certain primacy among the *baise* states of the Karnali basin' (Whelpton 2013: 32). Jumla withstood the onslaught of the Gorkhalis for two years before its capital, Chinasim, fell eventually in 1789. Accounts differ as to what then happened to its ruler, Shobhan Shahi; some say he was arrested and brought to Kathmandu, others that he escaped to Mugu, from where he mounted a revolt, which he lost, before mounting another revolt from Humla, which he again lost, before fleeing to Tibet, where he died (Adhikari 1998: 55-59). Jumla was finally pacified in 1793 and it was then governed by a *subba* sent from Kathmandu (Shrestha-Schipper 2013: 260).

By the end of the century, the western *chaubise* and far western *baise* hill principalities had all been subjugated or annexed, and the frontier of the Gorkhali state extended to the Mahakali River in the west. By 1808, the Gorkha army had expanded into Kumaon and Garhwal (today in Uttarakhand in India) and reached Kangra, across the Jamuna River. By this time, the Gorkhali state had more or less established its hegemony over a significant territory extending approximately 1,300 miles from the Sutlej River in the west to the Tista River in the east. This was the point, however, where the Gorkhali State came up against the Sikhs, and its expansion was halted by the armies of Ranjit Singh (as we shall see below).

During the early years of the 19th century, the expansionist Gorkhali state also came up against the expansionist British East India Company. There were increasing tensions and even conflicts over the respective jurisdictions of these two powers over the populations and territories in the western and central *terai,* which culminated in 1814 in the Anglo-Nepali War (1814-1816). This lasted for only three years, but culminated in the establishment of a definite frontier, after the defeat of the Gorkhali forces and the Treaty of Sugauli in 1816, and of a distinctive new relationship between the Gorkhali state and the Company.

One might best characterise the emerging Gorkhali state as 'a tributary state', accruing wealth essentially through its power, authority and jurisdiction over the subordinate states, which had vassal status and gave 'tribute' to Gorkha; and also increasingly by its own control over an increasing number of trade routes, from which it derived revenues, over the natural resources of the forests and, increasingly important, over an expanding cultivated area of settled farmers and peasants, from whom it extracted surplus in the form of rent and or tax.

As regards the last of these, Stiller tells us that 'one of the instructions of Prithivi Narayan (to two men appointed as *amalis* of Bhadgaon, a well-populated city), was that they should settle people and encourage agriculture' (Stiller 2017: 31). This implies that a policy of encouraging immigration into relatively sparsely populated areas was adopted by the rulers of the expanding Gorkhali state; and, indeed, the oral histories of many ethnic groups in the middle hills of Nepal today refer to their origins elsewhere, generally to the north in what is now Tibet, but in some cases from the south, from the *terai* and from India. They came originally to Nepal as immigrants. Kirkpatrick noted that 'even the Turrye or Turryani[3], generally speaking, would seem to be but indifferently peopled, the villages throughout being, as far as I can learn, very thinly settled, and in most places of a mean rank in point of magnitude, as well as in appearance' (Kirkpatrick 1811: 1982-83).

❁ ❁ ❁

---

3. What we refer to as the *terai.*

CHAPTER 2
Migration and Settlement

Over time, as 'unification' took place, settlement and cultivation increased, and the overall system came to resemble more what Marx and Engels referred to as 'the Asiatic mode of production', in which the state raises taxes through inter-mediaries (often local chiefs or headmen) from the peasant producers and local village communities. As settlement and cultivation increased, though, so too did the population and population density, creating in some areas an increasing tendency to emigrate. In part this was in response to new pressures imposed on the local landowners and peasants by the Gorkhali State, in the form of of increasing taxation (one of the ways in which the state intervened in the local economy) and rents, partly as a result of the subsequent indebtedness to local moneylenders.

Regmi remarks, for example, that 'people who left Nepal to settle in India did so primarily because they were unable to maintain themselves at the customary level of subsistence' (Regmi 1971: 197-98). Indeed, he argues that the condition of the peasantry more generally across the country deteriorated to a considerable extent after political unification and that 'at least in some areas, the situation had become so serious that peasants left the holdings they cultivated in search of more congenial surroundings, both elsewhere in the country and outside' (Regmi 1999: 99). Kansakar also suggests that 'the period of unification and expansion of Nepal's territory during the late eighteenth and early nineteenth century was (generally) accompanied by movement and settlement of the Nepalese in Darjeeling, Sikkim, Kumaon and Garhwal' (1984: 50).

Migration cannot, however, be attributed solely to push factors. The new regime of land tenure, with a promise of fixed rights over the land, introduced in 1793 by the British East India Company in Bengal (which at the time included Bihar), provided an attraction not available under the Gorkhali State at that time

(Regmi 1999: 132). Indeed, many were said to have brought new land under cultivation in Purnea, Bihar, with the hope of establishing rights to the land as settlers and 'tillers' (Regmi 1999: 141). Mandal suggests, for example, that 'many Nepalese emigrated to India because of their search for arable land for which North and Northeast India became the potential destinations. As a result, people from the hills of Nepal colonized the relatively poor, sparsely settled interior parts of Sikkim, West Bengal and Assam in the east and the Kangra Valley in the west' (Mandal, cited in Subedi 1999: 85).

Not all of those who migrated, however, were seeking land for re-settlement; some at least, even at this early period sought employment on temporary or longer-term basis. Buchanan's account of the district of Purnea in 1809-10, for example, refers to workmen that had 'been induced to come from Nepal, where the people are more skilled, living almost entirely in brick houses' (Buchanan 1928: 129). Who precisely these were, and whether they came from the Kathmandu Valley (which was often still referred to as 'Nepal') is not entirely clear, these were clearly not peasants seeking land; they were probably *dalits* of some kind, with skills for sale.

While there is no explicit mention of women that I can find in these early references to migration and re-settlement, it is certain that many of the migrants who left to cultivate or gaze their livestock in India went as families, the women accompanying their menfolk as wives, daughters and even mothers. Some of the 'workmen' who went to Purnea were probably also accompanied by their wives and families, and it is possible that some of them were women migrants, for, as we shall see, labour migration to India in the 19th century usually involved a significant minority of women. The earliest form of relatively large-scale emigration involving women from what is now Nepal was therefore probably the migration and re-settlement of whole families and even communities from the hill areas to adjacent territories at the time of the expansion and consolidation of the Gorkhali State, from the early to mid 18th century onwards.

Certainly, as Adhikari & Bohle suggest, after the Sugauli Treaty in 1816, 'villagers from Nepal went to India in large numbers either to enlist in the army or to work in factories, mines and tea estates. From India, they also migrated to Burma' (1999: 58). Part of the reason for this was the attraction of newly emerging economic opportunities. But while a few men might have found work in factories and mines, and a number in the informal service sector, as security guards (*chowkidars*) or domestic servants, the majority of Nepalis had experience only of farming and agricultural work, so most tended to seek employment of this kind. Nepalis also went to India to work as 'graziers' and dairymen (and women).

They settled in places like Assam and Meghalaya, where plenty of grazing land was available, and also in Bihar. Initially, the British encouraged them with incentives, like tax exemptions and special reserves for grazing. This often resulted in long-term or permanent settlement, and women and children were involved as well as men – whole families moved to re-settle and take up farming in India. The network of trails that led eastwards, through Sikkim and into India, enabled men and women from the eastern hills of Nepal to travel reasonably easily to places like Assam and Darjeeling.

Indeed, Davis (1951: 117) suggests that emigration from the eastern hills of Nepal for agriculture-related work in Darjeeling, Sikkim and Bhutan was considerable, even if, once there, migrants apparently often found the work and working conditions extremely onerous and restrictive. But it was not just from the hills that migration took place. Many local small-holders subject to the newly introduced *ijara* system left the eastern *terai* towards the end of the 18ᵗʰ century to escape oppressive taxation; they also left from mountain regions, such as Thak Khola in the west and Solu Khumbu in the east (Regmi 1999: 131, 140).

This process of what might be termed permanent emigration contributed to the establishment of significant communities of expatriates in the areas to which they moved and where they settled that have, over the last two hundred years, become part of an ever growing diaspora. But migration involved not only the re-settlement of families seeking land for cultivation and grazing, but also labour migration. Women as well as men were engaged as labourers. One source of employment was the growing tea plantation sector in north east India, in Darjeeling and Assam in particular.

In Assam, where the cultivation of tea had begun during the late 1820s (after the discovery of wild tea by Bruce and Scott in the early years of the decade), tea plantations developed during the 1830s, now that Assam was securely within the British Empire after the end of the first Anglo-Burma War (1824-26). In 1835, the Rajah of Sikkim ceded an area of about 140 square miles - Darjeeling - to the British as the site for a health resort and sanatorium. Initially, only a hundred or so *basti-wallahs* lived there, but within ten years, 'more than 10,000 houses had settled there. People from all parts of the country flocked there. It having become a great market, the slaves and menial classes of Sikkim, Bhutan and Nepal all took refuge there'[4]. Darjeeling soon emerged as the quintessential hill station for British military families stationed in India - a cool, well-ordered landscape dotted with pleasant tea-gardens.

In the 1830s, Chinese workers were brought into north east India to teach the planters and their labour force the art of tea planting on the hilly slopes of Darjeeling, Dooars and Assam (Chatterjee 1995: 45). Nepali immigration and settlement was encouraged, in part to help contain the Bhotias of Sikkim and Bhutan, and in part to provide labour, as casual labourers and porters and as workers on the newly developing tea plantations from the 1840s onwards. Both men and women were involved. Davis (1951: 117) indicates that seasonal and more long-term migration from the eastern hills of Nepal for agriculture-related work in Darjeeling, Sikkim and Bhutan remained a constant feature of the eastern hill economy and society for more than one hundred and fifty years, even though, once there, migrants often found the work and the working conditions onerous and restrictive, and some returned.

In the early phases of land clearance, mining and tea plantation, Nepali labourers were, according to some, in high demand (Dahal and Mishra 1987), although they were also characterised, by some, as unable to acclimatise to the tropical jungle clearing required to prepare the tea estates in what for them was 'an unhealthy district' (Chatterjee 1995: 50). The plantations in Darjeeling had the good fortune of a steady supply of Nepali labour 'without formalities and without the cost of importing it' (Xaxa 1985: 72).

Nepali migration to Darjeeling for agricultural work was also facilitated by the active recruitment of Nepalis for the British army in India. In Assam, however, by contrast, the major problem for many planters was the shortage of labour for the estates. Commercial production, however, began, with the first exports of tea from India being 12 tea chests in 1838. In 1839, the first English plantation, the Assam Company, was established, soon to be followed by settlements in North Bengal. The Assam Tea Company took over the East India Company's tea plantations.

Davis (1951: 117) indicates that the innovative practice of granting rice plots to tea estate plantation workers, as an incentive for them to settlement

---

4. Namgyal & Drolma, *The History of Sikkim*, ms 1908, cited in A. C. Sinha, Indian Northeast Frontier and Nepali Immigrants, in Sinha & Subba, *The Nepalis in Northeast India*. Indus Publishing Company, 2003

permanently in the area, seems to have augmented the number of Nepalis in Assam, and created new settlements. This also inadvertently prepared the land for rice cultivation by the Assamese. They also settled near urban areas, and practiced dairy farming and wet rice cultivation. Nepali workers were also used to clear forest for sugar cane production (Lloyd 1923: 42, cited in Kansakar 1984: 60). Predominantly male, but also female, labour from Nepal was used in both Darjeeling and Assam; men came with their families both to work and to settle.

Despite strenuous objections from the Nepali royal court (or *durbar)*, the British continued recruiting and encouraging settlement of migrant workers and small-holders in the new hill stations of Shillong and Darjeeling (Subba 1983: 128). The plantations in Darjeeling thus benefited from a steady supply of Nepali labour 'without formalities and without the cost of importing it' (Xaxa 1985: 72). This was by contrast with Assam, where the major problem for planters was the shortage of labour for the estates. Also, there were new emerging employment opportunities in the armies of the British East India Company and the Sikh state.

Something of the same kind occurred in the Kumaon area of India, to the west of Nepal, especially in the Kangra Valley, where the British government had now also established 'Gurkha' settlements without the settlers having to pay for the land (Subedi 1999: 86-87). These Nepali settlements included whole families (men, women and children). In Garhwal also, there was a significant Nepali presence. It is significant that Garhwalis, like those from Kumaon, were regarded by the British as 'Gorkhas' and were integrated into the British Army, fighting together with other 'Gorkhas' in the ranks of the first five 'irregular' Gurkha regiments, until as late as 1887 (as we shall see below). Indeed, a significant proportion of the women migrating to India in the 19th century were accompanying their husbands – and many of those were seeking employment as soldiers – or *lahures,* as they came to be called.

❀ ❀ ❀

CHAPTER 3
Lahures

For nearly two centuries, those men serving in foreign armies have been referred to in Nepal as *lahures*, because of the early association with the town of Lahore in present-day Pakistan. We believe this association began in the first decade of the 19th century, when Ranjit Singh, the Sikh ruler, began to recruit men from the Himalayas into his army. As Brook Northey and Morris in the 1920s, remarked: 'did not the Maharaja Ranjit Singh, of Sikh fame, enlist them at Lahore?' (1927: xxix). In fact, Ranjit Singh probably first enlisted them into his army after defeating the Gorkhali army at Ganesh Ghati in Kangra in 1809 and signing the Treaty of Sutlej with the British, thereby defining their respective territories the same year (Hasrat 1977: 357, cited in Des Chene 1991: 235).

As Patwant Singh remarks, 'with the Marathas in the southeast and the Kangra chieftains and the Gurkhas in the north and northeast, also eyeing Punjab's territories, in addition to the Afghans in the northwest, and encouraged by fratricidal conflicts between *misl* chiefs, the challenges that Ranjit Singh faced, when he crowned himself Maharaja of Lahore in April 1801, were considerable. But he was un-fazed' (2002: 106). By a combination of alliances forged by marriage and friendship, strategic military initiatives, and careful diplomacy, above all with the British, Ranjit Singh managed over the next decade to consolidate his position in the region.

A crucial encounter was that between the Sikhs and the Gorkhalis in Kangra in 1809. The confrontation between the Gorkhali state and the Sikhs had its genesis in the expansionist policy of the former. Having incorporated the Kingdom of Kumaon in 1791, the Gorkhalis planned to add the hill country to its west as far as the river Sutlej. In 1807, Kangra Fort, on the west bank of the

Sutlej, was put under siege by Gorkhali forces under Amar Singh Thapa. By early 1809, most of the land of Kangra had been annexed, although the fort still held out. At first, Ranjit Singh was reluctant to assist the ruler of Kangra, but a push by the Gorkhalis towards the Kashmir Valley changed his mind. Kashmir was effectively independent territory, riven by factions and coveted by both Sikhs and Gorkhali.

Ranjit Singh reached Kangra accompanied by a large army by the end of May. According to one estimate, there were about one hundred thousand horse and foot with the Maharaja at that time. The hill chiefs who were well-acquainted with the hilly terrain were ordered to block all routes in order to prevent the procurement of provisions and equipment for the Gorkhali army. A bloody battle ensued on 24 August at Ganesh Ghati in the Kangra Valley, in which both sides fought with ferocity. But eventually the Gorkhalis were forced to retreat back across the Sutlej for lack of provisions, and the Sikh army emerged victorious, albeit with heavy losses, and reclaimed control of the fort and surrounding area.

It has been suggested that the reliance on their short knives (*kukris*) by the Gorkhalis and the advantage of long swords, not to mention more firepower (rifles and artillery) on the other side, was another reason behind the failure of the Gurkhas. In any case, 'after he had witnessed hand-to-hand fighting between the Sikhs and the Gurkhas at Ganesh Ghati, Ranjit Singh's admiration for their fighting qualities resulted in the raising of a Gurkha contingent for his own army. He also took Bhopal Singh Thapa, son of the Gurkha commander Amar Singh Thapa, into his service, paving the way for the possibilities of close ties with Nepal – a kingdom which would not be too far from his territories after the Sikh conquest of Ladakh in 1834' (Singh 2002: 117-118).

From this time onwards, there was a flow of men from the hills of what is now Nepal, as well as from the regions of Garhwal and Kumaon, to Lahore to fight in the Sikh army as *lahures*. It is highly likely that some at least of these were accompanied by their wives and families. The Sikh Army was mainly Punjabi with a predominantly Sikh cadre, but it also had a significant multi-religious multi-ethnic composition: there were soldiers of different religious backgrounds (i.e. Muslims and Hindus) and there were soldiers of different ethnic or national backgrounds: Pashtuns, Dogras, Khatris, Jats, Kashyap Rajputs, Ramgarhias, Gorkhalis and even European mercenaries. As Allen remarks, 'nor were the men who made up the rank and file of Ranjit Singh's Khalsa Dal exclusively Sikhs: large numbers of Hindu Dogras and Gurkhas served in his infantry, which was organised, trained, dessed and armed very much along French lines' (Allen 2000: 29)

In less than 20 years, the Sikh kingdom expanded, largely through initial military conquest followed by the formal subordination of local rulers to the rule of Ranjit Singh, to include Kangra, Attock, Multan, Kashmir, Derajat and Peshawar. Eventually, in the 1830s, the flag of the Sikh Kingdom would fly in Ladakh and Kabul. In all of these campaigns, men from Garhwal, Kumaon and what by then can be called Nepal formed a small but significant part of the Sikh army. It is highly likely that some at least of these men were accompanied by their wives and children.

It was not only the Sikhs who recruited hill men from Nepal as soldiers early in the 19th century. The Treaty of Sutlej (1809) with the British defined the borders between the Sikh Empire and the territory of the British East India Company; but the Gorkhali State continued to press for greater control over its territories in the *terai,* as these were also a significant source of state revenue. This eventually led to increased tension and eventually, in 1814, conflict with the British East India Company, which was also ambitious about controlling and administering territories in the Ganges plains adjacent to the southern territories of the Gorkhali state.

For two years between 1814 and 1816, the British East India Company was at war with the Gorkhali State. The eventual defeat of the latter led to the Treaty of Sugauli, by which the Gorkhali State had to cede all those territories that had been annexed from the Raja of Sikkim to the East India Company. In 1817, in the Treaty of Titalia, the East India Co. reinstated the Raja of Sikkim (who had been driven out), restored all the tracts of land between the Mechi and the Teesta to the Raja and guaranteed his sovereignty.

However, impressed by the quality of their opponents during the Anglo-Nepali War, the British were concerned to recruit some of these impressive fighters – or at least the men - into their own army as soon as possible. They did not wait until the war was over and the Treaty of Sugauli signed. Recruitment started as early as 1815. According to an agreement between Amar Singh Thapa, Gorkha's western commander, and his British adversary in the field: 'All the troops in the service of Nepal, with the exception of those granted to the personal honour of Kagjees Ummersing and Rangor Sing, will be at liberty to enter into the services of the British Government if agreeable to themselves and the British Government choose to accept their services'. (Smith 1973: 9, cited in Hutt 1989: 1).

The process of recruitment began with the recruitment of 'Gurkhas' who then formed the Nusseree (Nasiri) battalions that would eventually become the 1st Gurkha Rifles. Also, in 1815, Lieutenant Frederick Young (who is regarded as the father of the 2nd Gurkhas) recruited some 3,000 'Gurkhas' in Sirmoor, which is in Garhwal, some 150 miles west of what is now Nepal, and they became known as the Sirmoor Battalion (1815-1823). The Simoor battalion was the first of these new 'Gurkha' units to fight on the British side. The British also recruited in Kumaon. So, at this time – and indeed for much of the 19th century - the 'Gurkhas' included Garhwalis and Kumaonis as well as Nepalis.

❀ ❀ ❀

CHAPTER 4

Fighting Women

The British were impressed, early on in the war, not only by the qualities of the fighting men of the hills, but also by those of their their women folk in defence of their homeland. In an early encounter between the Gorkhali army and the British - at the battle of Kalunga[5] in October 1814 – when the Gorkhali governor of Dehra Dun was obliged to retreat into the hills as the British East India Company moved troops in large numbers against them – the Gorkhali fighters were accompanied by women and children. Khanduri notes that, 'to Gorkhas, women were both wives and mothers, and also fighters. Some of them moved about dressed as men. The local women also joined them in fighting. Besides nursing the wounded and the dying, they built walls, collected stones to be thrown as missiles' (1997: 91).

Khanduri suggests that 'the strength which Captain Bal Bhadra Kanwar (the Gorkhali military commander) had on Kalunga proper was about 600, and included 200 Gorkhas, the same number of Garhwalis, the balance being women and children' (1997: 109). Khanduri states that 'perhaps the first example of women joining the men in fighting a modern enemy is found in this war (against the British)' (Khanduri 1997: 91). Colonel Shakespear wrote, of this encounter, 'this was our first stiff fight with the Nepalese, who here showed their grit, and not only the men but their women too. For there were a number of the latter in

---

5. The Kalunga fort was a strategic western outpost of the Gorkha empire on the chief route at that time from Dehra Dun to Tehri. It was made a key point in the defences against invasion. The forces at Kalunga were in total around 600, of which some 200 were Gorkha troops, some 200 Garhwalis and the remainder women and children (Khanduri 1997: 109). There were additional forces in outlying posts – "at Virat there were 150 and the remainder were scattered in penny-packets for collection duties, manning the stockades on the two passes and controlling the local villages" (Khanduri 1997: 109).

the fort, and these, true to the best traditions of their sex, helped man nobly, for they were seen at the assaults on the walls throwing heavy stones on our men' (cited in Khanduri 1997: 121).

Kennedy, Vansittart and Fraser recorded that 'during the assaults on the fort, women were seen hurling stones and undauntly exposing themselves; and several of their dead bodies and four wounded were subsequently found amidst ruins of the fort' (cited in Khanduri 1997: 91). A similar account is provided by William Fraser, who notes that, 'the defence was so desperate that I saw women actually throwing stones from the walls'. Khanduri himself remarks that, 'the women joined the men in defence as actively as combatants. The western modern army, which employed female folk as stretcher bearers or musicians, must have viewed these brave women with awe' (Khanduri 1997: 11)[6].

Interestingly, a memorial at Dehra Dun, now derelict, records a tribute both to the British soldiers who fell at Kalunga and to their adversaries; but nothing is said of the women who fought there. Indeed, it only mentions 'our gallant adversary, Bulbuddr. Commander of the fort' and his 'brave Gorkhas, who were afterwards, while in the service of Ranjit Singh, shot down in their ranks to the last man (sic) by Afghan Artillery' (cited in Khanduri 1997: 127).[7] However, there were women and children among the bodies buried and cremated after the battle at Kalunga: the British Colonel Mawbey cremated 97 men and women on 1 December; he also counted 90 already buried (Khanduri 1997: 124).

It was not only at Kalunga that Gorkhali women were actively involved in the Anglo-Gorkhali war. William Fraser – who was at the time raising irregular forces in the hills, moving from one British camp to another and seeing a wide range of encounters between the Company troops and those of the 'Gorkhas' – referred in 1815 to the enemy generally as 'arrays of rusticks, ploughmen, carriers, camp followers, women, boys and old men' (cited in Des Chene 1991:

---

6. Richard Holmes remarks, however, that, in the British Army, 'women routinely accompanied the army and some were killed or died of illness or exposure. One of them, the wife of Sergeant Reston of the 94th Regiment carried ammunition and supplies to the front line, at the siege of Matagorda Fort at Cadiz in 1810, and received no official recognition of her heroism, despite the efforts of her regiment' (Holmes, 2001: 99).

7. As mentioned earlier, after the Anglo-Nepali war of 1814-16, increasing numbers of men from the hill areas of Nepal (as well as from Kumaon and Garhwal) joined the armies of Ranjit Singh and of the British East India Company.

44). The women were, for the most part, camp followers, but in some cases they did fight. During the battle for Malaun in April 1815, for example, women and children were actively involved. Khanduri recounts how, early in the morning of 16th April (around 2 am),

> 'the fort was scampering with activities. Some 400 men had assembled. There were also the band and the flag bearers of the Kazi (Amar Singh Thapa). The women and the children were awake and helping the men draw their ammunition from the silos of the fort. Some girls and boys had dressed themselves in men's attire and were ready to march off with the attackers. They were, instead, told to get to the perimeter defences and be prepared to rush to the battlefield to evacuate and treat the wounded. A batch of them fetched the water and found some Firengis (Englishmen) nearby, but they still managed to draw the water' (1997: 189).

These camp-followers, many of them women, also therefore, played a heroic and active part in the defence of the fort at Malaun, as they were often to do, largely unsung, in the many campaigns in which the Gurkhas were deployed, not against the British, but in their service, over many decades. For it was not only the Gorkhalis who relied heavily on camp followers to support the troops. The British did also, in India, just as they did in other wars. As Richard Holmes remarks, in *Redcoat,* his study of 'the British soldier in the age of horse and musket', 'women routinely accompanied the army and some were killed or died of illness or exposure' (2001: 99).

What is not clear, however, is what facilities there were to look after the men and women who accompanied the troops in peace-time and on campaigns in time of war as camp followers. The British East India Company had established a hospital for soldiers as early as 1664, and certainly provided some medical facilities for military casualties. One suspects, however, that camp-followers were not afforded the same privileges. Indeed, as we shall see later, the casualties among the camp-followers often exceeded those of the troops themselves.

The direct involvement of women in military encounters would, however, not have been so strange to British army officers in India, at this period. As Julie Wheelwright points out, 'women have always played an important part in the British military.. they served aboard ships, although unofficially recognised, worked in cannon crews, nursed and even gave birth while at sea. Women also formed an integral part of camp life in early modern armies, performing a wide variety of tasks, including foraging for food, selling meats and wines, laundering, nursing or looting as well as working as prostitutes (Hacker 1981). At Britain's largest military battles in the eighteenth and nineteenth centuries women's presence is also well documented' (1990: 17).

As Charles Esdaile has shown (2014), women were very much involved in the Peninsular War (1808-1814), which was taking place at much the same time in Europe. While some local Portuguese and Spanish women actually fought or otherwise became directly involved in the conflict against the invaders, others turned collaborator, used the war as a means of effecting dramatic changes in their situation, or simply concentrated on staying alive. Esdaile provides information about the role of French sympathizers, camp followers, pamphleteers, cross-dressers, prostitutes, amorous party girls, and even a few proto-feminists; and we meet not just the women to whom the war came but also the women who came to the war—the many thousands who accompanied the British and French armies to the Iberian peninsula.

There were also women who fought alongside, but usually disguised as, men, as Julie Wheelwright has revealed (2020). An early example is provided by the life of Christian Davies (1667 – 7 July 1739), born Christian Cavanagh and also known as Mother Ross, who was an Irishwoman who joined the British Army in 1693 disguised as a man. She fought with the infantry in Flanders during the Nine Years War until 1697, then with the 4th Dragoons, later the 2nd Royal North British Dragoons and finally with the Scots Greys in the War of the Spanish Succession from 1701 to 1706. The author Daniel Defoe met her in old age when she was a Chelsea Pensioner and turned her story into a novel entitled *The Life and Adventures of Mrs. Christian Davies.* He also wrote about her in *Roxana; or, The fortunate mistress,* and in *The life and adventures of Mother Ross* (1855).

As Richard Holmes tells us, 'the best-documented female soldier (of this period) is Hannah Snell, who seems... to have served four and a half years in the marines and been discharged in 1750. She subsequently made a living by appearing on the stage in her regimentals to perform arms drills, and selling buttons, garters and lace. The diarist Parson Woodford saw her at the White Hart at Weston, near Norwich. He believed her assertion that she "was 21 years as a common soldier in the army, and was not discovered by any as a woman"' (2001: 99). When she was a young woman Hannah Snell moved to London and in 1744 married a man named James Summs. The couple had a daughter, but the child died at the age of one, and Summs disappeared. Hearing a rumour that he had been pressed into military service, Snell borrowed the clothes of her brother-in-law, James Gray, and assumed his identity to join the British army and locate her husband.

Although she later discovered that Summs had been convicted and executed for murder, this did not prevent Snell from pursuing an adventurous military career disguised as James Gray. According to her own account she became a soldier in the 6th Regiment of Foot, where she was stationed in Carlisle during the Jacobite rebellion in Scotland. During this time she was trained in military drill and the use of firearms. However after she prevented a sergeant from raping a local girl she was sentenced to 600 lashes of the whip for 'neglect of duty'. As she endured the first 500 lashes without making a sound her commanding officer ordered that she be spared the final 100 lashes.

She left the regiment after this and travelled to Portsmouth where she joined the British Royal Marines and set sail for India on the *Swallow*. In 1748, Snell fought in the naval Battle of Pondicherry where the British attempted to capture a French colony. She reportedly killed several Frenchmen before being wounded herself. She is also known to have fought in a battle at Devicotta, and was wounded a total of 12 times during her naval service, including suffering a musket shot to the groin. She operated on herself to remove the musket ball so that she wouldn't be identified as a woman by the ship's surgeon.

In 1750, Snell returned to Britain and decided to finally reveal her true identity to the other members of her unit during the sea voyage back home. With the encouragement of her shipmates she petitioned the head of the British army, the Duke of Cumberland, to grant her a military pension. Remarkably, the pension was granted and she was honourably discharged from the army. Snell's exploits became popular gossip around London and she eventually sold her story to a London publisher under the title '*The Female Soldier*'. She later toured England, appearing on stage in military uniform and performing drill. Eventually, she retired to Wapping where she opened a pub named The Female Warrior. She lived for another 40 years, married twice more and raised two sons. In her old age Snell began to suffer from dementia and, in 1791, she was admitted to the Bedlam asylum where she died 6 months later, in 1792.

The first known example of a fighting woman from America was Deborah Sampson. Born in Massachusetts in 1760, she enlisted during the American

Revolution as an infantry soldier in 1782, adopting the name Robert Shurtleff, and served for 18 months. She was nearly 'outed' when she was hospitalised and had to be treated; but the medical staff kept her secret and she continued, eventually receiving an honourable discharge for her military service, and a full military pension. She then returned to her home town in Massachusetts and spent a happy married life with her husband, Benjamin Gannet, and three kids. When she died at the age of 66, her husband petitioned for financial support as a spouse of a military person, which was generally awarded only to female widows. However, Congress made an exception this time and approved his petition because of Sampson's act of heroism and courage in the war.

At about the same time, Joanna Żubr (1770–1852), a Polish woman who followed her husband into battle as a camp follower, then enlisted as a male soldier and saw action as such. She eventually was awarded the highest Polish military award for bravery – the Virtuti Militari. Jeanne Louise Antonini (1771—1861) was born in Corsica. She was orphaned at the age of 10 and joined the crew of a frigate posing as a boy. She maintained her disguise through various military experiences, and eventually joined the French army to fight in the Napoleonic Wars. She was wounded nine times but managed to keep up appearances throughout her military career.

There was also Dr James Barry (1792/5-1865), born in Ireland as Margaret Ann Bulkley, who assumed a male identity initially to study medicine at university but entered the British army as a male hospital assistant in July 1812, was appointed assistant surgeon two years later and rose eventually to become Inspector General of the Army Medical Department in 1858. While serving in the Cape, she was described as 'the most skilled of physicians but the most wayward of men', as her quarrelsome temper had led her to fight a duel at some point. It was only after her death in 1865 that it was discovered that she was a woman and has apparently given birth to a child.

The Russians had their Nadezda Durova, a female cavalry officer who served in the Napoleonic wars as 'Cornet Aleksandrov', and whose celebrated memoirs, *The Notes of a Cavalry Maiden* have been popular with Russian readers since their publication in 1836. They remained inaccessible to the English-speaking readers until, in 1988, not one but two translations appeared in the US. The daughter of an army major, she left home in Sarapul, a small city in the Urals, at the age of 23. By this time she had already married and born a son. However, in 1807, accompanied by her ferocious horse Alkid, she enlisted and joined the Russian army's lancer regiment, the *Uhlans,* posing initially as a mail officer.

Understandably concerned with maintaining her cover, she had most likely chosen this regiment as its officers were famously clean-shaven. For years, she served with this and other regiments disguised as a man using the pseudonym Aleksandr Sokolov. Durova performed unusually well in combat, and as a reward for her bravery, she was summoned to St Petersburg for a formal audience with the Tsar Aleksandr I himself. Whether he was impressed with her bravery in battle or worried that the news of female soldiers enlisting would be bad public relations for the Russian army, the Tsar suggested she continue to serve in the army and take on a new alias, Aleksandrov, derived from his own name.

Published in *The Contemporary,* a literary journal founded and edited by Aleksandr Pushkin, her memoir, '*The Notes of the Cavalry Maiden',* became the toast of the Russian literary society. In a manner conventional for the period, the leading Russian literary critic Vissarion Belinskii even suggested the text was so full of 'masculine power and strength' that it must have been written by Pushkin himself! Durova herself became a welcome guest in St Petersburg literary salons. Fortunately for contemporary researchers, there are a great number of vivid, if unflattering, recollections of her in some of the most well-known literary memoirs of the period.

For example, Avdotya Panaeva, a writer and hostess of *The Contemporary*'s literary salon in the 1840s-1860s, wrote in her *Memoirs/Memories* that Durova 'was of medium height, with a face the colour of soil, and mottled, wrinkled skin; her face had a long-ish shape, with features devoid of beauty; she kept squinting, even though her eyes were already quite small... Her hair was cut short and styled as a man's. Her manners were also manly: she sat on the sofa.... with one elbow on her knee, in her other hand she held a long cigarette holder and kept smoking...' (Panaeva 1889).

When Peter Hagberg, a career soldier in the Swedish army, was called away to fight in the 1788 war against Russia, his wife Brita, unwilling to bear life without him, cut her hair, dressed as a man and followed her husband off to war. She enlisted under her married name. A veteran of numerous battles, she was eventually was unwittingly transferred into her husband's own regiment. According to the story, when one day, during roll call, the commander yelled 'Hagberg', both Brita and Peter stepped forward. Reunited at last, the two kept her true identity secret; until Brita was wounded while serving as a marine at the Battle of Vyborg Bay. When a surgeon discovered her sex, she was discharged, but not before being awarded a medal for bravery and a full pension for her service. When she died in 1825, she was honoured with a full military funeral.

Finally, the song 'Polly Oliver', known in America as well as in England, which describes a young woman who decides to 'enlist as a soldier and follow her love', is just one of several songs of the period (18th-19th century) that refer to a woman enlisting as a soldier. There are several different versions. In all of them she dresses as a man; in some she lies with the man she knows is her love, but only reveals herself as a woman to him the next morning, in others she ends up nursing him, but eventually reveals herself to him. In all the versions, she ends up marrying him[8].

But these were all individual women who disguised themselves as men. It was far more rare to be openly involved in military service, still less to be able to fight as a soldier or a marine without a male disguise and persona. In Mughul India, at least in Hyderabad, there were other examples of women as warriors – something which at least some of the British stationed there would have known about.

During the campaign of spring 1795, when the army of the Nizam of Hyderabad took to the field against the Marathas, it included a whole regiment of female infantry, dressed in British-style red-coats, as well as the Nizam's harem women, who also came along on the trip in a long caravan of covered elephant *howdahs*. The first clash was between the two rival battalions of French-trained infantry, the recently raised Corps Francais de Raymond on the Nizam's side and the famous de Boigne brigades fighting under French Bourbon emblems, on the side of the Marathas.

After they had engaged, with Raymond's troops having taken advantage of their position at the top of the ridge known as Moori Ghat, they were followed downhill by the Mughal Women's Regiment - the Zuffur Plutun or Victorious Battalion - who advanced steadily with their muskets and managed to hold their own against the Maratha right wing. Dalrymple comments that 'British commentators who saw the Zuffur Platun on parade tended to make snide remarks about their 'ridiculous appearance'. Those who saw them in

---

8. Several versions of "Polly Oliver" survive as undated broadside ballad sheets in the Bodleian Library, University of Oxford.

action, however, were always surprised by the women's ferocity, discipline and effectiveness' (Dalrymple 2003: 94).

Despite the military success of the Nizam's army, of which evidently the Zuffur Platun were an integral part, however, a crisis developed when an intermittent cannonade by the Marathas had apparently panicked the Nizam's women, who had accompanied the troops, and especially Bakhshi Begum, his most senior wife, who threatened to unveil herself in public if the Nizam did not take his entire harem back into the shelter of the small and half-ruined fort of Khardla. During the confusion of the Nizam's retreat, a small party of Marathas looking for water stumbled across a picket and the brief exchange of fire was enough to throw the remaining Hyderabadi troops into a complete panic. They rushed back to the Khardla fort, leaving all their guns, baggage camels, ammunition wagons, stores and food behind them.

The Marathas, though surprised by this, took full advantage of the situation and effectively surrounded the army of Hyderabad. After three weeks of extreme privation and considerable loss of life, the Nizam was obliged to accede to all of the Marathas' demands, which included key fortresses and great swathes of Hyderabadi territory, leaving the Nizam with a fragment of his former lands, an indefensible frontier and a substantial sum required as 'war reparations'. Not too long after this, in August 1801, Edward Strachey described the 'run-down' appearance of the city of Hyderabad, but ruminated that 'in better times it must have been in a high degree splendid and magnificent' (cited in Dalrymple 2003: 284).

A month later, Mountstuart Elphinstone described the Hyderabad durbar in some detail, and made special mention of what he referred to as 'several female women sentries, dressed something like Madras *sepoys*. More were on guard before the doors and about 20 or 30 more women were drawn out before the guardroom in sight. Many women sat in the back part of the room where we were'. Dalrymple comments that 'the description is...interesting for what it shows of the sudden and unexpected power and prominence of women in the Hyderabad durbar at this period, and the degree to which Mama Barun, one of the two senior *aseels* - former wet nurses of the royal family who had also been commanders of the Zuffur Platun women's battalion at Khardla five years earlier – now acted as the principal master of ceremonies, while their women *sepoys* acted as the Nizam's body guards' (2003).

Henry Russell, who reported on the situation in Hyderabad somewhat later, in March 1816, quoted an officer 'of high rank in the King's Army' (who) once said, on seeing a party of them (the Zuffur Platun) in action, that 'they would put half the native corps in India to the Blush' (reprinted in *Indian Archives*, vol. ix, no. 2, July-December 1955, p. 134). Sir Henry Russell, 1st baronet (1751-1836) served as a judge in the Calcutta Supreme Court from 1797 to 1813. His eldest sons, Henry (later Sir Henry) Russell (1783-1856) and Charles Russell (1786-1856) both worked for the East India Company for many years in India. Interestingly, it appears that Henry junior had a liaison with an Indian woman in Hyderabad, which resulted in a child. In his collection of letters are some that relate to this illegitimate daughter[9]. We shall return to this in a later chapter.

❀ ❀ ❀

---

9. www.ourmigrationstory.org.uk/uploads/Correspondence%20between%20Sir%20 Henry%20Russell%20(1783-1852)%20Major%20Robert%20Pitman%20and%20 Mary%20Wilson.pdf – cited by Margot Finn, 'Migrating home: 'mixed children' and the return of the nabobs of India', www.ourmigrationstory.org.uk/oms/migrating-home-the-return-of-the-nabobs-of-british-india.

CHAPTER 5

Campaigns and Camp Followers

We have referred above to the involvement of Gorkhali women in the fighting at Kalanga and Malaun, and how impressed the British were at this. These may have been relatively unusual events, associated with the desperate defence of their homeland from British invasion. There are no other accounts of women actually involved in the fighting during the Anglo-Gorkhali War; and certainly, as far as we know, neither the Gorkhali army nor that of the Sikhs actually contained female soldiers – although we cannot be certain. As far as we know, the British Army in India never actually employed women as troops, but they certainly did engage them as camp followers.

The phenomenon of camp-followers, however, is widely documented in accounts of military campaigns from the time of the ancient Greeks onwards. Many of these were women. These usually 'served' in an ancillary capacity, as nurses, cooks, porters and sexual companions, but it also seems that a minority at least were more actively involved in a military capacity. We have already remarked on this phenomenon. In many regiments in the British Army, over the centuries, wives lived with their menfolk in their barracks, whether these were in Britain or abroad.

The Crimean War was probably the last major conflict in which wives accompanied the British army on campaign. Prior to this, in any campaign overseas, there were usually women and children in camp, on the line of march and sometimes even on the field of battle (Holmes 2001: 364). The women provided a variety of services – including cooking and washing - as well as companionship; on the other hand, they were often felt to present disadvantages to the troops, particularly on the line of march and during campaigns, even if, ultimately, they were a welcome presence. As George Bell of the 34th comments of the situation as he experienced it during the Peninsular campaign:

'averse to all military discipline, they impeded our progress at time, particularly in retreat. They were under no control. They were ordered to the rear, of their donkeys would be shot, to stay with the baggage under the discipline of the Provost Marshal. Despite the warning, next morning they would pick up their belongings and set off, lamenting their bitter fate, ahead of the column, marauding, preparing their men's meals before their arrival, plundering the battle-field or searching it for their dead; they were wounded, killed or died of exposure and hunger. Collectively and individually, they formed cameos of the Peninsular campaign, a colourful kaleidoscope of the romance and tragedy, devotion and self-sacrifice, the hardships and endurance of women at war' (cited in Holmes 2001: 366).

Welsh women followed The Royal Welch Fusiliers (23rd Regiment of Foot) ever since the earliest days of the Peninsular War. Swansea University historian Dr Gerry Oram explains that 'officially six women were permitted to travel with each company of a hundred men; these were drawn by lot. But of course far more than this accompanied the army unofficially, and commanders' attitudes towards them varied according to the situation. They could prove extremely valuable, cooking, sewing and tending to the wounded, but at times - such as the evacuation of Corunna - they also became a major hindrance'. Some - such as Jenny Jones of Talyllyn - are even believed to have fought alongside their men (www.bbc.co.uk/news/uk-wales-33080507).

In the case of the British Army in India, the wives of the 'native' troops often accompanied their husbands – as of course did a significant number of single women who 'serviced' the soldiers in a variety of ways when they went off on campaign. As Holmes in *Redcoat*, demonstrates with numerous examples (2001: 367-70), and as we shall later, 'women themselves were killed, wounded and captured' (ibid 369). The scale of the possible camp-follower presence in a line of march is given by an estimate of the average monthly strength for operations of the Company's Indian Army during the Anglo-Gorkha or Anglo-Nepali War: about 19,000 British troops, 30,000 Indian troops, 42,000 'private' followers, 17,500 *banjara* bullocks, 14,000 bullocks, 12,250 camels and 1,500 elephants (*History of ASC*, vol 1., 1760-1857, p. 83; Massé, Lt-Col. C. H. (1948). The 'private' followers here included men, women and children.

Many women were also involved as wives and camp followers in the early campaigns in which the Gurkhas fought for the British, in India and beyond. Even before the Anglo-Nepali war had ended, some 4,650 men had already been enlisted in four irregular 'Gurkha' battalions – the 1st and 2nd Nussuree (Nasiris)[10], the Sirmoor and the Kumaon – stationed at Sabathu in the Simla Hills, at Dehra Dun and at Almora in Kumaon respectively (des Chene 1991: 54). Over the next forty years, the 'irregular' corps of 'Gurkhas' were deployed by the Company to great effect in numerous campaigns, as the British consolidated and expanded their control over northern India, even embarking on major expeditions (in which 'Gurkha' troops were involved) to subdue neighbouring states, such as Burma to the east and Afghanistan to the north west.

Some of these men would have been accompanied in their stations and during their campaigns by their wives, mistresses and sweethearts during their campaigns – a tradition widespread among the 'native' infantry of the Company army - and, as the flow of men from the hills increased during the next few decades, and the recruits were organized more formally into their own 'Gurkha' battalions, so too, thousands of women from the hills came down to find employment in and around the army camps. Within less than a decade after the Anglo-Nepali war of 1814-16, more than ten thousand 'Gorkhali' men had been recruited into the British army in India – affecting ten thousand 'Gorkhali' households – including women and children - back home in the hills. For while some women migrated abroad, most 'Gorkhali' women remained at home, to 'keep the home fires burning' as it were, as their menfolk fought for the British.

The story of those women and their families, whose menfolk often spent years abroad, is one that we cannot tell in any detail for lack of information. We can only imagine their trials and tribulations. As Shrestha and Conway (2001: 156) put it, in somewhat dramatic terms, referring to a much later period,

> 'theirs is a story written in tears that flow from the pain of separation from their migrant husbands; these are tears of silent waiting wailing that wet the pillows night after night in a lonely room where not even the nightly stars can witness their heartache and sorrow. Theirs is a story of endless emotional endurance, one that is only matched by the physical punishment meted out by the harshness of the ruthless hills'.

Pratyoush Onta has written vividly, mainly in regard to the involvement of the Gurkhas in the First and Second World Wars, about the privations and the pain (*dukha*) experienced by the soldiers on the Western Front and other theatres of those terrible conflicts (Onta 1994). Conway and Shrestha have also

---

10. Meaning 'loyal' or 'friendly'.

emphasised that 'countless have died serving as mercenaries for the British and Indian armies, some leaving behind only shreds of memories among parents, widows and orphan children' (2001: 1790). But it is also the case that, whatever the 'pain' of the ordinary Gurkha soldier, the suffering of the camp followers, many of whom were women, was at least as great during the many campaigns of the 19ᵗʰ century.

Gurkhas from the Sirmoor and Nussuree battalions fought in the Pindari campaign (1812-1817) and the third Anglo-Maratha war (1817-19), which saw the British extend their power to the borders of the Punjab and Sind)[11]. At least one other 'Gurkha' battalion was raised over the next few years[12]. Renamed the 8ᵗʰ Sirmoor Local Battalion in 1823, the first battle honour achieved by the Sirmoor regiment was at Bharatpur (Bhurtpore) in 1825/6. Between December 1825 and January 1826, the heavily fortified town of Bharatpur in the princely state of Bharatpur (now part of Rajasthan) was the target of Lord Combermere's army of 21,000 men and 100 guns comprised two divisions of infantry, one division of regular cavalry, a brigade of irregular horse, a large train of battering ordnance, several brigades of field artillery (horse and foot), along with a corps of engineers, sappers and other requisite troops.

The infantry included the 8th Sirmoors. It is likely that they, like the other regiments deployed, were accompanied by camp followers who included women and even children. The town was first besieged and then mined, with the loss of 600 men; but the wall was breached and the Gurkhas fought through alongside their British comrades. The following year, they were renumbered as the 6th (Sirmoor) Local Battalion.

The First Anglo-Burmese War (March 1824-February 1826) was the first of three wars fought between the British and the Burmese. The war, which began primarily over the control of northeastern India, ended in a decisive British victory (in 1885), giving the British total control of Assam, Manipur, Cachar

---

11. The first war against the Maharattas, whose confederacy sprawled across north central India had taken place in 1779-81 and the second in 1803-05. In the second, the decisive battle – at Assaye in 1803 - had been commanded by Arthur Wellesley, the future Duke of Wellington.

12. The modern Indian Army's 9ᵗʰ Gorkha Rifles dates back to 1817, when it was raised at Infantry Levy at Fategarh; in 1823, it became a regular unit, as part of the Bengal Native Infantry. The 8ᵗʰ Gorkha Rifles, known as the Shiny Eight (also now part of the Indian Army), had its origins in the 16th Sylhet Local Battalion, raised in 1824, which participated in the Burma War of 1824-26.

and Jaintia as well as Arakan Province and Tenasserim. The Burmese eventually submitted to a British demand to pay an indemnity of one million pounds and sign a commercial treaty. This war was, however, the longest and most expensive war in British Indian history. The high cost of the campaign to the British contributed to a severe economic crisis in British India which eventually cost the East India Company many of its privileges.

Some 40,000 British and 'Indian' troops were involved, of whom 15,000 died. Only a minority of these were killed in action; almost 70 per cent were the result of tropical diseases. The troops involved included the Bengal Native Infantry – the 13th (Light Infantry) and the 38th and 40th Regiments – but not, apparently, any of the Gurkha regiments. Sir Robert Sale, however, the commander of the 13th (1st Somersetshire) Light Infantry during the Burma campaign, was later to hold a command in the First Afghan War (1839-1842), in which all five of the Gurkha regiments in existence by that time were involved.

In the meanwhile, over the years between 1810 and 1834, the Sikh Empire expanded vastly to include Kangra, where the 'Gorkhali' forces (of men, women and children) had once made their heroic stand, as well as Attock, Multan, Kashmir, Derjat and Peshawar; eventually the Sikh flag would fly over far Ladakh and over Kabul. 'Gorkhali' troops were involved in most of these campaigns by the Sikh army; they undoubtedly fought with the Sikhs during Ranjit Singh's campaign in Kashmir in 1819 and 1820, his 1821 campaign across the Indus in Dera Ghazi Khan and the Dera Jat region, then under the vassalage of Kabul and the Sikh-Afghan war of 1822. In fact, Balbhadra Kunwar was killed by Afghan artillery in Naushera, in the Peshwar region of Afghanistan in the last month in the Hindu Lunar calendar (March/April in the Roman calendar).

In 1823, when Ranjit Singh defeated Azim Khan, the former governor or Kashmir, he almost certainly was accompanied by 'Gorkhali' troops. Bhimsen Thapa, the man who effectively ruled the new unified state of Nepal in the early part of the 19th century, had men sent to Lahore specifically to collect information about the progress of this war and about the death of his nephew, Balbhadra Kunwar, the most famous of the '*lahures*'. For a further ten years, the armies of Ranjit Singh, with their units of 'Gorkhalis' and in some cases their wives, carried the Sikh flag and helped to expand the Sikh empire as far as Ladakh and Kabul in Afghanistan.

In August 1835, however, Ranjit Singh had a stroke; and a second stroke in January 1837 half-paralysed him. By 1838, the year before he died, his army included an entire 'Gurkha' regiment (Osborne 1840: 105-08) and in 1839, a treaty was signed between the Nepali government and the Khalsa (Sikh) government (Yogi Narhari Nath and Basnyet 1964: 21-2, cited in Kansakar 1984: 50) to regularise recruitment.

These 'Gorkhalis' serving abroad – whether for the Sikhs or for the British - were now widely known as *lahures*, even when they were employed by the British. It is likely that most of these recruits were not accompanied by their women folk – after all, they were recruited to fight, and there was a good deal of fighting to be done during the early 19th century, as the British consolidated their hold on India and 'pacified' those who resisted. A man unencumbered with a wife or sweetheart was often considered to be a more reliable fighter. But, as we have already seen, it was not uncommon during this period for the troops to be accompanied, even during campaigns, by a horde of camp-followers, which often included wives, mistresses and sweet-hearts, as well as prostitutes.

The widespread existence of camp-followers in the British Army in India during the early part of the 19th century is well documented. Robert Waterfield, for example, on arriving at a European camp in India for the first time, was struck by the noise of the camp and remarked that

'the bustle attendant on a European camp in India was something strange to us all. The constant jabbering of the natives and the roaring of the camels, together with the elephants and the buffaloes reminds one of the striking contrast there is between India and peaceful England. It's an old saying that there's no stopping a woman's tongue, but the women of Bengal beat all I ever saw, for they will fight, and keep up such a chattering that they may be heard above the din of the Camp' (cited in Holmes 2001: 350).

An even more detailed picture is provided by one British colonel, writing of a somewhat later period (John Dunlop MD, *Mooltan,* 1849, cited in Robin Lane Fox, *Alexander the Great*, 2004, pp. 377-78):

'we need an extraordinary assemblage of men, women and children, ponies, mules, asses and bullocks and carts laden with all sorts and kinds of conceivable and inconceivable things: grain, salt, cloth, sweetmeats, shawls, slippers, tools for the turners, the carpenters and blacksmiths, goods for the tailors and cobblers, the perfumers, armourers, milk-girls and grass-cutters: *moochees* must work the leather, *puckulias* carry our water, while *nagurchees* will supervise the travelling canteen. What a sea of camels! What guttural gurgling groanings in the long throats of salacious and pugnacious males! What resounding of sticks, as some throw away their loads and run away, tired servants often getting slain or miserably losing the column, thousands of camels dying, not only from fatigue but from ill-usage and being always overloaded. Such is the picture of the baggage of an army in India; Smithfield market alone can rival it'

Many of the camp followers would have been married women accompanying their soldier husbands, others would have been women married to men who performed some function or service themselves in the 'baggage train' as camp-followers, and yet others would have been single women providing the usual range of 'services' to the soldiers far from home. This last was by no means always an easy form of employment even if it might have been lucrative; also, the British soldiers could not always distinguish between prostitutes and ordinary local women: Captain Hervey refers to the 'sometimes unwelcome attentions' the local women received from British soldiers.

Some of these women, however, were officially recognised as 'regimental wives', in some cases they were accompanied by their children; these were provided for by the army (see Holmes, where he refers to women and children in the barracks of several regiments (2001: 292-306) and comments that 'wives on the regimental strength received half-rations, and children a quarter ration' (2001: 281). For many commentators at the time, the presence of women and children was 'generally the greatest of nuisances'; but for others, families helped maintain morale and keep bounds on the behaviour of the soldiery.

Simply being on the married roll did not entitle a wife to accompany her husband and his regiment. Much depended on the character and morals of the women concerned, and Holmes remarks that 'regimental women were subject to a discipline scarcely less severe than that which bore upon their men' (2001: 295). But in many regiments a quota was applied, which limited the number of women per company or per hundred men (Holmes 2001: 294). On the other hand, women also managed to smuggle themselves into the barracks and remain covertly with their husbands.

Captain Albert Hervey refers in his *A Soldier of the Company: Life of an Indian Ensign, 1833-43,* to the families of the 'Indian' *sepoys* and the encampments in which they were permitted to erect their tents, 'promiscuously without any regard to regularity'. He notes, particularly, the difficulty with which the *sepoys* were faced when trying to safe-guard the privacy of their women-folk ('of which the Natives are peculiarly tenacious in all castes') from the intrusions of the British troops: 'They would often grumble: bully and tyrannize us as much as you like, but do not meddle with our families'. But 'it was only the poverty-stricken married soldiery who are so miserably provided for, and it is they who suffer principally all hardships and privations of a line of march' (p 132).

On the other hand, when their men were killed, John Pearman observed that, 'most women widowed in India had remarried soldiers of the regiment within the four-month period that they were allowed to remain 'on the strength' as widows. Some courtships were swift. A cavalry sergeant in India asked a pretty widow to marry him just after her husband's funeral. She burst into tears, not because of the suddenness of the proposal, but because she had just accepted an offer from the corporal who had commanded the firing party at the funeral: the sergeant would have been a better catch' (Holmes 2001: 369).

This reveals that one of the attractions of being a 'regimental wife' on the strength of the regiment was not just the rations they received - although it also appears that even this depended on the rank of the husband: in the words of one ditty that accompanied the bugle-call for dinner: 'Officers' wives get puddings and pies, and sergeants' wives get skilly; but a private's wife gets nothing at all to fill her poor little belly' (2001: 282) – but also on access to the pay and life style of a soldier. For, as Holmes observes, 'soldiers, and by extension their wives, were induced to tolerate the squalor of the barrack-room and the discomforts of campaign by the prospects of steady pay' (Holmes 2001: 307).

Indeed, he reminds us, 'the word soldier has its origin in the old French, *soude,* pay, and the Latin *soldati,* paid men' (ibid). In India, the pay provided by the British East India Company, and after 1857 by the Crown, was relatively generous, and evidently attracted large numbers of recruits and their womenfolk.

❀ ❀ ❀

CHAPTER 6

Companions and Concubines

Not all encounters between soldiers and women, however, were casual or short-term encounters for payment; or even marriages driven by largely mercenary motives. For there remained into the 19th century, the vestiges of an earlier social order in Mughal India, in which the British elite in India in the 18th century intermingled, on a personal as well as a social basis with the local population, as a matter of course and on a regular basis.

Such a practice, William Dalrymple emphasises in his book *The White Moghuls,* began in the early 16th century, shortly after the conquest of Goa in 1510 and continued well into the early part of the 19th century. He describes a whole range of possible relationships between 'white' men and local women, all the way from casual encounters to more enduring relationships all the way to marriage. In fact, his book is centred around the long and loving relationship between Lieutenant Colonal James Achilles Kirkpatrick, the British Resident at the court of the Nizam of Hyderabad between 1797 and 1805, and Khair un-Nissa ('the most excellent of women'), the great-niece of the diwan (prime minister) of Hyderabad, whom he married and with whom he had two children.

He also had a more covert relationship with a 'dark girl' with whom he had a child ('the Hindoostani Boy'), while James' counterpart as British Resident in Delhi, and an old friend of Kirkpatrick's elder brother William, Boston-born Sir David Ochterlony, had thirteen consorts who paraded every evening around Delhi when he did, each on the back of her own elephant. When he slept in a tent, a red silk harem tent was set up on one side for his wives, and another for his daughters (Dalrymple 2003: 30).

Every bit as assimilated into their Indian surroundings were those European mercenaries who fought for Indian rulers or those who were employed by the British East India Company. Dalrymple gives several examples of the former, including George Thomas, who succeeded eventually in carving out his own state in the Mewatti badlands west of Delhi, and was a possible model for Rudyard Kipling's *The Man Who Would be King*. Once established in his Haryana kingdom, Thomas, or Jehaz Sahbi as he was known, built himself a palace, minted his own coins and collected about him a harem, eventually 'going native' to the extent that he forgot how to speak English. His son, Jan Thomas, became a celebrated Urdu poet.

As regards the latter, Dalrymple remarks that, in Calcutta, where the young employees of the Company were lodged, the only way for one of them to 'come into close or intimate contact with Indians and Indian society was if he took an Indian *bibi*, or companion', or even married a local woman. In the second half of the 18th century, the majority of Company servants still seem to have done this: of the Bengal wills from 1780 to 1785 preserved in the India Office, one in three contains a bequest to Indian wives or companions or their natural children.

Dalrymple suggests that 'it can safely be assumed that many more kept Indian mistresses without wishing to leave a formal legal record of the fact'. But he adds that 'many wills from the period rather touchingly...(suggest) that ties of great affection and loyalty on both sides were not uncommon at this time (Dalrymple 2003: 34). The wills also show that in many cases the *bibis* achieved a surprising degree of empowerment. A few refer to contracts – something like eighteenth century pre-nuptial agreements – and many women inherited considerable sums and households full of slaves from their English partners on their death.

When Major Thomas Naylor died in 1782, for example, he bequeathed to his companion, Mukmul Patna, forty thousand rupees, a bungalow and garden at Berhampore, a hackery, bullocks, jewels, clothes and all their male and female slaves. The diarist William Hickey started a relationship with 'a lovely Hindustani girl'. What seems to have been at first a simple physical attraction soon became a serious relationship. Jemdanee, as she was called, lived with him, 'respected and admired' by all his friends 'from that day until the day of her death' (Dalrymple 2003: 37). She died in childbirth, giving birth to twins. It is not clear what happened subsequently to the twins; presumably they were brought up in India.

But in some cases at least, the offspring of these relationship were treated in a more ambivalent fashion. The older son of Sir Henry Russell, 1st baronet (1751-1836), who served as a judge in the Calcutta Supreme Court from 1797 to 1813, also named Henry (and later also Sir Henry) Russell (1783-1856), had a liaison with an Indian woman in Hyderabad, which resulted in a child. In his collection of letters are some that relate to this illegitimate daughter[13].

It seems that Henry sent this girl 'home' to England at the same time as he returned with his wife and children; but he sent her on a different ship, and gave her the name 'Mary Wilson' to hide her identity, placed her under the guardianship of his friend from India, Major Robert Pitman, and established a fund for her worth £60 a year. Mary was first sent to a school for girls in Clapham, in London.

In 1834, there was an exchange of letters between Russell and Pitman regarding Mary's possible future, and it was agreed that she should be sent to Devonshire as a governess in the household of the wealthy Mrs Eleanora Savile, mother of ten, to look after four of her children. She knew no-one there, and was very lonely. In 1837, still only a teenager, she had a nervous breakdown, and was sent back to Clapham to recover. In April 1838, Pitman mentions that she was 'much agitated' on the subject of her birth. He explains that

> 'Her enquiries during the two last years have been frequent and to quiet her as far as possible I felt myself obliged to say that whenever circumstances rendered it desirable for her, I should no longer keep her in ignorance. She has vivid recollections of the house in which she passed her early days [the British Residency in Hyderabad, India], the library to which she was occasionally taken and from her description I think also of her father and mother. At her age it is natural she should think deeply on a subject so interesting to her and I hope when you come to England you will agree with me in some means of setting her mind at rest regarding it. It will be satisfactory to you to hear that she has turned out as well as the fondest parent could desire and is in every respect deserving of every possible kindness and consideration that can be shewn to her.'

Russell was equivocal about revealing to Mary the precise circumstances of her birth, and wrote back (from Rome):

> 'With respect to communicating with her the circumstances of her birth, as in all matters, I wish, as I am bound, to do that which may be substantially the best

---

13. www.ourmigrationstory.org.uk/uploads/Correspondence%20between%20Sir%20 Henry%20Russell%20(1783-1852)%20Major%20Robert%20Pitman%20and%20 Mary%20Wilson.pdf – cited by Margot Finn, 'Migrating home: 'mixed children' and the return of the nabobs of India', www.ourmigrationstory.org.uk/oms/migrating-home-the-return-of-the-nabobs-of-british-india.

for her. We will talk the subject over when we meet, which I hope we may in the course of next winter, but although it seems unkind to deny her information on a topic on which she is naturally so solicitous, there are many difficulties in the other course which must be maturely weighed before we encounter them.'

In autumn 1838, Mr William Coxhead, a local Devonshire curate (a junior clergyman in the Anglican church) proposed marriage to 'Mary Wilson', and she accepted his proposal. This was a much more humble marriage partner than Russell expected for his legitimate daughters, but a much more respectable prospect than he had expected for Mary as a 'mixed-race' illegitimate daughter trained as a governess. This proposal however raised many issues. In November, Russell wrote at length to Pitman to set out what he proposed to do. As regards the marriage, he gave his consent. As regards a financial settlement, he explained that

'I am not justified in expecting to be able to assist Mr Coxhead in his preferment [that is, to obtaining a senior appointment, called a 'living', in a parish church]; if the occasion ever did offer itself, it would be as cordially my wish, as it would be my duty, to avail myself of it; but I will do at once what I think I can do prudently for Mary, to enable her to contribute something towards the support of their little establishment. I propose therefore to give her £1000, but that sum I should insist on seeing settled upon her and her children, in the usual way, instead of being sunk, as you justly observe, upon a living....The next point to be considered is when the marriage shall take place. It is important to avoid any delay, by which the prospect of so desirable an establishment might eventually be frustrated; and yet Mr Coxhead, before he marries, should have provided the means of sheltering and maintaining his Wife.'

'On the other topic, which has often been the subject of correspondence between us, namely the telling Mary whose daughter she is, natural as it may be that she should wish to acquire the information, there are many considerations, affecting even her individual happiness, which should make us slow to take so important and irretrievable a step. When we meet I shall probably be able to suggest many reasons to you for the reluctance I feel upon this subject. I cannot help fearing it would open the door to serious embarrassment of many kinds'.

Negotiations over the marriage dragged on for months, much complicated by Henry Russell's refusal to acknowledge that Mary was his daughter. She wrote to Pitman anxiously in September 1839, a few weeks before the marriage, which she hoped he would be willing to attend: 'I trust you will be able to come for every reason in the first place I shall be so glad to see you—and then in the register I see the father's name and profession are put down. I know neither.' It appears that Russell did not reply to her directly, but after negotiations with Pitman, he agreed to make a settlement of £1,200 on Mary, but he resisted Pitman's requests that he acknowledge his paternity.

In a letter to Pitman in October 1839, he explains why:

'For the present I am satisfied on reflection, that we cannot tell Mary, whose daughter she is...[and for] this there are two especial reasons. In the first place, I could not tell her who she is, without at the same time receiving her at least occasionally into my house, and I find, what is perhaps not only natural but proper, that Lady R. [his wife, Lady Russell] would object to this, at all counts while her own daughters are unmarried. In the second place we know as yet but little of Mr Coxhead. He may, and it is reasonable to expect, that he will prove a very respectable man; but if he should, in any particular, turn out to be otherwise, only think with what an encumbrance I should have embarrassed myself, by enabling him to refer to me as his father in law ....If anything on this subject should be said by Mary, I think you might safely tell her that the concealment, which is observed, is as much for her benefit as for any other reason, and that, if circumstances shall ever arise to make it necessary for her to know the secret, it will no longer be withheld from her.'

Henry Russell's acceptance of 'Mary's right to be maintained by him in Britain as a child and adolescent was matched by his determination that she (in sharp contrast to his 'legitimate' daughters) would work for her living as an adult. His refusal to acknowledge publicly that he was her father—or to entertain her in his family home—made her marginal status in his family conspicuously clear.

Henry, like his younger brother, Charles, had been an employee of the British East India Company when he developed the liaison that produced 'Mary Wilson'. One contemporary commentator, Thomas Williamson, remarked, of such young men, that 'in the early part of their career... (they) attach themselves to the women of this country and acquire a liking, or taste, for their society and customs, which soon supersedes every other attraction' (cited in Dalrymple 2003: 35). Dalrymple notes that 'the explorer Richard Burton echoed a similar idea a little later: an Indian mistress taught her companion, he wrote, not only Hindustani grammar, but the syntaxes of native Life' (2003: 35).

On the other hand, as Dalrymple is at pains to emphasise, 'not all the relationships recorded in the wills of the period make such happy reading, and there are many in which the Indian *bibis* are treated with a chilling carelessness: Alexander Crawford, writing his will in Chittagong in 1782, goes into extravagant details as to how he wants his executors to care for his dogs and horses (referring to them by name). After several pages of this sort of thing, he adds, almost as an afterthought: 'to my girl, I desire that two thousand rupees be given for her care of my children provided that she places them under your charge without further trouble'.

Also, judging by the wills they left, many Englishmen were serial philanderers, moving on from one partner after another, often at speed, while a substantial number kept two or more *bibis* simultaneously, limited only perhaps by the expense involved. Thomas Williamson writes of one Company official who kept no fewer than sixteen concubines; and when asked what he did with them all, replied: 'Oh, I just give them a little rice and let them run around', which even as a joke, likening them to chickens, is not very amusing.

From 1786, however, under the new Governor General, Lord Cornwallis, legislation was brought in excluding the children of British men who had Indian wives from employment by the Company. An order was passed banning the orphans of British soldiers from travelling to England for their education, so qualifying for service in the Company army. In 1791, an order was issued that no-one with an Indian parent could be employed by the civil military or marine branches of the Company. In 1795, further legislation was issued explicitly disqualifying anyone not descended from European parents on both sides from serving in the Company's armies – except as pipers, drummers, bandsmen and farriers.

One consequence of this was that the number of Indian *bibis* mentioned in wills and inventories began to decline: while between 1780 and 1785, *bibis* appear in one in three wills, between 1805 and 1810, the ratio is down to one in four, by 1830 it is one in six, and by mid-century they have all but disappeared. The second edition of Thomas Williamson's *East India Vade Mecum* (1825) had all references to *bibis* completely removed. However, what was true of Calcutta and the three Presidency towns, was not necessarily the case outside; if a young man was posted to Hyderabad or Lucknow, or one of the more lively Rajput courts, like Udaipur, he would by necessity and probably by preference have drawn his circle of friends and companions, including his sexual partners, from the Indian society all around him.

As we have seen, after the Anglo-Nepal War, as the Indian Army began increasingly to recruit men from the hills to special 'Gurkha' regiments, the number of women accompanying them also began to increase, whether as wives or companions or simply in casual liaisons, and as camp followers. It was not only the 'native' rank and file, and non-commissioned officers, who brought with them their women-folk, or found mistresses or temporary sexual relief with prostitutes, many of whom may also have been camp followers. The British soldiers also were able to take advantage of the availability of these or of local women, on a temporary or, sometimes, more long-lasting basis, sometimes unofficially, but also sometimes with official sanction.

The officers of the new Gurkha units like those of the British regiments were always British. The senior officers were usually married and some too their wives with them on campaign, as we shall see. But the junior officers were less likely to have wives, and these young men often took a mistress. These were not always Indian women. Indeed, 'Gorkhali' women were considered particularly attractive by many of the British officers, and were kept as mistresses or *bibis*. and it seems that certainly in the Gurkha battalions of the Indian Army, the *bibi* was likely to have been a 'Gorkhali' woman.

Farwell comments that in the early 19th century, many officers 'kept a delightful Gurkhali mistress in the *bibi-khana* (lady's house)'. In fact, Richard Burton, who wrote of his experiences in the 'Bombay Army' in the mid-1840s, and himself kept a mistress in Baroda, recalled that:

> 'the Bibi (white woman) was at that time rare in India; the result was the triumph of the Bubu (coloured sister). I found every officer in the corps, more or less provided for with one of these helpmates. We boys naturally followed suit: but I had to suffer the protestations of the Portuguese padre, who had taken upon himself the cure and charge of my soul and was like a hen who had hatched a duckling. I had a fine opportunity of studying the pros and cons of the Bubu system... (The Bubu) is all but indispensable to the student, and she teaches him not only the Hindostani grammar, but the syntaxes of native Life'.

> 'She keeps house for him, never allowing him to save money, or, if possible, to waste it. She keeps the servants in order. She has an infallible recipe to prevent maternity, especially if her tenure of office depends on such compact. She looks after him in sickness, and is one of the best of nurses, and, as it is not good for man to live alone, she makes him a manner of home' (cited in Fawn Brodie, *The Devil Drives*, p.51-2).

Not all were as faithful to their local companions or *bibis* as Burton suggests. Anton Gill, for example, cites Edward Sellon, an officer in the Indian Army at around the same time as Burton, oddly described by Gill as 'an anthropologist', describes how he

> 'now commenced a regular course of fucking with native women. They understand in perfection all arts and wiles of love, are capable of gratifying any tastes, and in face and figure are unsurpassed by any women in the world... It is impossible to describe the enjoyment I have had in the arms of these sirens' (1995: 37)

⊛ ⊛ ⊛

CHAPTER 7

Labour Overseas

In almost all cases, throughout the 19th and early 20th century, women from the Gorkhali state and subsequently from Nepal and adjacent parts of north India travelling, working and living abroad remained on the Indian subcontinent. As we have seen, they may well have gone as far afield as modern day Pakistan and Afghanistan to the west, Burma to the east and to the far south in India. But it was certainly rare that they went 'overseas'. Even for men, travel across 'the dark waters' was officially forbidden by Hindu religion and a special dispensation was required, involving a ritual (*puja*) - of *pani patiya* - performed by a Brahmin priest, for them to do so in the first place and for them to be 're-instated' to regain their caste on return (as we have seen above).

Although the Gurkha regiments tended not to take their women folk with them on the few overseas campaigns in which they were involved during the 19th century, there were forms of employment which did take Nepalis, both men and women, overseas, one of which was indentured labour. We have little information about female indentured labour, but we can occasionally catch a glimpse of a Nepali woman among the mass of 'Indian' men and smaller numbers of 'Indian' women caught up in this process, which would take them eventually half-way across the world to work like slaves in the West Indies and elsewhere.

The earliest example of 'Indian' indentured labour is from 18 January 1826, when the Government of the French Indian Ocean island of Réunion laid down terms for the introduction of Indian labourers to the colony. Each person was required to appear before a magistrate and declare that they were going voluntarily. This agreement was known as *girmit* and it outlined a period of five years labour in the colonies with pay of ₹8 (11¢ US) per month and rations, provided labourers had been transported from Pondicherry and Karaikal.

When, after slavery was abolished by the British and the slaves working in the West Indies and elsewhere were emancipated in the 1830s, the plantation owners began to seek replacement workers. At first, they tried the use of emancipated slaves, families from Ireland, Germany and Malta and Portuguese from Madeira. All these efforts failed to satisfy the labour needs of the colonies due to high mortality of the new arrivals and their reluctance to continue working at the end of their contract. Then they turned to indentured labour, and the importation of 'coolies' from India.

'Coolies' - a word that originated in India (Tamil - *kuli* = wages) to refer to a day-labourer - was the term they used for the indentured labourers they enlisted. Ultimately, over the course of eight decades, well over 1 million and possibly as many as 2 million 'coolies' were shipped from India to more than a dozen colonies across the globe. This resulted in the development of a large Indian diaspora in the Caribbean (especially in British Guiana, Trinidad and Jamaica), in Natal (South Africa) and in Réunion, Mauritius, Sri Lanka, Myanmar, Malaysia, Singapore, Surinam and Fiji.

1834 marks the beginning of the arrival of indentured labourers in Mauritius. That year, on 1 August, a vessel named *Sarah* berthed in the Port Louis depot – on its board, the very first 39 indentured labourers from South India. On 2 November, the *Atlas* arrived with an additional 36 'Indian' labourers, most of whom were this time from Bihar and were destined to the sugar estate of Antoinette, in the region of Piton. They had embarked in the port of Bhawaneepore, in Calcutta, next to Ghanta Ghar or the Clock Tower. The voyage from India to Mauritius had taken about 40 days. Today, 2 November is a national holiday in Mauritius, marking 'the arrival of indentured labourers'.

On 10 September 1834, 36 'hill coolies' of the Dhangar caste (originally from the hills of Bihar in eastern India who were then living in Calcutta) signed a five-year labour contract with George Charles Arbuthnot of Hunter-Arbuthnot & Company, a major British trading company in Mauritius. The contract was written in Bengali. They were under a five-year contract and had to work either in the sugar cane fields or the factories. Because the indentured labourers were recruited and employed through a contract, and were thus, in theory at least, volunteers, they were referred to as *girmitia*, meaning 'terms of agreement'.

Thirty of the 'signatories' were men and six were women. Indeed, throughout the many decades that indentured labour from India was contracted to work in

Mauritius, women always constituted a significant minority, travelling to a new life either as a male indentured labourer's wife or as a single woman. Photographs of indentured labourers to Mauritius include a significant minority of women. It is possible, although we cannot be sure, that some at least of these women were originally from Nepal. They, like the men, dreamed of better life conditions and fled the numerable trials and tribulations they faced at home.

The salary for the males was five rupees per month but for the females only four rupees per month. The *sirdar* (overseer) was paid ten rupees per month and the assistant *sirdar* eight rupees per month. They all received six months' pay in advance before boarding the Atlas. Hunter Arbuthnot & Company would pay for their journey from Calcutta to Port Louis. As a result, one rupee would be deducted from their monthly wages for the return passage to India, if they wished to return; and they were promised food, clothing, lodging and medical care. The funds saved through the monthly deduction (60 rupees) were returned to them if they chose to stay in Mauritius. The trip back to Calcutta cost £3.45 shillings, to Madras £2.19 shillings and to Bombay (Mumbai) £3.18 shillings.

The labourers worked from sunrise to sunset, six days a week and they were also required to perform light duties on Sundays. Thus, they worked side by side with the slaves of Belle Alliance in the sugar cane fields. In addition to their monthly wages the men each received two pounds of rice, half a pound of 'dhal', two ounces of coconut oil, two ounces of mustard oil and salted fish. At the end of year, their employer would provide them with a shirt, two sheets, a jacket, a cap, a '*dhoti*' – or a total of eight yards of 'kaliko' - and two covers. The ration for the women and children was smaller.

The first small 'wave' of migrants would swell with the abolition of slavery and the need for the British to recruit workers for the sugar cane factories and fields. In 1834, the Indian indentured labourers made up less than 4 per cent of the colony's total population but by 1860, they constituted more than 66 per cent. This is because, between 1834 and 1910, around half a million (451,796, of which 346, 036 were men and 105, 760 women) were brought to Mauritius from India. During that same period, around 300,000 (294, 257) labourers remained in the colony, while 157, 539 (128,761 men and 28,778 women) returned mostly to India (and Nepal), with some migrating to Natal in South Africa, British Guyana, Trinidad and Fiji.

Soon, the recruitment and deployment of indentured labour would become more strictly controlled and regulated. The British East India Company's

Regulations of 1837 laid down specific conditions for the dispatch of Indian labour from Calcutta. The would-be emigrant and the emigration agent were required to appear before an officer designated by the Government of British India, with a written statement of the terms of the contract. The length of service was to be five years, renewable for further five-year terms. The emigrant was to be returned at the end of their service to the port of departure. Each emigrant vessel was required to conform to certain standards of space, diet etc. and to carry a medical officer. This scheme was shortly afterwards extended to Madras.

The first ship to take indentured labourers to the New World, the *Whitby*, sailed from Calcutta for British Guyana on 13 January 1838, and arrived in Berbice on 5 May 1838. So, on 5 May 1838, the very year of final slave emancipation (Abolition of Slavery) in the British West Indies, a small batch of 396 Indian immigrants popularly known as the Gladstone Coolies landed at Highbury, Berbice in British Guyana aboard the *Whitby* (and the *Hesperus*). This was the effective beginning of the indenture system, which was not abolished until 1917, by which time a total of some 240,000 indentured workers from India had come to Guyana.

The term 'Gladstone Coolies' requires some explanation. On January 4, 1836, Sir John Gladstone, an absentee proprietor, merchant and slave owner, and father of England's future Prime Minister, William Ewart Gladstone, wrote a letter to Gillanders, Arbuthnot and Company, a Calcutta firm recruiting and exporting labourers to Mauritius. He asked for 100 able-bodied Indians on contracts for between 5 and 7 years. Gladstone's letter detailing the attractive features of plantation life highly exaggerated the truth. The letter promised light work, comfortable dwellings, abundance of food, legal protection, free education, free medical attendance and religious freedom. The letter skilfully omitted the penalties for non-completion of work or for other infringements of the immigration ordinances.

The firm envisaged no difficulty in procuring such labourers, 'the natives being perfectly ignorant of the place they agree to go to, or the length of the voyage they are undertaking'. This reply paved the way for the fraud and deceit which permeated the recruiting system. According to John Scoble, the vigilant secretary of the Anti–Slavery Society, it permitted 'every scoundrel in India to kidnap and inveigle into contracts for five years, in a distant part of the world, the ignorant and inoffensive Hindoo!' The stage was now set for Indian indentured workers to labour under conditions bordering on slavery.

As soon as the new system of emigration of labour became known, a campaign similar to the anti-slavery campaign sprang up in Britain and India. On 1 August 1838, a committee was appointed to inquire into the export of Indian labour. On 29 May 1839, overseas manual labour was prohibited and any person effecting such emigration was liable to a 200 Rupee fine or three months in jail. The planters in Mauritius and the Caribbean worked hard to overturn the ban, while the anti-slavery committee worked just as hard to uphold it. The Government of the East India Company finally capitulated under intense pressure from planters and their supporters; and on 2 December 1842, the Indian Government officially permitted emigration from Calcutta, Bombay and Madras to Mauritius.

In these early years, we have no indication of how many women, if indeed any women at all were involved, migrated overseas as indentured labour. But, as we shall see, as the system developed and the numbers of migrants grew, women became increasingly involved, and at least some of these may well have come from Nepal (as we shall see).

❁ ❁ ❁

CHAPTER 8

The Invasion of Afghanistan

In the meanwhile, the demand for soldiers to help control the territories and the populations under Company rule in India was also continuing to grow; and several major campaigns were undertaken by the Indian Army, which now comprised a number of Gurkha battalions, amounting to several thousand men. For, after the establishment of the first 'Gurkha' battalions, the British army in India continued to recruit hill men from Nepal and from Garhwal, and the 'Goorkas', or 'Ghoorkhas', as they were usually called, served in a number of major campaigns during the 1830s and 1840s, notably in the First Afghan War.

Even before the death of Ranjit Singh, the British had looked with interest and ambition at Afghanistan and now they prepared for a campaign to set Shah Shujah back on the throne in Kabul from which he had earlier been ousted. In 1838, Lord Auckland, Governor-General of India, launched 'the army of the Indus' on an invasion of Afghanistan. He himself travelled all the way from Calcutta, first by barge pulled by a steamer to Benares and then by road up through the Punjab to the newly established hill station of Simla - across the 'famine struck plains of Hindustan, from the Kingdom of Avadh to the British controlled North West Provinces' (Dalrymple 2013: 109).

On his leisurely journey 'up the country', he was accompanied by his two unmarried sisters, his political secretary, Macnaughten, and various other viceregal officials, attachés, wives and babies, as well as Macnaughten's wife and her entourage. One of his sisters (Emily) noted, as they prepared to set off, that, in addition to the two lines of troops, there were '850 camels, 140 elephants, several hundred horses, the Body Guard, the regiment that escorts us, and the camp followers. They are about 12,000 in all' (Dalrymple 2013: 110). And that was just the Governor General's establishment.

The army of the Indus itself was the usual mixture of British regiments and Company troops; among the latter were the 5th Native Infantry, the 27th, the 35th, and the 37th. In addition, there were the troops seconded to the service of Shah Shujah (the 44th Native Infantry, the 49th and the 54th) as well as the Shah's own troops, which included the 4th Regiment ('Goorkhas')[14]. From cantonments all over north west India they came, at the tail-end of the monsoon. Dalrymple comments that 'in Meerut and Roorkee, the cantonments were awash with mud as the Company sepoys packed up their kit and began the march up the Grand Trunk Road towards Karnal and Ferozepur, their bedraggled wives and mistresses streaming through the quagmire behind them' (2013: 147).

By now, the Army of the Indus consisted of around a thousand Europeans and 14,000 Company *sepoys* - excluding the 6,000 irregulars hired by Shuja – accompanied by no fewer than 38,000 'Indian' camp followers, many of whom were women and some of whom were children. William Dalrymple remarks that, during August and September 1838, 'every day, the scale of the invasion and the degree of British participation gradually increased until a full 20,000 British troops were committed: the largest military operation undertaken by Company forces for two decades' (2013: 141).

The army did not travel light. The baggage was carried on over 30,000 camels, and Dalrymple remarks that 'even junior officers travelled with as many as forty servants – ranging from cooks and sweepers to bearers and water carriers' (2013: 153). As they marched west, having crossed the Indus into the dry lands the salt marshes between Shikapur and the Bolan Pass, the troops suffered severely from the heat, in their tight-fitting woollen uniforms, and from thirst. But 'the poor heavily-laden camp followers, some carrying infants, were in a more pitiable state still, and the children's cries were heart rending' (Dalrymple 2013: 159).

Also, they were increasingly the subject of robberies and murders on a daily basis by local tribes of the area, who looked on the vulnerable columns as fair game. Neville Chamberlain, a young cavalry officer on his first campaign, saw his first casualty a week after leaving Shikapur: 'one woman lay – poor creature – on the edge of the water, with her long black hair floating in the ripples of the clear stream'. Her throat had been cut from ear to ear. The unburied dead were left rotting on the road.

---

14.   Evidently, Shah Shujah had also recruited Nepalis as 'Gurkhas', soldiers in his cause.

As they traversed the Bolan Pass, 'the Baluch tribesmen did not delay to snipe and plunder'. Thousands of pack animals, bullocks, camels, horses, elephants and their loads were lost. Beyond Bolan lay Quetta, and then a second difficult pass, the Khojak, where there was very little water, and what there was was filthy and putrid. Food had by this stage virtually run out among the camp followers: some 'were to be seen gouging carrion and picking grains of corn from the excrement of animals' reported one officer. Before the army had fought a single Afghan, it was already a wreck (Dalrymple 2013: 164).

Eventually, on 25 April 1839, the Army of the Indus reached Kandahar, where it remained, recovering, until 27 June, when it started out again, for Kabul, leaving a garrison of some 3,000 behind. It was a 200-mile march to Ghazni, which was reached on 20 July. The fortress there was well defended, but it was captured within 72 hours with very few losses. The army marched on towards Kabul, which it reached on 7 August, eight months after leaving Ferozepur. Shah Shujah was restored to the throne and it seemed that Afghanistan was now effectively under British control.

In Kabul itself, the army sought to consolidate its position by building a cantonment just outside the walled city to provide a barracks for the troops and a veritable horde – more than 12,000 - of camp-followers. Others were housed in lodgings within the city, and many more in a camp out on the Kohisan Road; while some troops were billeted in the Bala Hisar. This was necessary, for not only were several of the British officers accompanied by their wives and families, but the 'native' troops (including the Gurkhas in the service of Shah Shujah himself) had also been encouraged to bring their families – including women and children – and these numbered many thousands. The 37th Native Infantry alone had 5,000 registered camp-followers[15].

But there were restrictions on building a properly defensible new fortress in Kabul and the cantonment for the troops and camp followers was poorly designed, with an extended perimeter wall, a low, easily escaladed rampart and a narrow ditch, built outside the city in a fertile plain. Furthermore, the stores were located in an old fort, detached from both the main cantonment and the Bala Hisar, with only a hundred or so *sepoys* under a subaltern officer to protect them. Several observers, including Lady Florentina Sale, the wife of 'Fighting Bob' General Robert Sale, remarked on the poor placing and construction of the

---

15. According to Lady Sale (Sale 2002: 48).

cantonment and indeed, the inadequacy of the whole defensive system on which the army depended (see Dalrymple 2013: 221-223).

All remained reasonably quiet, however, for the next two years, and the movement of British troops between India and Afghanistan proceeded unhindered - largely because British Envoy Sir William Macnaughten was paying the Khyberis an annual toll for the safe movement of the Company's troops. In the meanwhile, the Army of the Indus was settling in. Several officers took local women as mistresses and some even married Afghan women; the British political officer Alexander Burnes, who, it was alleged, had brought his own troops of Kashmiri women, who were 'in his service', was also rumoured to have an Afghan mistress with whom he took baths where 'two memsahibs, also his lovers, would join them' (Dalrymple 2013: 225).

The troops took advantage of the flourishing prostitution industry that 'quickly sprang up to service the needs of all the single soldiers lodged around the town' (Dalrymple 2013: 223). Kabul already had a discreet red-light district in the quarter occupied by Indian musicians and dancers close to the walls of the Bala Hisar. But there 'were not nearly enough Indian *rundis* around to cope with the demand created by a garrison of 4,500 sepoys and 15,500 camp followers, and a growing number of Afghan women seem to have made themselves available for a short but profitable ride into the cantonment' (Darlymple 2013: 224-5). This was the source of growing concern on the part of the Afghans.

One senior leader and former Governor of Peshawar wrote in the summer of 1840 to his half-brother: 'I cannot tell you what oppression is committed by the Firangis. Some of the people have publicly turned Christians and others have turned prostitute. Grain has got very dear. May God turn this accursed set out of the country as their appearance has discarded both religion and morality' (cited by Dalrymple 2013: 237). In July, the local clerics began to omit the name of Shah Shuja at Friday prayers, on the grounds that the real rulers were the Kafirs (unbelievers).

The security situation across the country as a whole deteriorated throughout the rest of the year, and support for the ousted Amir of Afghanistan began to grow. British Envoy Sir William Macnaughten, who had been paying the Ghilzai and Khyber tribal leaders an annual subsidy or toll for the safe movement of the Company's troops, decided to end this payment in the spring of 1841 and ordered the return to India of one of the two brigades that had helped maintain the increasingly unpopular Shah Shujah in power (a 50 per cent reduction of his occupying force).

Allen notes that 'when the troops of the withdrawing brigade and the thousands of native camp-followers who accompanied them began to retire through the Khyber defile, they were blocked and pinned down for two weeks by Shinwari marksmen furious at the loss of their toll fees' (2001: 40). Many of the women and children who comprised the bulk of the camp followers of this force apparently perished. The decision to reduce the subsidies for the sake of a relatively small cost, was arguably the single biggest misjudgment of MacNaughten's career – it would have widespread and long lasting adverse consequences.

Despite this, the British dug in, and several senior officers in Kabul were joined by their wives, one of whom was the indomitable Lady Sale, wife of 'Fighting Bob', who arrived in the summer of 1841 with a grand piano and her youngest daughter, Alexandrina – who was soon being courted by half the officers in the cantonment. Another was MacNaughten's wife Frances, who brought her cat and parakeet and five attendant *ayahs*. In early October, however, 'Fighting Bob' Sale and his brigade of the 13th Light Infantry was ordered back to India.

The advance guard left Kabul on 9 October 1841, but was ambushed on the road only 15 miles out. The rest of the brigade was sent off in support, but they were also attacked and suffered numerous casualties, including the General himself. They struggled on, however, with 'Fighting Bob' directing his forces from a palanquin, despite a shattered leg, but within a few days they lost over 250 men, and their position was worsening fast. Eventually, on 12 November, Sales' brigade reached Jalalabad and took the town. They then came under siege and were unable to contemplate returning to Kabul.

In the meanwhile, less than a month after the departure of General Sale, it became increasingly apparent that a mass uprising was imminent across the country, including in the areas surrounding Kandahar and Kabul. So certain was he that his small garrison of Gurkhas at Charikar would be massacred, that Eldred Pottinger rode back to Kabul to ask for reinforcements. He was unsuccessful. MacNaughten appeared simply to be ignoring the rapidly deteriorating situation for which his own actions were at least in part responsible. In Kabul itself, however, at the very beginning of November, there was an outbreak of violence within the city, which rapidly spread.

By mid-day on 2 November 1841, the whole city was in commotion. Sir Alexander Burnes was one of the earlier casualties, having been, it seems, a specific target of the angry Afghans. The inadequacy of the British military defensive preparations soon became clear, as the forts and store houses surrounding the cantonment came under attack. In the Bala Hisar, where he and his own troops were stationed, Shah Shuja, who had already sent some of his troops into Kabul to support the British, was baffled by the failure of MacNaughten to counter-attack. By early afternoon, however, MacNaughten had decided to retreat rather than counter-attack, despite having some 5,000 troops, ample horse artillery and a year's store of ammunition at his disposal. Abandoning the Mission Compound he withdrew his civil headquarters into the cantonment, where General Elphinstone ordered the guard along the walls to be doubled and counselled a 'wait and see' policy. Lady Sale remarked in her diary that 'all was confusion and indecision'.

On the morning of 3 November, Eldred Pottinger was becoming very concerned about his prospects. With only a hundred or so Gurkhas in a small fortified enclosure some 60 miles north of Kabul near the British barracks at Charikar, his position was already threatened by growing numbers of hostile tribesmen. The following night, he and his men secretly moved to their main base at Charikar, where 750 Gurkhas and around 200 women and children were stationed. In the meanwhile, the numbers of hostile tribesmen continued to grow – to perhaps 20,000 – and the siege of Charikar began.

Two British officers were able to make their escape and eventually reach Kabul, but the remainder, including the garrison commander, were killed, some of them apparently by their own men, who felt they had been betrayed. It is not known precisely what happened to the remainder of the garrison at Charikar, or to the women and children who so 'encumbered' them, but presumably they were captured or killed. Lady Sale wife of Sir Robert Sale and a member of the officers' wives contingent in Kabul remarks that the site of the cantonment at Charikar had been badly chosen: 'in addition to there being no water, which of itself rendered the site unfit for a military post, their position was completely commanded on two sides by the enemy, who, having cut off their supply of water from above, gave the defenders no rest by day or night'. (Sale 2002: 45)

She notes that 'added to these trying circumstances, the garrison were encumbered with their wives and children, who had been encouraged to come up from Hindostan in great numbers. It is affirmed that they did so by permission of Lord Auckland, it being supposed that they would have no wish to quit the country (Afghanistan) with their families settled along with them' (Sale 2002: 45). The idea that if soldiers had their wives and families accompanying them, this would increase their commitment to the army and reduce the threat of desertion, was later to be much discussed in the context of Gurkha 'settlements' or regimental homes in India. But the problem of camp followers impeding the troops when on campaign was widely recognised.

At Charikar, as in Kabul, there were contingents in the service of the Shah, including his own 4th Regiment of 'Gurkhas'. Lady Sale refers explicitly to their poor morale, noting that 'the Ghoorkhas...harassed by the enemy and encumbered by their families...sank into a state of perfect apathy'[16], while some of the Punjabi (Sikh) artillerymen actually deserted to the enemy. It was a similar story all over eastern Afghanistan; the British forces were unprepared and overwhelmed as the region rose in revolt. In Kabul, in the meanwhile, the siege of the forts containing the commissariat stores around the cantonment was intensifying; but no troops were sent in support, although there were 5,000 armed sepoys in the cantonment, 'idly awaiting orders' (Dalrymple 2013: 318).

The Afghans eventually took and pillaged the commissariat stores. Lady Sale commented in her diary that 'it was very like the scenes depicted in the battles of the Crusades. The enemy rushed on and drove our men before them like a flock of sheep with a wolf at their tails' (Holmes 2001: 304). One group, under Colin Mackenzie, moving under cover of night, managed to reach the cantonment. This group included wounded soldiers, woman and children, as well as fighting men. Mackenzie recorded how 'many poor women, contrived to slip out with loads of their little property on their shoulders, making their children walk, whose cries added to the danger of discovery' (cited in Dalrymple 2013: 321).

He mentions in particular, a beautiful young 'Gurkha' girl: 'a picture of life, spirit and energy'; but he never saw her again and feared that she was either killed or taken prisoner on the night march. He himself, bringing up the rear of his little group, found himself alone and under fire, 'with a *chaprasi* and two *sowars* in the midst of the wailing crowd of women and children'. They were then attacked, but he managed to get away, on horseback, leaving many behind, and reached the cantonment. 'During the night' he records, 'many stragglers of my party, principally followers, dropped in. From first to last I had about a dozen killed' (cited in Dalrymple 2013: 322). Later, he was praised for having brought

16. Sale 2002: 45-46.

back 'all his men and the crowd of women and children safe'; but it seems that those who reached safety did so more by luck than anything Mackenzie did.

The troops were now reduced to three days' food inside the cantonment, and urged their commander, Lord Elphinstone, to take the offensive. He, however, together with the other senior officers, seems to have virtually given up. Although there remained sufficient ammunition to withstand a twelve-month siege, Elphinstone decided that they were running out of ammunition. He warned MacNaughten that some arrangement with the enemy might be required. Macnaughten sent a message to General Sale at Jalalabad asking him to march post haste to Kabul to take over command. But Sale was still surrounded by Afghan forces and, even though Lady Sale and his daughter were in Kabul, he felt he could not risk attempting to break out. The garrison in Kabul would have to fend for itself.

On 15 November, Eldred Pottinger and his colleague John Haughton, broke through the ring of besiegers; they were the only survivors of the 750-strong Gurkha garrison of Charikar. They made it because they had horses; and only a handful of their men managed to escape and follow them. Most of the rest were killed, but the 300 or so wounded, who were left behind, and any of the soldiers or their wives captured alive, were distributed among the tribal leaders, and sold as slaves. Among those captured and enslaved was the Gurkha Havildar Moti Ram who, uniquely, left an account of the whole affair (which is partly recounted by Dalrymple – 2013: 315-316, 329-330)[17].

The siege of the cantonment continued as winter deepened and by the beginning December the outlook appeared quite bleak; the Afghan forces were now estimated at over 50,000, outnumbering the British garrison by more than ten to one. The senior officers and the British Envoy – Elphinstone, Shelton and MacNaughten – were barely on speaking terms; and there was no leadership. Eventually, Macnaughten agreed to meet the Afghan leader, Akbar Khan, to discuss terms of a surrender. Eventually, on 11 December, an agreement was reached: the British were to make a substantial payment to Akbar Khan, and then would be allowed to withdraw from Kabul three days later (on 14

---

17. Moti Ram was captured not far short of Kabul, but was released on professing to be a Muslim; then, as he headed off, this time on the road to Jalalabad, he was captured again, but protected from those who wanted to kill him. His 'personal narrative' was eventually published as an appendix to an account of the siege and fall of Charikot by Colonel John Haughton, who survived the war (Haughton 1878).

December) with a guarantee of safety. Shah Shuja could choose either to leave with the British or remain in Kabul as a private citizen. Shah Shuja, however, was not part of this agreement.

14 December came and went. Akbar Khan increased his demands. MacNaughten now urged his military colleagues to abandon the 'agreement' and come out fighting; but they opposed this and seemed committed to surrendering and marching out to safety. MacNaughten continued to try negotiation as the way forward, approaching other tribal leaders with a view to forging an agreement behind Akbar Khan's back; but when Akbar Khan invited him to a final meeting, on 23 December, he accused MacNaughten of betraying the agreement and first shot him, then had him beheaded and dragged through the streets of Kabul.

Cowed by this, Elphinstone agreed to Akbar Khan's demand that the British now evacuate the area and return to India. Consequently, on 6th January 1842, with snow a foot thick, some 4,500 British troops, together with some 12,000 non-combatants (men, women and children), marched out of Kabul. Lady Sale describes how the contingent was 'perfectly disorganised, nearly every man paralysed with cold, so as to be scarcely able to hold his musket or move', and how, even as they left the cantonment they were attacked, and 'the whole road was covered with men, women and children, lying down in the snow to die' (Lady Sale's diary 2002: 97).

The column had barely travelled more than a few miles when 'the officers of the rear-guard report that the road is strewn with baggage; and that numbers of men, women and children are left on the road-side to perish' (ibid 2002: 99). Not only Akbar Khan's own forces, but tribesmen from every area they passed through, took part in the harassment of the column as it retreated towards Jalalabad. It was said that even Afghan women and children hacked down the helpless British soldiers and butchered them in the snow. The fate of the camp-followers was equally dismal.

On 8 January, Lady Sale records that '500 of our regular troops, and about 2,500 of the camp followers, are killed' (2002: 107); on 10th January, only two days later, she concludes that 'about 12,000 persons have perished!' and refers to 'the remnant' as 'about 4,000 people of all descriptions' (2002: 115-116). By 12th January, the numbers were down to around 2,000 (2002: 122) and on 13th January, as the remnant of the column moved towards Gundamuk, 'the force now consisted of twenty officers...fifty men of the 44th, six of the horse artillery, and four or five Sipahees[18]. Amongst the whole there were but twenty muskets; 300 camp followers still continued with them' (2002: 125). She notes that 'eighteen officers and about fifty men were killed at the final struggle at Gundamuk' (2002: 126).

The retreat was particularly hard on the women, including the wives of the officers, most of whom were travelling in camel panniers which were mixed up with the baggage column. Lady Sale describes how they struggled to survive, often having the abandon their camels and walk through the snow, with their children (Holmes 2001: 305). Apart from a small group of married British officers and their families (including Lady Sale), who were given protection by Akbar Khan, and a tiny group (of one British officer and seven or eight men) from the main column who were taken alive and eventually returned, only one person survived the retreat to reach Jalalabad – Dr William Brydon of the Company's Army Medical Service, seconded to Shah Shujah's service in his 6th Regiment.

All of the rest were killed or captured on the way. Some of the women taken, like the Persian widow of Sergeant Deane, were taken by force and married to Afghan tribesmen; others, like Mrs Wade, the wife of another sergeant, decided to join the Afghans voluntarily. It was not until 19 January 1842 that the women were able to wash properly, for the second time only since leaving Kabul six weeks before. Lady Sale re-joined her husband shortly afterwards, only for him to be killed in 1845, fighting the Sikhs.

❀ ❀ ❀

---

18.   *Sepoys* or 'native soldiers'.

CHAPTER 9

The Anglo-Sikh Wars

Following the death of Ranjit Singh in 1839, even more Nepalis and others had trekked to Lahore to join up; and the Sikh army grew considerably, in part as a result of the recruitment of non-Sikhs, from around 29,000 at the time of his death to over 80,000 by 1845. It is highly likely that some of those Nepalis who volunteered were accompanied to the Sikh army barracks in Lahore by their womenfolk, but we have no information on this.

The death of Ranjit Singh was followed also by a struggle for power between his sons and divisions within the army itself. The British saw the combination of political division and military expansion as a potential threat to its own territories, and the Company also began to build up its military strength, particularly in the regions adjacent to the Punjab, establishing a military cantonment at Ferozepur, only a few miles from the Sutlej River which marked the frontier between British-ruled India and the Punjab. In 1843, they conquered and annexed Sindh, to the south of the Punjab,

After mutual demands and accusations between the Sikh Durbar and the East India Company, diplomatic relations were broken off, and the Company army commanded by Sir Hugh Gough, the Commander in Chief of the Bengal Army, began marching towards Ferozepur, where a division was already stationed. The Company forces consisted of formations of the Bengal Army, with usually one British unit to every three or four Bengal infantry or cavalry units. When, in December 1845, units of the Sikh army crossed the Sutlej, the Company immediately declared war on the Sikh State – to initiate the first Anglo-Sikh War.

The British recognised that the Sikh forces constituted a formidable opposition. Trained by French and Italian officers, 'the Sikh army was the most efficient, the hardest to overcome, that we have ever faced in India' (Gough

& Innes 1986: 43). It was also the case that 'the backbone of the Indian army consisted of the British troops; but, unfortunately, there were very few of them and too much reliance was placed in those days on the sepoys' (ibid 1986: 70).

As usual, the 'native' troops were accompanied by the baggage train and numerous camp followers. At Ferozapore, for example, the 63rd Regiment Native Infantry occupied the entrenchment 'into which all the ladies, women, children and sick... were sent' (ibid 1986: 84); while at Ludhiana, the barracks were blown down in a violent storm one night, as a result of which 80 men, women and children were killed and 135 were seriously injured (ibid 1986: 133). The Indian army included the two 'Goorkha' regiments, the Nussuree and the Sirmoor, the former amounting to 586 men and the latter to 781. We cannot be sure, but it is likely that these units also had their complement of camp followers, including women and children.

In fighting around Mudki and Ferozapore, both sides suffered heavy losses and the result was inconclusive. On Christmas Day, the Governor-General of India issued a proclamation encouraging desertion from the Sikh ranks, directed particularly at the non-Sikh elements in the Sikh army; but we have no information as to how successful this ploy was. Another battle took place on 26 January 1846 at Aliwal, which was lost by the Sikhs. A final battle took place some two weeks later on 10 February at Sobraon, by which time the British army had been reinforced with new troops and with supplies.

The Gurkha units, including the Nussuree (Nasiri) or 1st Gurkha Rifles and the 6th Sirmoor or 2nd Gurkha Rifles, took part in these battles, at Aliwal and Sobraon as well as at Bhudaiwal, on the British side. 'At Aliwal... the two Goorkha regiments, not yet enrolled among the regular regiments of infantry, much distinguished themselves ... particularly in the last two engagements and were specially mentioned by Sir Hugh George at Sobraon" (Gough & Innes 1986: 119). Five Gurkha infantrymen won the Indian Order of Merit in these encounters. The 1st Gurkhas were awarded two battle honours for their involvement in the Battle of Aliwal. There were also, doubtless, soldiers from Nepal, Garhwal and elsewhere fighting with the Sikh forces, about whom we know much less.

Defeated as much by intrigue among their leaders and lack of support – some simply fled the field - the Sikh soldiers fought heroically but desperately and were defeated. Undoubtedly, there were not only Sikhs on the Sikh side, but also men from what we can now call Nepal. When migration from Nepal to take up service in the Sikh army developed on such a scale, it is probable that some at least of those who volunteered were accompanied by their wives to the barracks in Lahore. We know little of the detail of women's involvement in the Sikh Army, but it seems highly likely that they accompanied the troops as camp followers on their campaigns.

In early 1848, when Diwan Mulraj Chopra, the governor of Multan (200 miles south west of Lahore) refused to pay his dues and resigned from his position, a military expedition, consisting of about 1,400 Sikh soldiers, a Gurkha regiment of some 500 infantrymen, a troop of some 700 cavalry and six guns with eight artillerymen, was sent, under two junior British officers, to escort a replacement, Khan Singh, to Multan. The two officers were murdered and the escort, having failed to defend them, largely deserted. Allen remarks that 'this is the only instance in the course of the long relationship between the British and the Gurkhas in which the Gurkha troops (albeit in the service of the Sikh Durbar) deserted their British officers – and it is an episode few historians of the alliance have cared to mention' (Allen 2000: 149-50).

Within a short time the Sikh troops joined in open rebellion. Governor General of India, Lord Dalhousie, agreed with Sir Hugh Gough, the commander-in-chief, that the British East India Company's military forces were neither adequately equipped with transport and supplies, nor otherwise prepared to take the field immediately. He also foresaw the spread of the rebellion, and the necessity that must arise, not merely for the capture of Multan, but also for the entire subjugation of the Punjab. He therefore resolutely delayed to strike, organized a strong army for operations in November, and himself proceeded to the Punjab.

Despite the successes gained by Major General Herbert Edwardes against Mulraj, and Gough's indecisive victories at the Battle of Ramnagar in November and at the Battle of Chillianwala on 13 January 1849, the stubborn resistance at Multan showed that the task required the utmost resources of the government. Eventually, on 22 January, Multan was taken by General Whish, who was thus set at liberty to join Gough's army. On 21 February, Gough won a complete victory at the Battle of Gujrat. The Sikh army was pursued to Rawalpindi, where it laid down its arms, and their Afghan allies retreated from the Punjab.

The new Nepali Prime Minister, Jang Bahadur Rana (who had seized power in 1846 in a bloody coup d'état), actually volunteered the services of eight regiments under his personal command to assist the British in the Second Sikh

War, but the offer was not accepted – not because they did not wish to employ Nepalis as soldiers, but because they were convinced that they should continue to make efforts to recruit their own Gurkhas from the hills of Nepal.

The disastrous first Afghan war (1838-42) increased the concern of the British to secure effective and reliable 'native' troops for the army. The First Sikh war (1845-6) convinced the British of the value of the Gurkha battalions already raised and deployed. Even the experience of the First Afghan War (1838-42) and the disastrous 'Multan affair'- which precipitated the Second Sikh War (1848-49) - failed to discourage them.

❀ ❀ ❀

CHAPTER 10

Reliance on the Gurkhas

In 1832, while still assistant Resident, Hodgson had proposed the establishment of new and separate 'Gurkha' battalions, calculating that there were 30,000 men surplus to Nepal's annual requirements. He indicated the use that the government of India could make of these men, who - confined to Nepal, without employment or income, 'could not fail to provoke an uprising' - as recruits admitted to the Indian army, under the guidance of British officers, would easily find the opportunity to satisfy their warlike desires to the advantage of England (Pignède 1993: 19).

He argued that 'in my humble opinion they are by far the best soldiers in Asia; and if they were made participators in our renown in arms, I conceive that their gallant spirit, emphatic contempt of Madhesias (people of the plains) and unadulterated military habits might be relied on for fidelity; and that our good and regular pay and noble pension establishment would serve to counterpoise the influence of nationality, especially in the Magars and Gurungs, so far as that could injuriously affect us' (slightly different versions may be found in Hodgson 1874, Oldfield 1880, Pemble 1971, Hodgson 1972, Kansakar 1984: 51, Farwell 1984, Pignede 1993, Vansittart 1993: 56, and Rathaur 1995: 45; see also Des Chene 1991: 65, footnote).

Hodgson's plan was not approved. But ten years later, in 1843, after the First Afghan War, the British established a recruiting depot on the Indian side of the Nepal border, and an agent was sent into Nepal to seek new recruits. He was arrested, and the official ban on enlistment by Nepalis in the British Indian army widely publicised. The government of Nepal disliked such clandestine operations and took strong measures, even, according to some sources, putting to death some of the Gurkhas on their return home on leave and confiscating the property of those serving in the Indian army (Mojumdar 1973: 11, in Kansakar 1984: 51).

In December 1843, the Gwalior Campaign was fought between British and Maratha forces. The Maharaja of Gwalior had just died, leaving only a widow of 13; but the Governor-General, Lord Ellenborough had 'secured her position' by adopting an eight year old boy who was then appointed Maharaja with British support. However, the Marathas in Gwalior saw the failed British campaign in Afghanistan as an opportunity to regain independence and removed the young Maharaja. After attempts to negotiate failed, the British advanced in a two pronged attack and engaged with the Maratha forces in two battles on the same day, 29 December 1843.

The British did not foresee too much resistance: 'there was talk of 'horsewhips' being the only weapons required; and not only the Governor-General, Lord Ellenborough himself, but even a party of ladies accompanied the advance' (Gough & Innes 1986: 286). On this occasion it seems likely that the 'ladies' accompanying the troops would have been the wives of British officers. In the event, resistance was crushed within 48 hours with minimal losses on the British side. No Gurkhas, or their camp-followers, were involved.

Recruitment of Gurkhas was still not easy, however, in part because of the reluctance of the Nepali government to approve and support British recruitment policies, but also in part because of local constraints. In some areas - in the remoter parts of the western hills, such as Ghachok in Kaski District, for example, where, according to Adhikari & Bohle (1999) there were cases of men whose property was confiscated because of their temporary migration to India - there was always a shortage of labour and little emigration until the late 1880s. Also, in many parts of Nepal, even in the hills, land was still freely available and there was relatively little pressure to seek employment as a supplement or an alternative to farming.

This was to change, however, and even during the first half of the 19th century there is evidence that in some regions at least - in the eastern and western hills for example - population pressure and the demands of landlords contributed to a rise in the numbers of those emigrating, either on a temporary or a more permanent basis, from the hills of Nepal (Regmi 1971). Nepali migration to Darjeeling in particular was encouraged and facilitated by the active recruitment of Nepali men into the British army in India, particularly after the establishment of a military cantonment at Jalapahar in 1848.

During the 1840s and 1850s, the British were very occupied, not only with consolidating their military victories and the administration of their newly annexed territories but also with containing and suppressing a series of mutinies of increasingly significant scale within the Indian army itself. The loyalty and effectiveness of the Gurkhas during this critical period were to make a lasting mark upon the consciousness of the British in India. For example, when, in 1850, the whole of the 66th Bengal Native Infantry was disbanded following a mutiny over pay, it was replaced by the Nusseree Battalion, with a new designation - the 66th or Gurkha Regiment, Bengal Native Light Infantry[19].

This was the first regular Gurkha regiment in the Indian army; the other Gurkha battalions were given the pay, pensions and *batta* of regular troops at this time, but were not officially made regular troops of the line until the army reorganisation of 1861. The Commander-in-Chief of the British Army, Charles Napier, explained his choice of the Gurkhas of the Nusseree Battalion to replace the mutinous *sepoys* because 'they have a high military spirit, are fierce in war, of unsurpassed activity, and possess great powers of endurance'.

Furthermore, he added, 'the Goorkhas will be faithful, and for low pay we can enlist a large body of soldiers whom our best officers consider equal in courage to European troops. Even as a matter of economy this will be good, but the great advantage of enlisting these hill men will be that, with 30,000 or 40,000 Goorkhas added to 30,000 Europeans, the possession of India will not 'depend on opinions', but on an army able with ease to overthrow any combination among Hindoos or Mohammedans, or both together' (Petre 1925: 34).

The same year, 1850, Jang Bahadur Rana, Prime Minister and ruler of Nepal, visited England. Following this, he felt obliged (and possibly sufficiently flattered with his reception and impressed by the evident wealth and power of the British Empire) to promise that he would help the British after all to obtain recruits for their army in India from Nepal; but he was not really keen to allow them to recruit directly. In November 1850, following this reluctant offer, a British recruiting party arrived in Kathmandu and a notice was issued by the Nepali government asking those wishing to enlist to come to Kathmandu to do so.

Out of the thousands who applied, however, only 32 were eventually recruited to join the British Gurkha battalions. This confirmed for the British that their own procedures for recruitment were best. Adhikari suggests that,

---

19. It was later re-designated the First Gorkha Light Infantry.

'even though the Nepalese government was against the idea of recruitment for service in the British army, many villagers were eager to enlist, mainly because of the difficult economic conditions in the hills. The idea of joining the British (India) army or what is locally called *lahure jane*, thus became popular among village youths in the hills' (1996: 81).

He remarks that some young men actually 'fled the country to settle in India near the Nepalese border, so that they could more easily enlist for army service. As a result of such migration, undertaken as a step towards enlistment, settlements of Nepali people were established in Kangra, Nainital, Dharmasala, Darjeeling, Dehra Dun and Shillong' (1996: 81). While this account might suggest that the development of these settlements was essentially spontaneous, other sources indicate that they were, in effect, established by the British as a way of encouraging and promoting volunteers to come of their own accord to join the British Gurkhas.

For, as Kansakar argued, a decade earlier, 'owing to the harassment meted out by the Nepali government to the families of those serving in the Indian army, and to make the recruitment easier, emigration of young men from Nepal with their families was encouraged by the establishment by the British of 'Gurkha settlements' in the hills of India, such as Dharmashala (Bhagsu), Bakloh, Darjeeling, Dehra Dun and Shillong' (1984: 51). Adhikari also recognises that 'at the same time, the British administration encouraged the migration of Gurkhas from Nepal with their families. It also provided incentives to ex-army personnel to smuggle out people for recruitment' (1996: 81); and Regmi notes that 'in the absence of a formal arrangement with the government of Nepal, the East India Company faced considerable difficulty in finding suitable recruits.

This led to the founding of a number of Gorkhali settlements near regimental stations in north-western India, which created an additional inducement to emigration from Nepal' (Regmi 1999: 194). It is likely that that other women also, and not just wives of soldiers, migrated from Nepal, as well as from the surrounding regions of India, to these new settlements, which rapidly developed a variety of businesses and services to cater for the settlements, including the provision of sexual services for single soldiers far from home.

In the meanwhile, the irregular Gurkha troops (and the new 66th or Gurkha Regiment, of the Bengal Native Light Infantry established in 1850) continued to distinguish themselves in action, consolidating the frontiers of British India and helping maintain internal security. The British were particularly keen to recruit more Gurkhas; at this period they were not much concerned about distinguishing between 'genuine' Gorkhalis and others for purposes of recruitment at this time; all they knew was that they wanted more 'Gurkhas'. As one social historian has noted, 'it was not until the 1880s that definitions of Gurkhas had become so fixed, and that political negotiations with Nepal had been so arranged, that the 'Gurkha' battalions became composed entirely of 'genuine Gurkhas' from Nepal' (Des Chene 1991: 55-6).

Indirect recruitment through the government (Durbar) or Nepal had proved unsatisfactory. The British much preferred to recruit their 'men' direct from the hills, even though it was officially illegal and strongly resisted by the rulers of Nepal. They had their preferred recruitment areas and 'martial tribes' from which they wished to recruit; in fact, however, not only the 'preferred' Magars and Gurungs of the western hills, but also Newars and so-called 'untouchables' were recruited into the army - a factor which did little to encourage the approval of the government of Nepal. Indeed, one historian suggests that this 'enraged the Nepal Durbar' (Rathaur 1995: 49).

Consequently, despite Jang Bahadur's promise to facilitate the recruitment of Nepali troops to the British army, little progress was made by the Durbar towards a more open policy. He agreed to relax some of the stringent restrictions imposed on Nepali subjects serving in the British army, but continued to insist that they should wear civilian dress when in Nepal, not uniforms, they should not visit Kathmandu and neighbouring military stations, they should not enter Nepal via the direct Sugauli route. In other words, they should remain as nearly invisible as possible. In the meanwhile, British recruitment continued unofficially.

It was now almost half a century since the first recruits had been deployed in support of the British campaigns across India and beyond. In all this time, we have little information of the casualties suffered; about those who died and those who were left behind; or about what happened to those who returned home to their villages in the hills disabled as a result of their injuries. If we assume that somewhere between 150,000 to 200,000 served in the British Army of India throughout the 19th century, then casualties could have been at least as high as between 30,000 and 40,000.

There were no medical facilities across the country at this period, and no basis for rehabilitation or care other than by 'traditional 'healers and family members, although Dr. H. A. Oldfield, the doctor at the British Residency from

1850 to 1863, refers in his book to the major health problems of Nepal such diseases and conditions as smallpox, malaria, cholera, tuberculosis and problems related to childbirth (Oldfield 1880, 1973). The Khokna Leprosy Asylum was the first health institution established by the state in 1857. As regards sanitation generally, even the capital Kathmandu was said to be 'built on a dung hill in the middle of latrines' by Daniel Wright in 1877 (Wright 1877). There was little support for those who returned home with disabilities or ill-health, other than traditional healers and family members.

In 1856, Lord Dalhousie, the Governor General of India, strongly recommended a major expansion of Gurkha forces in the Indian army. A year later, the 'Indian Mutiny' of May-July 1857 proved, yet again, the value of the 'Gurkha' troops.

❀ ❀ ❀

CHAPTER 11

The 'Great Rebellion' & its Aftermath

The origins of the Great Rebellion or Great Mutiny – what some see as the first major uprising against British rule in India - are complex and have been much debated. An accumulation of concerns and grievances undoubtedly lay behind the dramatic events of 1857, but the accelerated rate of change in the regions of Bengal from which the bulk of the Bengal Army had been recruited for the previous half century as the impact of British imperialism increased provides a broader context for the more immediate 'causes' of mutiny in the army itself.

The conquest of the Punjab, the annexation of the kingdom of Oudh on the pretext of misgovernment, new land reforms, the withdrawal of 'foreign allowances' for military service in Sind and the Punjab, the General Service Enlistment Act of July 1856 (which meant that Brahmin and Rajput troops now risked caste pollution by being sent 'across the black water' to places like Burma), the increasing recruitment of non-Hindu Sikhs and Dogras and 'Gurkhas', and the 'final straw' of the issue of cartridges supposedly smeared with the polluting pig fat or beef fat, all combined to produce severe disquiet and unrest within the predominantly Hindu Brahmin and Rajput troops of the native Bengal Army.

In any case, in March-April 1857 there was a series of disturbances among a number of native regiments of the Bengal Army in Barrackpore and elsewhere in Bengal. On 24 April, a parade of some 85 soldiers of the 3ʳᵈ Bengal Light Cavalry at Meerut were ordered to load their rifles, they refused. They were arrested, court martialled and sentenced to ten year rigorous imprisonment. On 9 May, they were brought to the parade ground stripped and shackled, and surrounded by other troops to intimidate and humiliate them. The next day, there was an uprising as the Indian troops broke into revolt. By evening, 50 Europeans, including civilians, had been killed and the 85 soldiers freed from jail along with some other detainees.

As Shrabani Basu graphically describes what followed: 'the flame lit in Meerut spread across the plains of Bengal and United Provinces like a bushfire' (2016: 27). Three mutinous regiments marched to Delhi, won over the soldiers garrisoning the Red Fort there, and seized control of the city. At this stage, as Allen remarks, 'the mutiny appeared to be confined to the predominantly Hindu Brahmin and Rajput soldiery... mainly from the Gangetic plains' (Allen 2001: 360). Rapidly, however, the troops in other major centres throughout north west India joined the uprising and very soon the crisis was general across the region.

The British East India Company was surprisingly slow to respond to the uprising: it was two months after the first outbreak of rebellion at Meerut, that they were able to put together a large enough force to combat the rebels. The combined force, including two Gurkha units serving in the Bengal Army, fought the rebels' main army at Badli-ke-Seraj and drove them back to Delhi. The Company's army established a base on the Delhi ridge to the north of the city and the Siege of Delhi began.

When news of the fighting reached Jhansi, Lakshmibai, the Rani of Jhansi, asked the British political officer, Captain Alexander Skene, for permission to raise a body of armed men for her own protection; Skene agreed to this. The city was relatively calm in the midst of the regional unrest, but the Rani conducted a *haldi kumkum*[20] ceremony in front of all the women of Jhansi to provide re-assurance to her subjects, and to convince them that the British were cowards and not to be afraid of them. In June 1857, rebels of the 12th Bengal Native Infantry seized the Star Fort of Jhansi containing the treasure and magazine, and after persuading the British to lay down their arms by promising them no harm, broke their word and massacred 40 to 60 European officers of the garrison along with their wives and children.

Until this point, Lakshmibai had been reluctant to join the rebellion against the British; and her involvement in this massacre is still a subject of debate. An army doctor, Thomas Lowe, however, wrote after the rebellion characterising her as the 'Jezebel of India ... the young rani upon whose head rested the blood of the slain'. Four days after the massacre the *sepoys* left Jhansi, having obtained a

---

20. '*haldi kumkum*, or the *haldi kumkum* ceremony, is a social gathering in India in which married women exchange *haldi* (turmeric) and *kumkum* (vermilion powder), as a symbol of their married status and wishing for their husbands' long lives'.

large sum of money from the Rani, and having threatened to blow up the palace where she lived. Following this, as the only source of authority in the city, the Rani felt obliged to assume control and wrote to Major Erskine, commissioner of the Saugor division explaining the events which had led her to do so. On 2 July 1857, Erskine wrote in reply, requesting her to manage the District for the British Government until the arrival of a British Superintendent.

The Rani's forces defeated an attempt by the mutineers to assert the claim to the throne of a rival prince, Sadashiv Rao (nephew of Maharaja Gangadhar Rao) who was captured and imprisoned. There was then an invasion of Jhansi by the forces of Company allies Orchha and Datia; their intention was to divide Jhansi between themselves. The Rani appealed to the British for aid, but it was now believed by the Governor-General that she was responsible for the massacre and no reply was received. She set up a foundry to cast cannon to be used on the walls of the fort and assembled forces including some from former feudatories of Jhansi and elements of the mutineers which were able to defeat the invaders in August 1857. Her intention at this time was, it seems, still to hold Jhansi on behalf of the British.

In the meanwhile, Colonel Thomas Seaton, who had previously served in Afghanistan, arrived in Delhi and found that he was ordered to escort a convoy of grain and stores through the Doab, the land between the Ganges and the Jumna, to the commander-in-chief's camp. With a force of 2,300 men, Colonel Seaton was to guard 4,500 bullock-carts, 8,000 camels, 1,500 camp-followers and 16,000 bullocks: it was said that 'the whole might cover some eighteen miles of road'. This reveals the fact that even a relatively small force was accompanied by a large baggage train and nearly as many camp followers – almost certainly including women - as there were soldiers. (Seaton was successful in his mission and promoted to brigadier. He had hoped to be able to participate in the relief of Lucknow, but was appointed to command the Futtygurh District instead. He eventually resigned in 1859).

The siege of Delhi lasted roughly from 1 July to 21 September 1857, when the British successfully retook the city. In the meanwhile, fighting was also taking place elsewhere across north India. Further mutinies in Bengal on 18 November 1857 saw the 2nd, 3rd and 4th companies of the 34th Bengal Infantry Regiment storming the Chittagong Jail and releasing all prisoners. The mutineers were eventually suppressed by Gurkha regiments. In the meanwhile, early in 1858, a previous offer of assistance made by Jang Bahadur Rana, the prime minister of

Nepal, was accepted by the British, and he crossed the Indian border at the head of his own army of six regiments, numbering about 5,800 men, mustered over the previous months in Kathmandu.

It is highly probable that this force also included the usual baggage train and thousands of both male and female camp followers. General Dhir Shamsher Kunwar Rana, the youngest brother of Jung Bahadur, also led some 3,000 Nepali troops, no doubt with their accompanying baggage train and horde of camp followers, to provide further support to the British at Lucknow, Benares and Patna. These Nepali forces joined with the British at the beginning of March and helped bring an end to the siege of Lucknow. They also fought against the rebels at Gorakhpur, Azampur, Jaunpur, Allahabad and Awadh (Oudh).

The Rani of Jhansi was not the only woman involved in the fighting at the time of the 'great rebellion'. Another was the Begum Hazrat Mahal. Mahal became a *begum* after being accepted as a junior royal concubine of the Nawab of Awadh, Wajid Ali Shah, a Shi'ite Muslim of Iranian descent. The title 'Hazrat Mahal' was bestowed on her after the birth of their son, Birjis Qadra. The British had annexed Awadh (Oudh) in 1856 and Wajid Ali Shah was exiled to Calcutta. After this, Begum Hazrat Mahal took charge of the affairs of the state of Awadh, despite her divorce from the Nawab.

In 1857, Begum Hazrat Mahal's band of supporters, led by Raja Jalal Singh, rebelled against the forces of the British; later, they seized control of Lucknow and she declared her son, Birjis Qadr, the ruler of Awadh. One of her principal grievances against the British was that the Company had casually demolished temples and mosques to make way for roads. In a proclamation issued during the final days of the revolt, she mocked the British claim to allow freedom of worship:

> To eat pigs and drink wine, to bite greased cartridges and to mix pig's fat with sweetmeats, to destroy Hindu and Muslim temples on the pretence of making roads, to build churches, to send clergymen into the streets to preach the Christian religion, to institute English schools, and pay people a monthly stipend for learning the English sciences, while the places of worship of Hindus and Muslims are to this day entirely neglected; with all this, how can people believe that their religion will not be interfered with?

When the forces under the command of the British re-captured Lucknow and most of Awadh, she joined forces first with Nana Saheb against the British, and then joined the Maulavi of Faizabad in the attack on Shahjahanpur. Ultimately, she was forced to take refuge in Nepal, where she was initially refused asylum by the Rana prime minister Jang Bahadur but was later allowed to stay. She died in Kathmandu in 1879 and was buried in the grounds of Kathmandu's Jama Masjid (Friday Mosque). After her death, on the occasion of the jubilee of Queen Victoria (1887), the British Government pardoned her son Birjis Qadr and he was allowed to return home.

In the meanwhile, from August 1857 to January 1858, Jhansi under the Rani's rule was at peace. The British had announced that troops would be sent there to maintain control but the fact that none arrived strengthened the position of a party of her advisers who wanted independence from British rule. When the British forces finally arrived in March they found it well-defended and the fort had heavy guns which could fire over the town and nearby countryside. According to one source, Sir Hugh Rose, commanding the British forces, demanded the surrender of the city; if this was refused it would be destroyed.

The same source claims that after due deliberation the Rani issued a proclamation: 'We fight for independence. In the words of Lord Krishna, we will if we are victorious, enjoy the fruits of victory, if defeated and killed on the field of battle, we shall surely earn eternal glory and salvation'. Other sources make no mention of a demand for surrender. Be that as it may, the Rani defended Jhansi against British troops when Rose initiated the siege of Jhansi on 23 March 1858. The bombardment of Jhansi began on 24 March but was met by heavy return fire and the damaged defences were repaired. The defenders sent appeals for help to Tatya Tope, who brought an army of more than 20,000 to relieve Jhansi.

The relief force engaged the British on 31 March. During the battle with Tatya Tope's forces, the British forces continued the siege and on 2 April four columns assaulted the defences at different points. Those attempting to scale the walls came under heavy fire; but two other columns had already entered the city and were approaching the palace together. Street fighting continued into the following day and no quarter was given, even to women and children. The Rani withdrew from the palace to the fort, and after taking counsel decided that since resistance in the city was useless she must leave and join either Tatya Tope or Rao Sahib (Nana Sahib's nephew).

The Rani escaped in the night with her son, surrounded by a personal escort and decamped to the town of Kalpi, where she joined the rebel forces, including

Tatya Tope. On 22 May 1858, British forces attacked Kalpi; the defenders were commanded by the Rani herself and were again defeated. The leaders fled once more, this time to the strategic Gwalior Fort where they joined with other rebels and proclaimed Nana Sahib as Peshwa of a revived Maratha dominion with Rao Sahib as his governor (*subedar*) in Gwalior. The Rani was unsuccessful in trying to persuade the other rebel leaders to prepare to defend Gwalior against a British attack which she expected would come soon. General Rose's forces took Morar on 16 June and then made a successful attack on Gwalior the next day, engaging the Rani's forces and slaughtering them.

There are several slightly differing accounts of how the Rani met her end. According to one account, she put on a *sowar's* (cavalry officer) uniform and attacked one of the hussars; she was un-horsed and also wounded, probably by his sabre. Shortly afterwards, as she sat bleeding by the roadside, she recognised the soldier and fired at him with a pistol, whereupon he dispatched her with his carbine. According to another tradition, she was badly wounded while fighting as a cavalry leader, and not wishing the British to capture her body, told a hermit to burn it. After her death, a few local people cremated her body.

Whatever the truth of her demise, when the British captured the city of Gwalior after three days, Sir Hugh Rose commented in his report on the engagement that Rani Lakshmibai was 'personable, clever and beautiful' and 'the most dangerous of all Indian leaders. He also reported that she had been buried 'with great ceremony under a tamarind tree under the Rock of Gwalior, where I saw her bones and ashes'.

British operations to suppress the uprising were divided into three parts. First came the desperate struggles at Delhi, Kanpur, and Lucknow during the summer; then the operations around Lucknow in the winter of 1857–58; and finally the 'mopping up' campaigns of early 1858. By the end of the summer of 1858, the last remnants of the rebellion had been quashed and the 'Great Indian Mutiny' or Great Rebellion was over. So too was the administration of India by the British East India Company. The British government moved swiftly now to ensure its effective control of the empire in India from London, establishing an India Office and instituting a more direct form of rule. The British Raj replaced the Company. The Bengal army had dominated the Indian army before the uprising and a direct result of The Great Rebellion was the scaling back in the size of the Bengali contingent in the Indian Army as a whole.

In 1857, the Bengal Army had numbered 86,000 men, of which 12,000 were British, 16,000 Sikhs and 1,500 'Gurkhas'. Fifty-four of the Bengal Army's 74 regular Native Infantry Regiments mutinied, and all ten of the Bengal Light Cavalry regiments. Some of those units that mutinied were immediately destroyed or broken up, with their rank and file drifting away to their homes. A number of the remaining 20 regiments were disarmed or disbanded to prevent or forestall mutiny. In total, only twelve of the original Bengal Native Infantry regiments survived to pass into the new Indian Army. The Bengal Army had also contained 29 irregular cavalry and 42 irregular infantry regiments. Of these, a substantial contingent from the recently annexed state of Awadh mutinied *en masse;* and another large contingent from Gwalior also mutinied.

The remainder of the irregular units were raised from a wide variety of sources and were less affected by the concerns of mainstream Indian society. Some irregular units actively supported the Company: three Gurkha units and five of the six Sikh infantry units, as well as the six infantry and six cavalry units of the recently raised Punjab Irregular Force. The Bombay army had three mutinies in its 29 regiments, whilst the Madras army had none at all, although elements of one of its 52 regiments refused to volunteer for service in Bengal. Most of southern India remained passive, with only intermittent outbreaks of violence.

The Brahmin presence in the Bengal Army was significantly reduced because of their perceived primary role as mutineers. By contrast, the Sirmoor Battalion of Gurkha irregulars was honoured by Queen Victoria with a unique Truncheon in recognition of their bravery and loyalty at the siege of Delhi. The Queen herself, Empress of India, 'disbarred by her gender from military service, none-the-less appeared when a young woman, in a fetching uniform of a round black hat with a red and white plume, a general's tunic (turned down at the collar to show white blouse and black cravat) and dark blue riding habit. She rode side-saddle on a horse with field-marshal's badges on its saddle-cloth and holsters. Victoria took her military duties very seriously, presenting medals with evident pride.' (Holmes 2001:84).

Not only were the Gurkhas honoured in this way, but the Nepali troops deployed by Jung Bahadur Rana in support of the British returned home laden with booty (Parker 2000: 63 refers to 'a heavily laden wagon train of 3,000 or more bullock carts bursting with their booty'). This must have been well received by the 9,000 or so Nepali families back home, encouraging further demand for recruitment into the British army – even though hundreds at least of these families had lost loved ones and many more had seen them return injured and disabled. Jung Bahadur Rana himself was awarded the Order and Jewels of the Knight Grand Cross of the Order of the Bath, and with the Treaty of 1860, the areas of the far western *terai* commandeered after the war of 1814-16 (*naya muluk*) were handed back to Nepal. Jang Bahadur gave his promise, in return, that if ever the British needed his help in the future, they had only to ask (Parker 2000: 63).

This Treaty, however, also allowed foreigners to purchase and sell land in the *terai,* and Jang Bahadur even invited businessmen, traders and land-owners from India specifically for the 'development' of the *terai* (Adhikari & Gurung 2009: 33). This was followed by unrestricted movement, both ways, across the border, of raw materials and of people from Nepal and of manufactured goods into Nepal, both welcomed by the British, if not the government of Nepal. The migration of men and women, from Nepal increased significantly from the 1860s onwards, partly as a result of the growth of economic opportunities in India, and partly as a result of increasing population pressure and lack of comparable opportunities in Nepal, especially in the eastern hills. Permanent migration and settlement outside Nepal accelerated, particularly across the border to Assam, Bengal, Bhutan, Burma and Darjeeling (Caplan 1970; Nakane 1966; Poffenberger 1980 – all cited in Adhikari & Gurung 2009: 54).

The government of Nepal continued, however, to restrict the recruitment of Nepali nationals into the British Indian Army. In August 1858, Jung Bahadur had issued an order in which the four classes and thirty six castes of Nepal were forbidden to go on their own account to India to join the British Army. All Nepali subjects interested in joining the British Army officially needed prior permission from the Durbar. It was also made clear that the Nepali government would not cooperate with the British in tracing the families and heirs of any Nepali soldier who died while serving in the Gurkha regiments (cf Rathaur 1995: 54-55). It was also clearly stated that any Nepali disobeying this order would have his house and land confiscated. He would, furthermore, give up certain cherished rights.

A soldier who violated this order, for example, would not be entitled to punish his wife's lover, if she had one, and would be liable to capital punishment if he were to kill the lover of his wife. This particular right reflects the deeply-felt concern on the part of Nepali men leaving home for employment abroad – whether in the army or in civilian occupations - regarding the possibility of adultery on the part of their wives while they were away. This issue of adultery and the fear of adultery was clearly a matter of concern throughout the many decades prior to this period, during which men had left their families; it continued to be a matter of concern through the coming decades, right up until the First World War, and thereafter, as we shall see.

Although direct recruitment into the Gurkhas was officially banned by the government of Nepal, it continued to take place. Indeed, it has been suggested that after the 1860s, 'recruitment agencies openly travelled from village to village to recruit Nepalese youth' (Adhikari & Bohle 1999: 59). And if Nepal would not provide, there were still other sources for 'Gurkhas'. As an example of this, a fifth Gurkha Battalion was now raised from the 'Goorkhas' of the Sikh army at Abbottabad. These troops included men not only from Kumaon and Garhwal, as well as from the hill areas of Nepal, but also from different regions of the Punjab and even Afghanistan. First as the 25th Punjab Infantry, the Hazzara Field Force or the Hazzara Goorkha Battalion, and then as the 5th Gurkhas, this was to become one of the most famous (and most decorated) of Gurkha regiments, serving on the North West Frontier for 90 years.[21] Later it was to be known as the 9th Bengal Native Infantry, with one of its companies formed by 'Gurkhas' (Nepalis) and other hill men.

But the loyalty of the Gurkhas had been tested and proved in the heat of the Great Mutiny. There was growing pressure now to increase the size of the 'Gurkha' force and to regularise it. The old Bengal Army, however, much of which had mutinied in 1857, was disbanded. Frederick Roberts (late Lord Roberts), who had earned a Victoria Cross during the Great Mutiny, was concerned to recruit the new Indian Army from those who had proved their worth and their loyalty during that uprising. Shrabani Basu cites a source that suggests Roberts also believed that there was a crucial distinction between 'martial races' and others: "no comparison can be made between the martial value of a regiment recruited amongst the Gurkhas of Nepal or the warlike races of Northern India, and of one recruited from the effeminate peoples of the South' (Basu 2016: 29).

In 1861, the re-organisation of the Indian Army designated the existing Gurkha Battalions as Five Gurkha Regiments, within the regular army, but separate from the other regiments, of Sikhs, Pathans, Dogras and others. The Secretary of State argued that it was 'highly desirable that these corps should retain in a marked manner, their national and distinctive character' (quoted in

---

21. Re-named in 1923, the 5th Royal Gurkha Rifles (Frontier Force), which it remained until 1957 when it became part of the Indian army (Farwell 1985: 57).

Saxena 1974: 200-201, f.4; see also Petre 1925: 68). The Nusseree Battalion, raised in April 1815 and made the 66th Gurkha Regiments of the Bengal Light Infantry in 1850, was now re-organised into the First Gurkha Regiment. The Sirmoor Battalion, raised in April 1815, was made the Second. The Kumaon Battalion, raised in June 1815, was designated the Third; the extra Gurkha Battalion raised in 1857, was made the Fourth; while the Hazzara/Gurkha Battalion raised in 1858 was established as the Fifth Gurkha Regiment.

Increasingly, there was concern to recruit only 'genuine' Gurkhas – Brahmins and Khas recruits were now passed over in favour of Magars and Gurungs, and the 'non-martial Newars' were eliminated by attrition. Garhwalis were also no longer able to join Gurkha regiments. When a second battalion was raised from among Garhwalis for the 3rd Gurkhas, there was sufficient outcry from Gurkha officers that three years later these troops were renamed the 39th Garhwali battalion, and a new 2/3rd Gurkha battalion composed of 'genuine' Nepali Gurkhas was raised (Woodyatt 1922).

This must have had a significant impact on the involvement of different ethnic groups and castes, and in the financial rewards that accrued to those employed in the British Army. It had always been financially beneficial for households in the hills to have a member of the family working abroad and sending remittances back home. Employment in the British Army now became even more sought-after, particularly among those ethnic groups that were favoured by the British, notably the Gurungs and Magars of western Nepal. This concentration on a more limited and closely defined pool of potential recruits in a particular area of the hills would become the basis for increasing differentiation both between regions and within regions between different social groups, within Nepal.

This new concentration of recruitment on specific social groups or 'races' (as the British tended to regard them) contributed to the development of the idea of the regiment as a 'family'. Now 'usually from the same region and often from the same village, they spoke the same language and worshipped together, giving them a strong sense of community' (Basu 2016: 31) even when abroad and 'away from home'. 'The traditions of the regiment were taught to them at the temple, the mosque, the gurdwara and at church parades... The concept of 'being loyal to the salt' or loyal to the one who had provided for them ran deep' (Basu 2016: 31).

With formal integration within the regular forces of the Indian army, and a greater degree of ethnic and social coherence, there was now also increasing pressure from the men employed in the Gurkhas to bring their wives and children to India, to live with them in their stations, as well as to accompany them as camp-followers. As early as 1856, the men of the Sirmoor battalion had petitioned their commanding officer for permission to convert some disused barracks at Dehra Dun into homes for soldiers' families – implying that it had been difficult prior to that for their women folk to accompany their soldier husbands, and live with them in 'the lines', at least officially. He approved, but the government of India refused his request.

The 2nd Goorkhas (as they became) persisted, however, and finally in 1864, it was agreed that each of the first four Gurkha regiments should have their own 'station', with provision for families - the 1st at Dharmasala, the 2nd at Dehra Dun, the 3rd at Almora in the Kumaon Hills, and the 4th at Bakloh. In a subsequent letter (which came to be known as 'the Charter'), the commander-in-chief of the Gurkhas gave permission for these 'stations' to be granted in perpetuity. The Charter issued by the British Indian Government in 1864 provided for them to buy land for their respective permanent stations and so begin to develop official Gurkha settlements or 'colonies' in those areas[22].

❀ ❀ ❀

---

22. Later, in 1894, the 2/3rd battalion established its 'home' at Lansdowne; the 5th and 6th made their 'home' at Abbottabad, the 1/8th at Shillong, the 2/8th at Lansdowne, the 9th near that of the 2nd at Dehra Dun, and the 10th at Maymyo - Farwell 1985: 145).

CHAPTER 12

The Expansion of Overseas Employment

During the second half of the 19th century, opportunities for employment overseas, outside India, that had emerged in the 1830s and '40s, began to take off in earnest. On 16 November 1844, the British Indian Government had legalised emigration to Jamaica, Trinidad and Demerara (Guyana). Transportation to the Caribbean stopped in 1848, due to problems in the sugar industry, but resumed again in Demerara and Trinidad in 1851 and Jamaica in 1860. Importing labour became viable for plantation owners because newly emancipated slaves refused to work for low wages, and the influx of Indian workers diminished the competitive leverage and bargaining power of the freed slaves. The planters in the West Indies and in Mauritius also pressed consistently for longer indentures.

In 1847, in an effort to persuade labourers to stay on, the Mauritius Government had offered a gratuity of £2 to each labourer who decided to remain in Mauritius and renounce their claim to a free passage. On 3 August 1852, the Government of India agreed to change the conditions whereby if a passage was not claimed within six months of entitlement, it would be forfeited, but with safeguards for the sick and poor. It was also considered that if the labourers had a family life in the colonies they would be more likely to stay on.

The proportion of women in early migration to Mauritius had historically been small; the first systematic effort to correct this imbalance was when, on 18 March 1856, the Secretary for the Colonies sent a dispatch to the Governor of Demerara that stated that 'for the season 1856–7 women must form 25 per cent of the total, and in the following years males must not exceed three times the number of females dispatched'. It was more difficult to induce women from North India to go overseas than those from South India, but the Colonial Office persisted; and on 30 July 1868, instructions were issued that the proportion of

40 women to 100 men should be adhered to. This remained in force of the rest of the indenture period.

In the meanwhile, the regime for indentured labour in Mauritius became significantly harsher. The British colonial government of Mauritius passed laws which sanctioned the double cut system (or a system under which a worker lost two days' pay for being absent from work for one day), restricted the freedom of movement of the Indian labourers, enacted a pass law, allowed for corporal punishment, and extended their labour contract. By the 1860s, an extremely repressive system was in place, enforced by the colonial police for the benefit of the sugar planters.

Between 1860 and 1885, however, the sugar estate labourers filed 110,940 complaints with the stipendiary magistrates and Protector of Immigrants against their employers or an average of 4,437 per annum, with 72 per cent of these complaints concerning non-payment of wages. Most of the employers were found guilty by the stipendiary magistrates and forced to pay. The Indian labourers themselves actively resisted their repression by organizing strikes and filing complaints against their employers or the sugar estate owners.

Gradually, from the 1870s onwards, the repressive apparatus of the indenture system in Mauritius was officially dismantled. Between 1872 and 1873, a Royal Commission of Inquiry was appointed by the British imperial government in London and sent to Mauritius. For many months, it carried out a lengthy investigation into the working and living conditions as well as the grievances of the island's Indian labourers. In 1875, in their voluminous report, the Commissioners made several recommendations to alleviate the terrible plight of the colony's labourers.

In the meanwhile, transportation of indentured labour was extended to the smaller British Caribbean islands; Grenada in 1856, St Lucia in 1858 and St Kitts and St Vincent in 1860. Emigration to Natal in South Africa was approved on 7 August 1860, and the first ship from Madras arrived in Durban on 16 November 1860, forming the basis of the Indian South African community. The recruits were employed on three-year contracts. Permission was granted for emigration to Queensland in 1864, but no Indians were transported under the indenture system to this part of Australia.

Slavery was eventually abolished in Surinam on 1 July 1863, although slaves were only released after a ten-year transitory period, in 1873. This spurred the immigration of indentured labour from British India after a treaty to that effect had been signed between the Netherlands and Britain 1870. Indians began migrating as indentured labour to Surinam in 1873, mostly from the modern-day Indian states of Uttar Pradesh, Punjab, Haryana, Bihar and Tamil Nadu. However, among the immigrants there were also labourers from other parts of South Asia, such as Afghanistan and Nepal.

The first ship transporting Indian indentured labourers to Surinam, the *Lalla Rookh*, arrived in the Paramaribo. Newly freed slaves who witnessed Indian workers disembarking at the harbour, reportedly stated, "*jobo tanbasi*", meaning "the white man is still the boss", suggesting that they viewed the development as a continuation of the slave trade. Initially, the transport and living conditions of Indian labourers in Surinam were arguably worse than they had been prior to the abolition of the Dutch slave trade. The British Viceroy of India described it as 'a new system of slavery' . During the 1870s, however, conditions were improved greatly following the passage of new protective legislation.

The Government of the United Kingdom and the colonial British Government in India feared comparisons to slavery would hurt their reputation, and enacted several laws to make transportation of Indian workers safer and improve working conditions in plantations. They also appointed agents to oversee the process. Eden Vansittart, for example, who would later be a recruitment officer for the Gurkhas, was appointed Emigration Agent to Surinam in 1876 on joining the Indian Service, and, in that capacity, according to his own words 'came into contact quite soon with many Nepalis' (Vansittart 1993: introduction 4).

In order to reduce the mortality rate among workers being transported from India, the colonial British government required the presence of at least one doctor on every ship. As regulations required the doctor to be of European-origin, the regulations also required that one Indian indentured labourer be appointed as a translator and that he would be paid for his services at the end of the journey. Other regulations mandated that every ship have distilling apparatus with a capacity to produce at least 500 litres of drinking water from seawater daily, and also required ships to have a sickbay, male and female nursing staff, adequate food and medicine, and artificial ventilation in the passengers' quarters.

Another regulation prohibited any ship transporting Indian indentured labourers from setting sail between the end of March and the beginning of August. Any shipping company that violated the regulations would be prohibited from transporting contact workers in the future. The Dutch government, which had signed the agreement to recruit workers with the British after long and difficult negotiations, also feared jeopardizing the arrangement and meticulously followed the regulations imposed by the British Indian Service. The Dutch were also concerned that they would be accused of reviving the slave trade.

By 1870, the indenture system, transporting Indian labour to the colonies, was an established system of providing labour for European colonial plantations and when, in 1879, Fiji became a recipient of Indian labour it was this same system with a few minor modifications. Indian indentured emigration to Fiji was started by Sir Arthur Gordon, the first substantive governor of the colony (1875-80), to meet the shortage of labour caused by the prohibition of commercial employment of the Fijians and by the increasing uncertainty and cost of the Polynesian labour trade.

Between 1879 and 1916, a total of 42 ships made 87 voyages, carrying Indian indentured labourers to Fiji. Initially the ships brought labourers from Calcutta, but from 1903 all ships except two also brought labourers from Madras and Mumbai. A total of 60,965 passengers left India but only 60,553 (including births at sea) arrived in Fiji. The Nepali community in Fiji today are the descendants of indentured labourers (known as *girmityas*) brought in by the British colonial rulers of Fiji together with Indian labourers. They settled first in Suva, the capital of Fiji, and then moved around the island to Navua, another large town, and eventually to Kavanagasau, now home to largest Nepali community in the islands.

Here they lease farmland from the native Fijians and grow sugar cane and vegetables for the market. There is no record as far as we know of Nepali women in the early days, and it appears that initially only men came as labourers. But later, it seems there were Nepali women who came as well, although we know little about these women.

The vast majority of those leaving India as indentured labour were men, as we have already noted; but women were a significant minority, and it appears that not all of the 'Indian' women were in fact Indian. There is, however, only one explicit mention in all of the literature on indentured labour – as far as I can discover – of a Nepali woman being part of the human 'cargo'. In a fascinating discussion of Indian indentured labour, involving predominantly Indian women being shipped to the West Indies and elsewhere, by Gaiutra Bahadur (Bahadur 2016), mention is made of a 'Nipalese woman', named Morti:

'When *The Rohilla* landed in British Guiana in 1883, the immigration agent-general reported that "the Nipalese [sic] woman Morti refused to acknowledge Amirbun as her husband". If in fact they had been married, it was probably a hastily-struck depot or shipboard marriage. I say this because they weren't from the same part of India, not remotely' (2016: 72).

As far as I know this is the only recorded instance of a woman from Nepal travelling overseas until much later. But there were certainly Nepalis among the 'Indian' indentured labourers travelling to work far afield during the last two decades of the 19th century, and some of these were probably women.

In the period from 1834 to 1916, a total of well over 1 million Indian and Nepali labourers were shipped to various parts of the world to work as indentured labourers: the largest number (452,000) went to Mauritius, the next largest (239,000) to British Guyana; 152,000 went to Natal in South Africa, 144,000 to Trinidad, 87,000 to Reunion, 80,000 to the French Antilles, 61,000 to Fiji, 36,000 to Jamaica and 34,000 to Surinam. From 1906 to 1910, only 1,736 labourers arrived in Mauritius from the Indian subcontinent. In May 1924, the last batch of 'Indian' immigrants set foot on Mauritian soil.

✤ ✤ ✤

CHAPTER 13

The Second Afghan War

After tension between Russia and Britain in Europe ended with the June 1878 Congress of Berlin, Russia turned its attention to Central Asia. That same summer, Russia sent an uninvited diplomatic mission to Kabul. Sher Ali Khan, the Amir of Afghanistan, tried unsuccessfully to keep them out. Russian envoys arrived in Kabul on 22 July 1878, and on 14 August, the British demanded that Sher Ali accept a British mission too. The Amir not only refused to receive a British mission under Neville Bowles Chamberlain, but threatened to stop it if it were dispatched. Lord Lytton, the Viceroy of India, ordered a diplomatic mission to set out for Kabul in September 1878 but the mission was turned back as it approached the eastern entrance of the Khyber Pass, triggering the Second Anglo–Afghan War.

The first campaign began in November 1878 when a British force of about 50,000 fighting men, including several Gurkha regiments, was distributed under the command of Sir Samuel J. Browne into three military columns which penetrated Afghanistan at three different points. In all three, the various military contingents were supported by the usual baggage train, including the hospital carriage, and carts containing ammunition, food for the men, and grain for the camels, the draught bullocks and the cattle which accompanied the troops to provide meat, and by camp-followers, who included women and children, as usual. Even before reaching Afghanistan, the march to Quetta proved arduous for all concerned, and particularly so for the camp-followers, who numbered about the same as the all of the military personnel combined, had little shelter, insufficient food and no-one to carry them when too ill to walk. They were poorly equipped and clothed, and many fell by the wayside and died.

The Multan Field Force, which was assembled at Multan, and would also march on to Kandahar (after which it was referred to as the Kandahar Field

Force), included 200 officers, 6,600 men of all ranks, 1,800 horses and 42 guns. The two infantry brigades included the 1st and 3rd Gurkhas. Their camp-followers (comprising men, women and children) constituted a second 'army' of nearly equal size. There was a separate column which was initially under General Biddulph (Biddulph's Force), and subsequently under General Stewart, who eventually took command of all the British forces in southern Afghanistan.

The second main column was constituted by the Kuram Field Force under Major-General Roberts, who had earned his spurs at the siege of Lucknow during the Mutiny, was awarded the Victoria Cross in 1858 for action at Khudagunj, and was soon to be knighted for his role in the siege of Kandahar in 1878. This column comprised 150 officers, 5,500 men, 950 horses and 17 guns. The two infantry brigades in this column included the 5th Gurkhas, Punjab Frontier Force. Finally there were the two divisions of the Peshawar Field Force - which was a British field force of around 12,000 men involving a mix of British and 'Indian' regiments (including both the 2nd and the 4th Gurkhas).

As with the other columns there was an almost equally large array of camp-followers. Few of the accounts refer specifically to women when they refer to the camp-followers, but experience of other campaigns, including those of the first Afghan War, as we have seen, suggests that many were in fact women, and those accompanying the five Gurkha brigades now involved in the Second Afghan War would have been mainly Nepali women, some them also with their children. Certainly some of the officers and even non-commissioned officers were accompanied by their wives.

For example, Brigadier McPherson relates (according to Colonel Hanna, who was there) in one of his letters home, how, at Attock, he took the wife of a sergeant-major, sick of fever, out of a bullock cart in which she was travelling and putting her into his *gari* (carriage), sat himself in the doorway, putting his feet on the step, and in this position, passed his own regiment, the 2nd Gurkhas, and had great fun watching the men as he gravely salaamed to them, grinning as they tried to salute. Also, Surgeon-Major Evatt (in his *Recollections of the Afghan War*) tells the story of an officer's wife, who, having had the good luck to procure a carriage to take her from Jhelam to Rawalpindi, was asked by the post-master at the former place to allow a native officer to travel on the top of her carriage (reported in Hanna 1899).

Colonel Hanna describes in detail the first major military encounter across the Frontier, in the second volume of his account of the second Afghan War

(Hanna 1899). This involved 'the taking of Ali Masjid', a massive Afghan fortress above the Khyber River. This action involved the Peshawar field force, and included both of the Gurkha brigades. The British forces were eventually successful in taking the fortress, but Hanna remarks, in his critical assessment of the fighting, that the troops were 'hampered' by camp followers. Later he refers to one senior officer as having adopted 'the unusual course of giving to each regiment the charge of its own baggage, thus interposing camp followers and baggage animals between the different units of the column, a disposition which must have interfered with the mobility of his troops and with his power of control over them as a united body'.

After the taking of Ali Masjid, the advance further into Afghan territory took place with different dispositions and routes for different commands of the British forces, under Sir Sam Browne, General Maude and General Roberts respectively. The second division of the Peshawar Field Force (with the 2nd Gurkhas), for example, moved on to Jalalabad, while Roberts advanced through the Kuram Valley with the Kuram Field Force (which included the 5th Gurkhas). The key encounter for this section of the British forces was at Peiwar Kotal, a high pass in the Peiwar mountains. Despite some strategic errors by General Roberts, they were eventually successful in defeating the Afghan resistance. Here again, however, Hanna refers to at least one occasion when troops and baggage, soldiers and camp followers 'were mingled in one confused and struggling mass'.

British victories at the Battle of Ali Masjid and the Battle of Peiwar Kotal meant that the approach to Kabul was left virtually undefended by Afghan troops. An alarmed Sher Ali attempted to appeal in person to the Russian Tsar for assistance, but their insistence was that he should seek terms of surrender from the British. He returned to Mazar-i-Sharif, where he died on 21 February 1879. With British forces occupying much of the country, Sher Ali's son and successor, Mohammed Yaqub Khan, signed the Treaty of Gandamak in May 1879 to prevent a British invasion of the rest of the country. According to this agreement and in return for an annual subsidy and vague assurances of assistance in case of foreign aggression, Yaqub relinquished control of Afghan foreign affairs to Britain. British representatives were installed in Kabul and other locations, British control was extended to the Khyber and Michni passes, and Afghanistan ceded various North Western Frontier Province areas and Quetta to Britain.

The summer of 1879 saw the spread of cholera throughout much of northern India, reaching even into Afghanistan. The order to retire by the Kabul River route was given at the end of May, and the British Army began to withdraw. The 'native' regiments marched separately, with their own baggage train and camp followers. Colonel Hanna describes the return from Afghanistan as 'the march of death': 'at each camping ground, every regiment and corps left its toll of dead'. The heat, the dust, and the disease, meant that every contingent suffered serious casualties, with barely a shot being fired; even the medical personnel fell ill and died, and were buried along the route.

Hanna records that 'the march of death extended over a period of five weeks, from the end of May to the beginning of July, and during that time there were three hundred and fifty four deaths from cholera among the European troops. Their 'native' comrades suffered less severely, yet even in their ranks, the mortality was heavy, and numbers of camp followers fell victims to the disease'. In Kandahar, 458 camp followers fell ill, and 259 of these died. In the Khyber and the Kuram, the numbers were not recorded, but in both of these, Hanna reckons the losses were 'undoubtedly very heavy'.

The Treaty of Gandamuk was always 'a beginning', not the end, of British plans for Afghanistan. The Kuram, for example, showed no sign of returning to peace and order; indeed, 'all along the lines of communications, soldiers and camp followers were still frequently murdered, baggage animals stolen, camels carried off by deserters...' In July, Sir Louis Cagnari took up his post as British envoy at the court of the Amir in Kabul. His safety was a matter of concern, so he was given an escort; even so, one Lord Lawrence warned that 'they will all be murdered, every one of them'. Indeed, on 3 September 1879, an uprising in Kabul led to the slaughter of Sir Louis Cavagnari, along with his guards, and staff – provoking the next phase of the Second Afghan War.

Major General Sir Frederick Roberts now led the Kabul Field Force – comprising some 6,500 troops, of which 2,558 were British, 18 guns and 6,000 camp followers (supported by a further 3-4,000 to maintain his lines of communication) - over the Shutargardan Pass into central Afghanistan, defeated the Afghan Army at Charasiab on 6 October 1879, and occupied Kabul two days later. The 5th Gurkhas were a part of this force, and their baggage and camp followers accompanied them. It was during the engagement at Charasiab that Private MacMahon of the 72nd Highlanders led a handful of Gurkhas in a bayonet charge that earned him the Victoria Cross.

The occupation of Kabul did not end the fighting, and attempts to open up the Khyber route to Kabul to support General Roberts led over the next two months to several engagements, which involved the 2nd and 4th Gurkhas among others. In December, Ghazi Mohammad Jan Khan Wardak and a force of 10,000 Afghans staged an uprising and attacked British forces near Kabul, first threatening then besieging the Sherpur Cantonment. He failed to maintain the siege, however, shifting focus to Roberts' force which was deployed to draw the Afghans off; and this resulted in the collapse of this insurrection. Yaqub Khan, suspected of complicity in the massacre of Cavagnari and his staff, was obliged to abdicate.

The British considered a number of possible political settlements, including partitioning Afghanistan between multiple rulers or placing Yaqub's brother Ayub Khan on the throne, but ultimately decided to install his cousin Abdur Rahman Khan as Amir instead. Ayub Khan, who had been serving as governor of Herat, rose in revolt, defeated a British detachment at the Battle of Maiwand in July 1880 and besieged Kandahar. Roberts then led the main British force from Kabul and decisively defeated Ayub Khan on 1 September at the Battle of Kandahar, bringing his rebellion to an end.

In the meanwhile, in 1868, the 2nd Gurkha Regiment (former Sirmoor Rifles) were in action on the North-West Frontier against the tribes of the Black Mountain in Hazara, and in 1871 they were at the other extreme of the country, in Assam. Assam was attracting British tea planters, but the local tribes resisted their settlement. One planter couple were killed and their little daughter, Mary Winchester, kidnapped. An expedition under the command of Brigadier-General Brownlow set out in the autumn of 1871. The aim was to suppress the troublesome tribes and rescue the girl. In one encounter, two men (Major Donald Macintyre and Rifleman Inderjit Thapa) scaled the stockade and fought their way through the desperate tribesmen before they were joined by the rest of the Gurkhas. Macintyre received the VC and Thapa the Indian Order of Merit 3rd Class – the highest award for bravery available to 'native Indians'[23].

❁ ❁ ❁

---

23. To achieve IOM 1st Class, a soldier had to perform 3 acts of bravery; only six men ever achieved this in the 74 years that the medal existed. This iniquity was abolished in 1911 when Indians and Gurkhas could be awarded the VC. As for Mary Winchester, she was found alive and unharmed.

CHAPTER 14

New Rules for Gurkha Recruitment

Until the Sugauli Treaty of 1816 that ended the Anglo-Nepal War and clearly marked off the territories of Nepal and the English East India Company, there was little sense of an international border, and there were few effective restrictions on leaving the country. Following the war, however, under Bhimsen Thapa, the state placed strict formal restrictions on Nepalis leaving the country; although never fully enforced, this form of border control remained in place until 1885, when the British were given permission to begin recruitment within Nepal itself, and the official 'open border' system was re-established.

The death of Jung Bahadur in February 1877 changed little with respect to the official position of the government of Nepal regarding the direct recruitment of Gurkhas - which was to oppose it; but clandestine direct recruitment continued to take place. There was always a demand for men from the hills of Nepal for the Gurkha brigades. Indeed, within a year or so after his death, the British had need of men, as the Second Afghan War began. However, efforts by successive British Residents to put pressure on the Nepali government to allow direct recruitment of Gurkhas failed, and even requests to provide 1,000 recruits on the outbreak of the Second Anglo-Afghan War (1878-80) resulted only in 559 men after six months of persuasion; and 339 of these were rejected because they were declared 'the lame, the halt, the maimed and the blind' (Rathaur 1995: 61).

Commanding officers of the Gurkha regiments were concerned that they might face the unwelcome choice between dropping standards in recruitment - including accepting so-called 'inferior' tribes like Sunwars and Rais - and letting the regiments fall below full strength. But it is not entirely clear whether many of them could have distinguished between the different ethnic groups in any case, despite the ethnological efforts of Brian Hodgson some decades earlier. As we have already seen, Eden Vansittart, who joined the Indian service as Emigration Agent to Surinam in 1876 and came into contact quite soon with many Nepalis there, declared that he doubted whether anyone could tell the difference between Magars, Gurungs, Rais and Sunwars (Vansittart 1993: introduction 4).

Others also, like the British Resident Gridlestone, recommended in any case that the recruitment of soldiers from those ethnic groups considered 'less martial' be entertained, as well as the possibility of recruiting from Kumaon, Garhwal and Punjab hill states (Rathaur 1995: 61). In fact, men from Kumaon and Garhwal had served in the Gurkhas for some 70 years before they were institutionally separated within the Indian Army from 'the Gorkhalis'. Indeed, it was not until after 1887, when a separate regiment was created for them, for example, that Lansdowne was built as a cantonment station for the Garhwal Rifles Regiment (Basu 2016: 1).

As Shrabani Basu remarks, 'the Garhwalis and Gurkhas who has surrendered in 1815 were absorbed in the British Indian Army and until 1887 fought together in the ranks of the first five Gurkha regiments. It was General Lord Roberts, the Commander-in-Chief of the Indian Army and the hero of the siege of Kandahar, who in 1886 raised the proposition that the Garhwalis should have their own regiment. 'The men would be of an excellent fighting class', said the General...' (Basu 2016: 4).

He also favoured the Pathans, the Baluchis, the Sikhs, the Punjabi Muslims, the Rajputs, the Dogras and the 'Gurkhas', whether from Garhwal, Kumaon or Nepal. 'Lord Roberts had a clear policy: he preferred to recruit from the martial races of India and also from those classes that had been loyal to the British during the Mutiny. According to Roberts: 'no comparison can be made between the martial value of a regiment recruited amongst the Gurkhas of Nepal or the warlike races of Northern India, and of one recruited from the effeminate peoples of the South' (Basu 2016: 29).

Colonel Sail Hill, however, a veteran officer of the 1st Gurkhas, worried more about 'fitness' than ethnic origin: 'if the Nepal Durbar supplies us with recruits similar to those lately received, we shall either have to reject them at an expense to the state or to flood our ranks with a class of men that will deteriorate Gorkha Regiments' (cited in Rathaur 1995: 61). One proposal in response to this from Resident Gridlestone was to offer 'head money' to the Durbar for every fit recruit. He also suggested that all Nepali recruits should be allowed to take their wives and children with them, and that pensioners be given 'healthy encouragement' to settle in British territory, so as to create a source of new recruits in the future.

These suggestions were not acceptable to the high command for various reasons – expense, dilution of 'martial tribes', and danger of creating an inappropriate 'family' context for fighting men. But, as we shall see, the development of family 'lines' and 'settlements' for the 'Gurkhas' had already begun in reality. At the same time, however, the government of Nepal was making it very difficult to recruit new soldiers. A census was taken among the so-called military tribes and the village headmen were ordered to prevent anyone leaving without Royal permission. House to house enquiries were carried out and names of all adult males noted. The families of those who had 'sneaked' into the British Army were, it is reported, 'tortured' (Rathaur 1995: 62).

Retired Gurkha soldiers found it difficult to draw their pensions. Recruiting agents operating into Nepal from across the borders were liable to execution, if caught. Resident Gridlestone reported that, 'whereas formerly, men caught in Nepal recruiting for us were to be bound and sent to British territory, they are now to be cut in two. Men are sent about in disguise, badly dressed and apparently in great want, and if asked by a recruiting agent to enlist, they immediately turn round and seize him. He is kept in custody then, and gets anything but gentle treatment' (cited in Rathaur 1995: 63).

But the attraction of serving in the British Army was such that, by 1879, despite these restrictions, there were 4,685 Gurkhas in the British Indian Army, with 16 Gurkha officers and 85 *sepoys* or riflemen in each of the five Regiments and other men in the 42nd, 43rd and 44th Infantry Regiments[24]. In 1883, the Government of India ordered that Gurkhas be enlisted *only* in Gurkha regiments – this included not only the five numbered regiments of Gurkha infantry, but also the 42nd, 43rd and 44th regiments of the Bengal Native Infantry (which at the beginning of the 20th century became Gurkha regiments - the 43rd, the 6th Gurkha Rifles, and the 43rd and 44th, the 2nd/8th and 1st/8th respectively).

The next year, in 1884, the British Government in India decided to try to increase the number of Gurkha Battalions from five to ten, adding a second Battalion to each Regiment. The idea was to double the total number of Gurkhas. Negotiations on recruitment with the Nepali government under Prime Minister Ranoudip Singh proved difficult; but the bloody coup of November 1885, which

---

24. While all other Regiments would have 832 men, the Gurkhas would have 912 in each regiment.

brought Bir Shumshere Rana to power, also resulted in an effective liberalisation of the Nepali government's position on army recruitment. Bir Shumshere not only gave his approval to the plan to raise five more Gurkha Battalions but was prepared to assist in the process of recruitment and to accept the establishment of a central recruiting depot at Kunraghat, Gorakhpur, in the United Provinces not far from the frontier with Nepal.

In 1885, the Indian government purchased 'Goorkha Village', which was close to the railway station in Gorakhpur and could accommodate several hundred recruits. The area was sealed off so that "none but recruiting parties, recruits and the small bazaar (sic) establishment were on any account to be allowed to reside within the limits of the Village" (Mercer, cited in Farwell 1984: 74). Captain Mercer of the 1/4th Gurkhas, and in charge of recruitment, approved of Gorakhpur[25] as the centre for recruitment for western Nepal for it was within a few days of the hill areas and also the headquarters of the Bengal North-Western Railway, which allowed recruits to be easily brought in and then deployed to their respective stations.

Prior to 1886, there was no centralised system of Gurkha recruitment. Gorakhpur had been used as an unofficial recruiting post before it was made a major centre. Recruits would be housed in *serais* in the town, many of which were filthy dens in which healthy young men contracted diseases, many dying of cholera, before being sent on to their respective stations or barracks. This would eventually change as new rules for Gurkha recruitment were introduced in 1886. In that year, regular recruitment under the new dispensation was started (Morris 1963: 38) and the Rana regime was formally recognised by the British Government in India.

But, if the new Prime Minister, Bir Shumshere Rana, was prepared to support recruitment by the British through a post located in India, he was not happy with the proposal, presented by Colonel Berkley, to permit the Gurkhas serving in the Indian Army officially to take their families with them, and thereby develop cantonments with the potential for a continuous supply of recruits - even though the British had now established 'homes' for their Gurkha regiments. Bir Shumshere also insisted on initial recruitment within Nepal. This proved only moderately successful.

---

25. The origins of the name of this town are not clear, but it is possible that its proximity to Nepal and population of Nepalis had given rise to the name 'Gorkha-town' – Gorkha-pur.

First, money was offered as an inducement and then each village was obliged to supply a fixed number of recruits. Out of seven or eight thousand men who appeared before the army doctor that year, as a result of this pressure from above, only 2,200 were found fit for recruitment. One consequence of these pressures on a somewhat reluctant local population was a tendency at this period for candidates for recruitment to come from less well-off families, and from a greater variety of social backgrounds (in terms of caste as well as economic status). It may well also have affected the 'quality' of those recruited.

Not only did this approach fail to produce the required number of recruits, however; it made the whole process extremely unpopular at the local level. When Captain Mercer assessed the results of the first recruiting season under the new system, he was not satisfied with their quality and concluded that, 'the system of Regimental Recruiting, with all its drawbacks, is infinitely superior to that of recruiting through Durbar officials' (Farwell 1984: 74). The increased collaboration between the Nepalese government and the British recruiting agents from 1886-87 onwards, however, was rewarded by a strong response. Force was not used and almost all of the recruits came of their own accord.

The British Resident noted '... a far higher return, numerical and proportional, for filling vacancies than that of any previous year; and by dint of the efforts used the percentage of Magars and Gurungs for the line battalions has been more than maintained' (Rathaur 1995: 76). The British government in India now became increasingly convinced that a policy of conciliation, compromise and collaboration might bear more fruit than one which effectively threatened the independence of Nepal and its government. Over the next ten years, in part as a result of the influence of Lord Dufferin as Governor General of India and Lord Roberts of Kandahar, Commander-in-Chief of the Indian Army from 1885, British policy towards recruitment evolved away from its earlier heavy-handed and oppressive character. This had the additional benefit of making life easier for the recruiting parties.

❀ ❀ ❀

CHAPTER 15

Sex and Marriage

There is little doubt that prostitution developed and flourished in 19th century India wherever there were large bodies of men away from home – that is, in the larger cities and near army camps and barracks. There are indications that, in some cases at least, the areas that later became 'red light districts' and home to civilian brothels began life as institutions designed, literally, to service the Indian Army.

For example the famous Kamathipura, a red light area in Mumbai which was built during this era specifically for the refreshment of British troops, was later taken over by Indian sex workers operating on the basis of private enterprise. It was first settled after 1795, with the construction of causeways that connected the erstwhile seven islands of Bombay. Initially known as Lal Bazaar, it got its name from the *kamathis* (workers) of other areas of the country, who were labourers on the construction sites. The name then became more generally applied to brothels across the country.

We have little information of living conditions in army barracks or regimental stations in India in the early part of the 19th century, but we know that *lal bazaars* – essentially regimental brothels – and associated lock hospitals (known as such after the London Lock Hospital, where prostitutes were confined) were common wherever the army was stationed. They were reserved exclusively for soldiers, in a segregated order: one set just for officers, another for white enlisted men and a third for '*Indian sepoys*'. A madam on the government's payroll selected the women.

In the meanwhile, in the second half of the century, colonial administrators sought increasingly, through legislation, to create a contained market of disease-free prostitutes, specially certified to operate in regimental bazaars within the boundaries of British cantonments in India. In 1864, the Cantonment Act had required those selected as official prostitutes to register with the authorities as sex workers. They also had to submit twice a month to painful and humiliating physical exams denounced by feminists in London as 'instrumental rape by a steel penis' and 'medical lust.' If infected, the women were incarcerated in lock hospitals for treatment, rendering them unable to work and support any dependents.

Four years later, in 1868, a copycat of existing British law, the Contagious Diseases Act (CDA), extended those rules to prostitutes serving the wider population in major towns and cities across India. Under the law, every prostitute in those jurisdictions had to carry a pass bearing her name, caste and address and confine herself to certain neighbourhoods. Every sex worker also had to declare herself to be one, an official avowal that removed, irrevocably, all grey areas in her life. Kept women, moonlighting factory workers, flower-sellers and milkmaids who did it on the side, high-class *baijis* who were divas of classical dance all had to embrace an identity that—even as it was being regulated as a necessary social evil—was becoming black-and-white and stigmatized.

Police conducted frequent raids and harassed women, who faced the prospect of jail, with hard labour, if they failed to register as prostitutes or be examined regularly for venereal disease. The CDA was a law to be resisted and fled, and many women did resist and flee. They resisted by bribing police, in some cases. In others, they produced false marriage certificates or presented evidence before magistrates that they were mistresses rather than professional prostitutes. Many fled to a French settlement north of Calcutta or to areas in the outlying countryside where the act was not in effect. Others sneaked into central neighbourhoods to work at night, commuting home to suburban safe zones during the day. As one feminist historian has put it, 'women in prostitution played a hide-and-seek of sorts with policemen'.

The concern of the authorities regarding the risk of infection as a result of large-scale multiple sexual encounters associated with brothels and red light districts were, of course, justified, in the sense that sexually transmitted diseases (STDs) were a real issue at this time. One of the major concerns was syphilis. In 1808, a British doctor in Mysore had ranked syphilis next to smallpox as one of 'the most destructive and most perilous disease[s] in India', and claimed that 'few middle-aged males were entirely free of it' (Arnold 1993: 3). By the early nineteenth century, when the British had gained ascendency over a large part of the subcontinent, syphilis was already widely disseminated, though the extent of its incidence can only be guessed at.

It seems likely that the disease was introduced by the Portuguese in the early 16th century. Evidence suggests that syphilis was unknown in India before the early 16th century; some of the earliest references are to be found in the Bhavaprakasa, a mid-sixteenth century text reputedly the work of an Ayurvedic physician in Benares (Varanasi). At that time and for a long time afterwards, the disease was known as *firangi roga* (the foreigner's disease) (Arnold 1993: 3-8).

In the first half of the nineteenth century STDs were known to be widely present among European soldiers. In 1805, for instance, an assistant surgeon of the East India Company in Trichinopoly in south India referred to the 'great havoc' wrought by venereal disease among European troops stationed in the town.'

Until the 1850s, however, the incidence of debilitating but rarely fatal STDs was overshadowed by heavy mortality from cholera, malaria, dysentery, and other causes. Though no clear distinction was yet made between syphilis and other venereal infections, the full extent of STDs in the army first became clear around the middle of the nineteenth century. According to David Arnold, 'in Bengal, the province in which the majority of European soldiers were stationed, 177 men out of every thousand were admitted to hospital in 1855 for the treatment of STDs' (Arnold 1993: 3). However, in the wake of the Crimean War and the reforms in army nursing and medical provision instituted by Florence Nightingale, the Indian Rebellion of 1857-8 highlighted the atrocious state of health among European soldiers in India.

The uprising also raised the political commitment to soldiers' health by increasing British reliance upon white rather than Indian troops for the maintenance of colonial power in South Asia. The Royal Commission on the Sanitary State of the Army in India, which reported in 1863, stressed the imperative need for drastic improvements in the health of European soldiers in India: venereal disease was an important element in this. Following the influx of large numbers of British troops during the Mutiny campaigns, the figure for hospital admissions for the treatment of STDs rose steeply to 359 admissions per 1,000 men in 1859, only to fall back to 167 in 1867.

The introduction of the short-service system into the British Army in 1870 resulted in an increased proportion of young, unmarried soldiers being sent to

India. By 1880, 41 per cent of British soldiers in India were under 25 years old, with a further 34 per cent between the ages of 25 and 29. Though officially 12 per cent of British soldiers were permitted to have wives with them 'on the strength', the actual proportion was far smaller than this: only 3.7 per cent in 1890, for example, with as few as 2.8 per cent in the infantry, according to David Arnold (1993: 3). The recourse to infected Indian prostitutes by young, unmarried soldiers was seen to be the primary explanation for the high incidence of STDs in the British army.

The number of hospital admissions (identified in almost equal proportion with primary syphilis and with gonorrhoea) rose to 205 per 1,000 in 1875 and peaked at 522 per 1,000 in 1895. This was equivalent to more than half the army being hospitalised each year and the loss of more than a million military man-days. Although the number of deaths directly attributed to STDs was very small (less than 1 per cent of the total in 1890, they were a significant cause of invaliding from the army (13.2 per cent). After 1895, however, the rate of admissions declined dramatically - to 276 per 1,000 in 1901, 117 in 1906 and 68 in 1909. By 1913 it was down to 53, virtually a tenth of the 1895 peak.

Among 'Indian' soldiers, interestingly, the reported incidence of STDs was far lower than among Europeans. In 1877, the rate of admissions per 1,000 was 27; in 1890, it was 41 and in 1895, 31. However, these figures should be treated with caution: Indian soldiers before the First World War were subjected to far less medical scrutiny than British troops, and venereal complaints among them were probably significantly under-reported (Arnold 1993: 4). Most of the women employed as prostitutes in India, whether in civilian red light districts or in regulated army brothels, were themselves Indians. But a certain number may well have been from Nepal.

For not all of the Nepalis now living in India were soldiers, ex-soldiers and army wives; many, as we have seen, were civilian migrants who had come to work or to settle where there were opportunities for employment and a congenial life among people of their own kind. We have no idea, however, of how many of these were women, as early census data for India (starting in 1872) did not include this level of detail. (The first 'complete' census was not take until 1881). It is not at all improbable, however, that some at least of these were Nepali women looking to provide sexual services to the 'boys away from home' who were not married or had not brought their wives and families to the station.

Relatively little is known about the early history of prostitution and trafficking from Nepal to India, but a study by Human Rights Watch in 1995 suggested that

> 'trafficking of women from Nepal's hill communities began in the nineteenth century, when the feudal Rana family, a line of prime ministers who ruled Nepal from 1846 to 1951, began recruiting Tamang girls from the Helambu (Yolmo) region of Sindhupalchowk, northeast of Kathmandu, to serve as concubines for the ruler and his family. Owning concubines, or "Helambu girls," became a mark of high social status. The oligarchical Rana regime was overthrown by the hereditary monarchy in 1951, but the recruitment of women and girls continued, only now they were sold to brothel owners in India's red-light districts.

> The internationalization of trafficking in girls and women was due in part to a political alliance forged between Nepal and India in the last days of the Rana regime that opened the border between the two countries for travel and trade. Nuwakot, Sindhupalchok and other hill districts in the Bagmati Zone around Kathmandu became particularly notorious for trafficking. But as Indian demand for Nepali prostitutes grew, and the threat of AIDS increased the demand for new girls, girls from many castes and communities and from other regions of Nepal were recruited for sale in Indian brothels'.

This suggests that the development of trafficking and of the prostitution of Nepali women in India is a relatively recent phenomenon, associated with the period after the overthrow of the Ranas. It says nothing about the earlier involvement of Nepal women in prostitution in India, or the relationship between civilian and army brothels. This remains an area that deserves serious research.

British Gurkha officers still had their own sexual and marital arrangements, and opportunities for discrete 'recreation'; Farwell remarks, for example, that 'from the post-Mutiny period, when India was again safe for British women, there were no more Gurkha mistresses, but there were temptations. John Masters, as a young lieutenant in charge of the regimental depot while his battalion was on the North-West Frontier was inspecting the married quarters when, he says, he encountered a beautiful, sexually hungry young Nepalese woman who turned his stomach to water as she looked longingly at him. He felt that he had only to say the word and she would be in his bed, but after wrestling with his conscience for several nights he remained unsullied – and saved his career' (Farwell p. 131).

Active service often kept men (whether British, Indian or Nepali) away from 'home' for months, even years.[26] When their men were away, the women left behind were naturally lonely and bored. As far as the Nepali wives were concerned, they were alone in a strange land; they usually spoke little Urdu or Hindi, and many spoke little or no Nepali, but only their own native language. It would be dangerous to generalise from John Masters' reported experience, but some of these women would surely have been tempted into sexual liaisons or sexual encounters with other men around the married lines.

Indeed, sometimes, when bachelor lines were too close to the married lines of a battalion on active service, there was trouble. This appears to have been particularly the case at the end of the First World War, when all the men returning from active service abroad were sent to Dehra Dun to regain their caste (lost by travel overseas) by the *pani patiya* ceremony, and some were quartered close to the married lines of a battalion still on active service. Some wives found solace with lovers from among the soldiers soon to be discharged, and a few left with them for Nepal. The commandant of the 2/2nd Gurkhas, for example, protested to the brigade major of the 17th Indian Division at 'much interference and annoyance by men of the stranger battalions' (Farwell p. 148).

It was not only in the cantonments and the married 'lines' that sexual liaisons and adultery took place. Back home, when men were away for months and even years on end, there were bound to be 'affairs' between *lahure* wives and other men who had remained in the village. This had always been the case, since the early 19th century at least; and there were in fact recognised rights for men who discovered they had been cuckolded and then killed their wife's lover. We shall see that, in the First World War, not only the serving men but also the Nepali authorities were at pains to ensure that these rights for such 'wronged husbands' were clarified and maintained.

Aware of these difficulties, the army now attempted as far as possible to ensure that soldiers were able to return to their families in the hills when they went on leave. From 1885, for example, the army gave soldiers proceeding to leave a free pass on the railway, and not long afterwards began to provide similar assistance – railway warrants - to wives wishing to visit their husbands in their stations. All of this was to encourage recruitment and to maintain continuity of

---

26. The 2/5th for example left its 'home' in Abbottabad in December 1915 and did not return until June 1919. They then had only one day at home before they marched out to take part in the Third Afghan War.

employment. The troops themselves undoubtedly found it good to have a 'home' in India, a familiar place to come back to after whatever action they had seen when stationed elsewhere.

Farwell records, for example, how 'when the 1/2th returned to Dehra Dun after the Tirah campaign, in which they had been engaged thirty-two times in battles with tribesmen and had fought nineteen rearguard actions, it was welcomed not just by the families of the regiment, but by the entire civilian population as well. A considerable sum had been collected from Europeans and Indians for a celebration, and the battalion was treated to a banquet and fireworks; a handsome piece of plate was presented to the officers' mess and a generous donation made to the Widows Fund' (Farwell 1985: 146).

Smaller donations were made by individuals, suggesting an important sense of 'place' attached to the regimental 'home'. At Abbottabad in 1905, for example, two bath-houses were constructed with Rs 896 given by the mother of Bugler Chuni Damai (a *dalit*) of the 5th Gurkhas to perpetuate the memory of her son, killed on the North West Frontier. Even in peace time, there were occasions when the values attached to the idea of the regimental home were demonstrated.

In April 1905, for example, a severe earthquake hit Dharmsala in the Kangra hills, 'home' of the 1st Gurkhas. Many of the barracks were levelled. Less than a month before, the 2/8th had arrived at Dharmsala, in time to suffer the loss of 139 men dead and 54 severely injured; many wives and children were also killed or injured. Lord Kitchener started a relief fund for injured men and their families to which other Gurkha regiments gave generously. So many behaved bravely during the crisis that one man from each company was selected to receive the Order of St John of Jerusalem on behalf of his company and all those attached to it (Farwell p. 173-74).

❀ ❀ ❀

Chapter 16

Nurses in the New Indian Army

Shrestha and Conway have remarked that the tradition of migration and recruitment into the British Army in India 'was fully cemented following Prime Minister Bir Shamsher's determined efforts in the 1880s to assist the British in rounding up hill recruits for their imperial army' (Des Chene 1993; Shrestha 1990, Shrestha & Conway 2001: 164). In parallel with this, there was a major revision of the structure and organisation of the Gurkha elements of the Indian Army in the 1880s.

In 1888, Eden Vansittart (of the 5th Gurkhas), was posted from Surinam (where he had served as Emigration Agent for the Indian Service) to the main recruiting centre at Gorakhpur, where he was to be assistant recruiting officer. He had entered the Indian Army in 1876, and served in the Mahsud Waziri Expedition (1881) and the Hazara campaign (1888). In the winter of that year, he was deputed to Kathmandu as assistant to the Resident, to arrange for a visit to Calcutta by Bir Shumshere Rana, and at the end of 1888, Bir Shumshere himself visited Calcutta to reassure the Governor General of India of the regular supply of recruits to the British Gurkhas. When he claimed for the expenses incurred in the process, he was promised a bonus of Rs 20 for every recruit approved and a Sinder rifle for every recruit, up to the limit of 5,000.

The first army handbook on the Gurkhas, published in 1890, was written by Vansittart, in his role as chief recruiting officer at the recently established Gurkha recruiting depot at Gorakhpur, just across the border from Nepal (Vansittart 1890)[27]. Recruitment now began to take off with a vengeance. In the period from 1886 to 1892, altogether 7,662 Nepalis were recruited. Later,

---

27. Vansittart visited Kathmandu for a second time in 1889, when he was military assistant in charge of arrangements for Prince Albert Victor's shooting trip, which took place in March 1890.

Vansittart was to note that 'up till 1888 cases of recruiters being ill-treated in Nepal were of common occurrence, but thanks to the firmness of our Residents and the broad-minded policy of successive Prime Ministers, such cases are now seldom heard of, and recruiters are allowed to carry on their work unmolested' (Vansittart 1993: 148). This was a new situation.

'In 1886, for example the 1ˢᵗ Gurkhas' became the 1st Goorkha Light Infantry and a 2nd Battalion was raised in February. In 1891 the Regiment was designated as the 1st Gurkha (Rifle) Regiment or 1ˢᵗ Gurkha Rifles. From 1887, Garhwalis were recruited to a distinct, newly created Garhwal Rifles Regiment. Over the next few years a cantonment, parade ground and post office were constructed for the new regiment, and in September 1890 it was named after the then Viceroy, Lord Lansdowne.

In the meanwhile, another development that resulted eventually from the take-over by the India Office from the British East India Company was the institution of a nursing corps. Miss Ada Hind, who had experience as a Sister-in-Charge at the Royal Victoria Hospital in Suez, Egypt, had been asked to form an Indian Army Nursing Service, but she declined because of her ill health. Instead, two nursing sisters, Miss Loch and Miss Oxley, were chosen by the India Office to supervise and train nurses in the military hospitals in India and to work with the men of the Army Hospital Corps. The two became Nursing Superintendents (their official title was Lady Superintendent), and in early 1888 they took eight nursing sisters from Britain to India to form the Indian Army Nursing Service (IANS).

Almost immediately, Miss Loch and four of the new sisters saw field service with the Black Mountain Expedition - also known as the 'Hazara Field Force 1888' - one of the first major campaigns on the North-West Frontier of India in the last two decades of the 19th Century (cited in Juliet Piggott's book *Queen Alexandra's Royal Army Nursing Corps (Famous Regts.* S). This may have been the first time that British Army nurses were armed, for these sisters carried revolvers to ward off enemy and robbers.

On 18 June 1888, two British officers and four Gurkha soldiers had been killed in an altercation between British reconnaissance patrols and local tribes. The tribes involved were given an ultimatum, with a deadline of 2 October 1888. When this deadline passed without satisfactory response, the Hazara Field Force was assembled and began its march on 4 October 1888. The first phase of the campaign, against the Hassanzai and Akazai, ended with an armistice on 19 October 1888. The second phase of the campaign targeted the tribes that lived north of Black Mountain including the Allaiwals. The campaign ended when the Allaiwal village of Pokal was occupied and destroyed by the British on 2 and 3 November 1888. The then Commander-in-Chief in India, General Sir Frederick Roberts, viewed the Expedition as:

> 'a success from a military point of view, but ... the determination of the Punjab Government to limit the sphere of action of the troops, and to hurry out of the country, prevented our reaping any political advantage. We lost a grand opportunity for gaining control over this lawless and troublesome district; no survey was made, no roads opened out, the tribesmen were not made to feel our power, and, consequently, very soon another costly expedition had to be undertaken'.

The failure of the tribes to honour the agreements that ended the 1888 campaign led to a further two-month expedition by a Hazara Field Force in 1891. British and Indian Army troops who took part in these expeditions received the India General Service Medal with the clasps Hazara 1888 and Hazara 1891 respectively. It is not clear what commendations, if any, the Army nurses received.

In 1892, Commander-in-Chief Roberts visited Bir Shimshere Rana in Kathmandu - the first time a high-ranking British officer had done so. The initiative was well received and as a result the recruiting operation was systematised. Recruiting parties were allowed to travel freely throughout the country, but new recruiting depots outside the country, in addition to Gorakhpur, were established at Pilibhit and Bahraich. The majority of those recruited were still Magars and Gurungs from the western hills (Rathaur 1995: 86), but a more systematic enlistment of Rais and Limbus (Kiranti peoples) from the eastern hills was also initiated.

A couple of years before, in 1890 - the year that the cantonment at Landsdowne was made available for the newly formed Garhwali Rifle Regiment - the British also began deliberately to recruit Kiranti for the 7th and 10th Gurkhas, and a new recruitment post was established in Darjeeling. At first, this was only a single room located in the bazaar, and recruits and recruiters lodged wherever they could find accommodation. This was the beginning of a major 'tradition' of Indian army employment for Rais and Limbus, which was to have a profound effect on local economy and society in the eastern hills for the next hundred years and more.

Darjeeling had been used for many years as a recruiting depot for the Assam and Burma Military Police battalions; from 1890, the police battalions were also recruited from the eastern hills of Nepal. In 1893, the recruiting parties for the Assam and Burma police, and for the Assam Rifles, were placed under the orders of the District Recruiting Officer for Gurkhas for the first time (Farwell 1984: 76). Darjeeling was to grow significantly in importance over the next few decades – and not only as a centre for army recruitment, but also for civilian migrant workers from Nepal, including, notably, Sherpas from Solu Khumbu.

❀ ❀ ❀

CHAPTER 17

Destination Darjeeling

From the 1850s onwards, as the British began building roads and tea plantations in North East India[28], both Darjeeling (only ten miles from the Nepalese border) and Assam also began to see a rising tide of immigration (English 1985). Most were from the hill areas of eastern Nepal (O'Malley 1907: 43; Shrestha & Conway 2001: 169). The establishment of the first tea plantations on a commercial basis was in 1856, in Aloobari and Lebong. By 1866, there were about 39 gardens in the region. The clearing of the forests, opening out of land to people, the introduction and establishment of machinery, the establishment of the tea industry, agriculture all required more labour. Already by 1870, tea-garden 'coolies' and their families constituted some 70 per cent of the total Nepali population in Darjeeling (Pradhan 1982, cited in Onta 1996: 42).

The migration of Nepali labourers was specifically encouraged by the British in Darjeeling as early as the 1870s and J. W. Edgar, the Deputy Commissioner of Darjeeling at the time, reported the presence of numerous Nepali migrants in south-west Sikkim (Balicki 2008: 49-50, footnote 20). The Darjeeling Himalayan Railway was opened in Darjeeling in 1881. Darjeeling became a major 'hill station' for the British expatriates. All of this 'development' stimulated the growth of the population as a whole; by 1891, some 88,000 out of a total population of 223,314 in Darjeeling reported their place of birth as Nepal. The 1921 Indian census states that 'in 1891, nearly two fifths of the population of the Darjeeling district had been born in Nepal, and the proportion of Nepalese born in Sikkim in 1901... is about the same' (1921: 95).

Figures for 1901 show that the vast majority of the population of Darjeeling (135,000 out of 249,000) were people of Nepali origin from the eastern hills,

---

28. Subba (1992: 45) estimates that there were 39 gardens in 1866, 56 in 1870, 113 in 1874, 153 in 1881 and 177 in 1891.

including 33,133 Rais, 24,465 Tamangs, 14,305 Limbus, 11,912 Magars, 11,597 Chhetris, 9,826 Kamis, 8,378 Gurungs, 6,470 Brahmins, 5,770 Newars, 4,643 Damais, and 4,428 Sunuwars, etc. (Pradhan 1982: 34, cited in Onta 1996: 42 note 7). While undoubtedly some of these were from the literate Nepalese 'middle' classes (from Kathmandu and from elsewhere) – who made Darjeeling a famous centre of Nepali literature in the 1920s (Onta 1996) – the majority, however, were certainly men and women of modest peasant farming and agricultural labouring origins who were working in a variety of largely menial forms of employment, for whom Nepali was a *lingua franca* rather than a mother tongue (Nakane 1996; Regmi 1978).

Migration for agricultural and other economic purposes was only part of the story of emigration eastwards at this period. Between 1890-91 and 1903-94, a total of 1,734 men, of which the majority were Limbus and Rais, were recruited into the British Army from the eastern hills (Vansittart 1993: 174). Recruiting for the army, or for the military police, in Darjeeling district itself was, however, strictly prohibited, as it was considered to interfere with the labour of the surrounding tea-gardens, and all those enlisted through Darjeeling had to be brought in either from Nepal or from Sikkim, where there was also now a large Nepali colony.

Some (eg Major Nicolay) did not believe that army recruitment would affect the supply of labour to the tea plantations; firstly, he noted, there was an ample supply of migrant and immigrant labour in Darjeeling district itself - over 130,000 'Gurkhas' from Nepal (Vansittart 1993: 172) - and he believed that 'tea labour would always be forthcoming if the work was sufficiently attractive and paying'.

However, Vansittart remarked that 'many garden coolies attempt to get enlisted' and added that 'every endeavour should be made to detect them, and the recruiters who bring them in should be severely punished' (Vansittart 1993: 157). In any case, they were not considered 'early such good material as the raw lads brought in direct from Nepal' (ibid).

On the other hand, it was recognised that there was 'considerable demand among the Behar planters for the services of ex-Gurkha pensioners of good character to act as *chowkidars* over indigo-cake houses, grain godowns, etc. The work is light, there being little or no night work. The pay given is generally Rs 7 a month, with free quarters and fuel, and the employer pays the railway fare of the pensioner and his wife, if he is a married man, from Gorakhpur to the nearest railway station' (Vansittart p. 167). It was suggested, by Vansittart, that officers commanding Gurkha battalions should make it generally known to men who had decided, of their own free will, to remain in India on being transferred to the Pension establishment, or on taking their discharge, that there was a possibility of work being found for men of good character, on application to the recruiting staff officer for Gurkhas (Vansittart 1993: 167-68).

It was emphasised that the object of such a notice was not to induce Gurkha pensioners to take civil employment in India, but merely to assist men who had already decided to do so. That a good number did so, and settled in India with their families, is certain. Many clearly settled in Darjeeling. Some became Christians. Loreto Convent was founded in Darjeeling as early as 1846 by Mother Teresa M. Mons who is described in a 1922 history of Darjeeling as 'one of three Irish pioneer ladies who laboured in the cause of education in this distant land'. In 1841, a small group of nuns had travelled from Dublin to Calcutta where they set up the first Loreto school in India—Loreto House on Middleton Row—and did charitable work. In 1846, 'three of the nuns went to Darjeeling and Loreto Convent was built on land donated by three local notables'.

By 1870, William MacFarlane, a Church of Scotland missionary, had begun the Eastern Himalayan Mission, which was active in education, Christian literature, Bible translation, and village evangelism, in Darjeeling. The Church of Scotland's move to Darjeeling, and thereafter to Sikkim and the Dooars, each of which had an expanding Nepali population, heralded the beginnings of the modern-day Nepali church – a church which started in and expanded throughout the diaspora, and extended from there back into the homeland.

According to her thesis, *The History of the Expansion of Protestant Christianity among the Nepali Diaspora,* Dr. Cindy Perry, the history of the protestant Christian church in Nepal started in effect among the migrant and diaspora community across the eastern border in Darjeeling. The Gorkha Mission, an indigenous Nepali mission, was founded by Darjeeling Christians in 1892 to evangelize the local Nepalis, who were by now quite numerous, as many of those who had migrated from Nepal to Darjeeling to find temporary work had managed to secure more permanent, if low paid jobs for the most part and had settled there (Perry 1994).

Incidentally, it was not just in the east that the Christian Church had established itself; by the late 19th century, Christian missionaries had established their churches in many Indian towns along the border with Nepal, including Dharchula, Jhulalghat, Tanakpur, Rupaidiya, Nautanawa, Gorakhpur, Raxaul, Ghorehinshe and Jogbini. Many of these towns already had substantial Nepali diaspora populations, and some of them, significantly, were also army recruitment centres.

Employment in the army and military police, and one may envisage an increasing number of Rai and Limbu women migrating to accompany their husbands and to set up 'house' in Darjeeling and other stations. Many of these women also obtained employment, usually as porters or domestic servants. Many women as well as men, especially those from *dalit* or ethnic backgrounds, were attracted to Christianity in large part because of its 'egalitarian' message.

As Nepalis from the eastern hills of Nepal (Limbus, Rais and others) migrated to India in significant numbers, the Sherpas - who had immigrated into the mountain region of Solu-Khumbu around the 16th century from the eastern Tibetan province of Kham and were settled in small numbers across the region in the early 19th century (Ortner 1989) - also began to send migrant workers southwards, to Darjeeling in particular.

Anthropologist Christoph von Furer-Haimendorf (1964) argued that the introduction of the potato into the Khumbu region in the 19th century provided an agricultural surplus that stimulated population growth among the Sherpas; Ortner, also writing on the Sherpas of the Khumbu region, remarks that 'locally, the cultivation of potato, introduced around the mid-1800s, increased the total food crop production of the small people, which allowed the wages earned in Darjeeling to be used more as a surplus than for purchasing food' (Ortner 1989: 158-59, Fitzpatrick 2011: 10). Much the same thing was said by others who were familiar with the Sherpa economy and society. Fisher, for example, notes that, 'beginning about the 1850s, Sherpas had begun travelling to Darjeeling to seek their fortunes after the British began building roads and tea plantations there'.

Thus Sherpas were both 'pushed' and 'pulled' to emigrate". Undoubtedly, the remittances of Sherpa men and women working in Darjeeling contributed to the evolution of the Sherpa economy and society back in Solu Khumbu. Fisher suggests that 'in most respects, life after the introduction of the potato and the availability of new employment opportunities in Darjeeling must have gone on much as before, but these economic shifts allowed Khumbu to support a larger population, some of whom could be spared the burden of pursuing traditional means of livelihood' (Fisher 1990: 59).

Ortner emphasises that, during the first half of the 20th century, an appreciable number of Sherpa women ran away from home to take up these opportunities: 'they did so in fewer numbers than the men, but they did so' (2000: 236). Ortner remarks that 'running away to work in Darjeeling or – later – Kathmandu, was done more by women from poorer (but also middle-status) families', whether from Sherpa or from other ethnic groups. The Sherpas of Darjeeling lived and worked with other 'Bhotias' (from Tibet, Sikkim and Bhutan). They lived mainly in Toong Soom Busti, a shanty town close to the main shopping areas, but at the back of the ridge without a view of the mountains.

Tibetans with enough money to own a horse could offer pony rides to tourists on the mall, but few 'Bhotias' were that well off. They had difficulty in securing the better-paid and easier jobs as house servants and hotel workers; these tended to go to Nepalis and Indians. The Sherpas mainly specialised in the menial tasks of carrying loads and pulling rickshaws. While an increasing number of those Nepalis (Sherpas and others) living and working in Darjeeling now regarded themselves as towns-folk, there were still many who sent money back to the village, and arguably, remittances therefore also contributed to the on-going, long-term intensification of agriculture.

It was not just the development of potato production that transformed the rural economies of the eastern mountains and hills of Nepal, but also the production of cardamom. Basnet (2002), who studied Soyang VDC in Ilam district, in the eastern hills, describes a number of contradictory versions of the early history of cardamom in the village. One version tells of a Mr Thapa who brought cardamom from Darjeeling as long ago as 1864; another suggests that cultivation began around 1869, when seedlings were brought from Sikkim, but did not take off until 1919, when the Rana government opened a cardamom warehouse in Patna and began to supply the foreign market with Nepalese cardamom. As a result of this initiative, it was suggested, production increased and Indian businessmen used to come to Fikkal, in Ilam and to Dharan, in Sunsari, to buy cardamom[29].

❀ ❀ ❀

---

29. A more recent report (George et al 2007) describes, without mentioning sources, how cardamom was introduced into Ilam in 1865 by Nepalese migrant workers returning from Sikkim; but it suggests also that it was not until the establishment of the Cardamom Development Centre in Fikkal (Ilam) in 1975, that production in the eastern hills really took off.

CHAPTER 18

Migration to Sikkim & Burma

There is evidence that population pressure was already becoming a problem in some areas of the eastern hills towards the end of the 19th century. Caplan notes that for east Nepal, 'pressure on land was recognised as the principal cause of migration as early as the 1890s. At that time, one visitor to Sikkim remarked, of the Nepalis… 'it is because every bit of land in their country is taken up that there is such a steady emigration into Sikkim' (Donaldson 1900: 208)' (Caplan 1970: 6). In some remoter areas, including Taplejung, 'there was both an abundance of land and an acute shortage of labour'; but even there, 'extensive land grants made by the Limbu eventually led to conflicts between them and the Hindu populations when land was no longer in abundant supply' (Fitzpatrick 2011: 37).

Emigration to Sikkim seems to have reached such proportions eventually that laws were passed by the Sikkim authorities to check the in-flow (Nakane 1966: 260). It was not only Sikkim, however, that attracted Nepalese migrants. At the census of 1901, two-fifths of the inhabitants of Sikkim recorded Nepal as their birthplace; immigration and natural increase resulted in a further 50 per cent increase in the population of Sikkim between 1901 and 1911. It was remarked that 'many of the earlier Nepalese settlers are now dead, and most of their children are Sikkim-born, but in spite of this the number of persons who have returned Nepal as their birthplace (place of origin) is greater now than it was ten years ago.'

Migration eastwards from Nepal, however, was not only to North East India and Sikkim, but also further afield, to Burma. The British had started to penetrate into Burma early in the 19th century, and gradually, during the first two Anglo-Burmese Wars (1824 – 1826, 1851 – 1852) had conquered the southern parts of the country. Gurkha regiments were a part of the Indian Army at this time and many served in these wars. After the conquest of southern Burma, there was an increase in migrant labour from India, and to a lesser extent, from Nepal to Burma.

Initially, much of the migrant labour was seasonal, moving to Burma according to the demands of local rice production; but soon it developed on the basis of a three-year cycle of indentured labour. Since many of the labourers travelling to Burma in search of employment on farms or in mills were poor and often indebted, they relied heavily on recruitment agents and intermediaries *(mistris)*. These served the labour contractors, going village to village to find cheap labour which was then handed over to the contractors who would sometimes provide them with documents and contracts, but more often treating them as indentured labour, as free and independent labourers, not under contract. Some have argued, however, that the *mistri* system eventually became an exploitative system of bonded labour (Kaur 2006).

The *mistris* preferred male labourers to female. Also, given that the work was hard and living conditions were poor, the men who migrated to Burma, mostly from poor backgrounds, preferred to leave their families behind. This vastly skewed the gender ratio of the 'Indian' migrant community: from an initial ratio of about 8 males to 1 female, this ratio eventually declined to as low as 250 males to one female (Kondapi 1951). Most of these were settlers in the eastern state of Rakhine. It was not only labourers from Nepal who went to Burma during the latter part of the 19th century; soldiers were deployed there also.

In the Third Burma War - the last of three wars fought in the 19th century between the Burmese and the British - took place over two weeks (7–29 November 1885), with sporadic resistance and insurgency continuing for over a year, into 1887. The total effective force available was around 3,000 British troops, around 6,00 'Indian' *sepoys* and 67 guns, and for river service, 24 machine guns. The river fleet which conveyed the troops and stores was composed of more than 55 steamers, barges, and launches. By 28 November 1885, in less than a fortnight from the declaration of war, Mandalay had fallen, and King Thibaw was taken prisoner, and every strong fort and town on the river and all the king's ordnance and thousands of rifles, muskets and arms had been taken.

The British now poured reinforcements into the country, and it was in this phase of the campaign, lasting a couple of years, that the most difficult and arduous work fell to the lot of the troops. The resistance was finally broken by meting out collective punishments on villages. Villages were burned and the property of villagers either confiscated or destroyed. The British also organized the looting of the palace and city of Mandalay; the proceeds were sold off at a profit of 900,000 rupees. The war saw the final loss of sovereignty of an independent Burma under the Konbaung dynasty, whose rule had already been reduced to the territory known as Upper Burma, the region of Lower Burma having been annexed by the British in 1853, as a result of the Second Anglo-Burmese War.

On 3 May 1895 the name of the 10th Regiment (1st Burma Rifles) of Madras Infantry was changed to 10th Regiment (1st Burma Gurkha Rifles) of Madras Infantry to reflect its now all-Gurkha composition.

On 13 September 1901, as part of the broader re-organisation of the Indian Army, it became the 10th Gurkha Rifles and the regiment maintained its assigned recruiting areas in the Limbu and Rai hill areas of eastern Nepal. A 2nd Battalion was formed in 1903 although it became the 1st Battalion, 7th Gurkha Rifles in 1907. A new 2nd Battalion of the 10th Gurkha Rifles was formed in 1908. From 1903 to 1912 the first battalion was stationed in Maymyo in Burma as almost a ceremonial unit. In the winter months of 1912 and 1913, the 1st Battalion was sent into the Kachin Hills to guard against a potential uprising that did not occur. Following the war, from 1887 onwards for more than half a century, Burma became part of the British Raj as a province of India.

As a result of this, there followed many decades during which migration and settlement took place in Burma, gradually changing the demographic composition of the country. After its effective annexation as part of the British Raj in India, significant numbers of people – men, and to a lesser extent women and children, and whole families – from India and Nepal migrated to Burma and settled there. Chaturvedi (n.d. www.mea.gov.in/images/pdf/Indian-Migrants-Myanmar.pdf) notes that there were approximately 140,000 'people of Indian origin' in Burma in 1872, 243,000 in 1881 and 421,000 in 1891. Most of these were from Bengal and were Bengali-speaking, but there was a significant minority of Nepalis, as well as other groups. This was largely the result of a substantial flow of skilled and unskilled labourers under the aggressive British policy of importing labour.

❀ ❀ ❀

CHAPTER 19

The Gurkhas at the Turn of the Century

By 1892, there were 10 Gurkha Regiments serving in India - reinforced during the period 1886 to 1892 by 7,662 new recruits, mostly Magars and Gurungs from the western hills, but increasingly including Rais and Limbus from the eastern hills. In the meanwhile, in addition to Gorakhpur and Darjeeling (for the west and the east respectively), new recruiting depots were established at Purnea, Pilibhit and Bahraich. In March 1892, Commander-in-Chief Roberts visited Bir Shumshere in Kathmandu - the first time a high-ranking British officer had done so. In May, Bir Shumshere was made Knight Commander of the Star of India, as a mark of British appreciation, and shortly afterwards the British administration agreed to give 8,000 Martiny-Henry rifles and six 7-pounder field guns to Nepal.

In the meanwhile, even as the British Raj was expanded in the far east (Burma), the Gurkhas continued to be deployed to maintain the integrity of the Raj and to put down insurgencies. One example of this is the Tirah campaign (or expedition), a frontier campaign undertaken in a mountainous tract of country in what is now known as Khyber Pakhtunkhwa province of Pakistan. The Afridi tribe had been receiving a subsidy from the government of British India for the safeguarding of the Khyber Pass for sixteen years; in addition to which the government had maintained for this purpose a local regiment entirely composed of Afridis, who were stationed in the pass. Suddenly, however, in September 1897, the tribesmen rose, captured all the posts in the Khyber held by their own countrymen, and attacked the forts on the Samana Range near the city of Peshawar.

One of the forts to fall to the local tribes was the outpost of Saragarhi where the defendants were twenty-one Sikhs, who chose to fight to the death, in what is considered by some military historians as one of the greatest last stands in history. All 21 men were posthumously awarded the Indian Order of Merit, at that time the highest gallantry award which an Indian soldier could receive. The Indian Army's 4th battalion of the Sikh Regiment commemorates the battle every year on the 12th of September, as Saragarhi Day. The British responded by sending a force under General Sir William Lockhart, commander of the Punjab Army Corps, consisting of some 35,000 men, both British and 'Indian', and 20,000 camp followers, including men, women and children.

Among the infantry were several battalions of all five of the Gurkha regiments, the 9th 'Goorkhas' and the 39th Garhwal Rifles, no doubt with their own camp followers. The force also involved a baggage train of some 60,000 camels, bullocks and other pack animals (Shadwell 1898: 72). After three months of hard fighting, the Afridis sued for peace, and the expeditionary force was dissolved in April 1898. Also, during the fighting, particularly in December, many camp followers were killed or died of exposure, and quantities of stores were lost.

The earliest publication in Nepali concerning Gurkha soldiers seems to have been a story entitled *Ratan Singh Gurungko Outpostko Kathi* (*The Tale of Ratan Singh Gurung at the Outpost*), first published in Banaras in 1914, which had actually been translated from an article in an English magazine. It recounted the valorous deeds of its hero in the Tirah campaign – Ratan Singh, a Gurung - and is now regarded by some literary historians, rather tendentiously since it is a translation, as an early example of the modern short story in Nepali. Its popularity at the time is evident from the number of editions which emanated in subsequent years from Indian military centres such as Dehra Dun.

A process of remodelling the Gurkha Regiments started in 1901 and continued over the next few years. In 1902, Eden Vansittart, previously posted to Gorakhpur, was selected to raise and command the new 8th Gurkha Rifles. In 1903, the Brigade of Gurkhas was formally established. Chandra Shumshere Rana (Bir's successor as Prime Minister) approved the British plan to add 2nd Battalions to all ten Regiments of the Brigade of Gurkhas. By 1904, the three

Gurkha battalions of 1816 had swelled to 16[30] and by 1908, the Gurkha Brigade had reached its 'final' full establishment of 20 Battalions, organised into 10 rifle Regiments.

Chandra Shumshere was offered the title of Honorary Colonel of the 4th Gurkha Rifles (as well as that of Major General in the British Army) and during his visit to England in 1908 he was received by King Edward VII and presented with the Grand Cross of the Order of the Bath. In 1910/1911, the new King Emperor of India, George V, visited the Nepalese *terai* for shooting - following the 'tradition' established by Prince Albert.

On 1 January 1913, a year before the outbreak of the First World War, there were 18,142 Gurkhas serving in the Indian army, with a further 1,028 in the Imperial Service and 5,135 in the Military Police of Assam Bengal and Burma – making a total of 24,305 men. Of this, the majority (22,348) were from Nepal. In addition, there was a Reserve, residing for the most part in Nepal, of 100 men per battalion, for the Gurkha regiments of the Indian Army, the Reserve having been initiated after a successful first training at Gorakhpur in 1909 and placed on a permanent footing in 1910.

The British were still not allowed to enter Nepal themselves, so recruitment parties of Gurkhas were sent out to scout for new recruits. As Vansittart remarks, 'recruiters almost invariably go straight to their own villages, and spend a few days with their people, at the same time keeping a look-out for any likely recruits. If unsuccessful in their own village, they work round the neighbouring villages and fairs, until they pick up a recruit, or run out of funds.' (Vansittart 1993: 152).

Keeping in contact with husbands in the army was a major pre-occupation for the wives left at home. Vansittart records how, 'besides the claimants to estates

---

30. The original five Gurkha regiments became the 1st, 2nd, 3rd, 4th and 5th Fifth Gurkha Rifles; the 42nd, 43rd and 44th Regiments became the 6th, 7th and 8th Gurkha Rifles respectively; the 9th Regiment of Bengal Infantry and the 10th Regiment of Madras Infantry became the 9th and 10th Gurkha Rifles respectively. In 1905, the 71st Coorg Regiment and 76th Carnative Clite infantry were replaced by two new battalions of Gurkhas, one consisting of Khas Gurkhas and the other of Gurungs and Magars (Rathaur 1995: 90). In 1906, the 1st Gurkha Rifles (the Malaun Regiment) became the First Prince of Wales Own Gurkha Rifles, and then in 1910, the First King George's Own Gurkha Rifles. In 1906, the 2nd Gurkha Rifles (Sirmoor Rifles) became the Second King Edward's Own Gurkha Rifles; in 1907, the 3rd Gurkha Rifles became the Third Queen's Own Gurkha Rifles, and in 1908, the Third Queen Alexandra's Own Gurkha Rifles (Rathaur 1995: 89).

and pensions, many hundreds and men and women come down every year, chiefly to Gorakhpur to communicate with their relatives in Gurkha battalions. These are called '*chiti-wallahs*' (because they require the sending of letters or 'wires' from Gorakhpur to wherever their husband or relative is stationed.). These people in many cases fail to get an answer to their letters or telegrams, and it then falls to the Recruiting Officer to see that arrangements are made for the journey of such women as wish to join their husbands' (p. 149). In many cases, wives were provided with railway warrants (p. 151).

In this way, the army assisted wives of Gurkha soldiers to keep in touch with their husbands and to travel to visit them if necessary. Many Nepali women travelled long distances in northern India to make contact, and sometimes take up residence, with their soldier husbands. This support for direct contact between wives and husbands was crucial, for it was not until the First World War that postal services were established that would enable those at home and those away from home, whether on campaign of not, to keep in touch. Even general news 'from abroad' was not available, except by word of mouth, for it was not until 1898 that the first newspaper – *Sudha Sagar* - was published., and the press did not really start until the publication of *Gorkhapatra*, as a weekly newspaper, in 1901.

Gurkha regimental 'homes' had been established in the 1860s-'70s, and it is clear that some young men came to the recruiting depots with their wives. The Nepali women undoubtedly provided a real support to their soldier husbands; Vansittart describes how the wives of the Gurkhas were not shy or reserved in comparison with Indian women, had more freedom and reciprocated the affection of their husbands, carefully looking after uniforms and all culinary and domestic matters (Vansittart 1993: 58; repeated by Farwell 1985: 147-48). Unfortunately, Farwell records, 'there were never enough quarters for the families of all the married men' and notes that 'until recently, government supplied only about a quarter of the living facilities needed' (1985: 145).

The quality of accommodation and sanitation was generally poor; Vansittart refers to the fact that in 1899 a 'Gurkha' woman died of cholera in the Gorakhpur depot (Vansittart 1993: 53). Clearly, however, some elements of a family life were available for some of those in army employment, even if most recruits were between 18 and 19 years of age and were probably not able to bring their wives with them, if they had one. That some men did so, however, is evident from the fact that children were born and grew up 'in the lines'.

Vansittart, like many other British officers, was wary of the idea of too easy a recruitment of any boys 'born and brought up in the regiment' ('line-boys'), although he recognised that the progeny of purely 'Gurkha' parents could make excellent soldiers, and also that 'the claims of line-boys to be provided for in the service are undoubtedly very great, as Government has always encouraged 'Gurkha' colonies, and their fathers and grandfathers having in many cases been all their lives in British employ, they have no other home than their regimental lines' (ibid, 92). The worst point against them was 'that, unfortunately they often prove to be men of very loose habits' (ibid, 92).

A somewhat similar concern with the dangers of recruiting from the settlements or 'regimental homes' was expressed by Major Nicolay. He referred to the number of Gurkhas serving in the army and in the military police who were living 'in British territory' as 'nearly 2,000'. He observed that 'if it were considered desirable more enlistments could no doubt be made in the Gurkha settlements in British India', but considered that 'it is not desirable to encourage the Gurkha to settle in the neighbourhood of his regiment instead of returning to Nepal at the end of his service'.

On the other hand, he recognised 'that certain men do lose all connection with their own country while in our service, and if they cannot go to a Gurkha settlement they drift into an existence about Gorakhpur, Nautunwa or even Benares' (Vansittart 1993: 173). He remarked that 'the numbers of 'Gurkhas' in India are becoming considerable; in 1911, there were approximately 8,000 males' (p. 173). This was almost certainly an underestimate, even if only soldiers and ex-soldiers were included. Even at this time, the total number of men, women and children of Nepali origin living in India must have been at least 100,000. The number of Nepali women living in India at this time, with their serving husbands or with Nepalis who had settled in India, or working on their own account, however, remains unknown.

Indeed, all that we know of Nepali women migrants abroad for the period just described – whether as labour migrants, settlers, army wives or camp-followers is patchy and at second-hand. As Farwell remarks, 'no Nepalese woman has ever written about her life as an army bride. This is not surprising, perhaps, but it is curious that no Englishman or English-woman ever tried to discover and record the thoughts and feelings of these young women' (1985: 150). The same can be said of the voices of *all* Nepalis, men as well as women, there being virtually no record of their experiences, their feelings, their lives, in their own words, at least before the Second World War.

The conflicting views of the British government and the officers of the Gurkha regiments and battalions regarding the desirability of promoting more permanent settlements or 'colonies' in British India are interesting. This was an issue from the outset, but it was to become more significant after the First World War, when many who were discharged decided not to return to their homes in Nepal but to find work or even to settle in India. Whole communities of 'Gurkha' civilians began to develop around the regimental 'homes', some of whom were Gurkhas (and their families) who had retired and chose to stay near their old regiments instead of returning to Nepal.

The number of these became more significant over time. Whereas in the early 1890s, the figure given was 'around 2,000' and 'by 1911, there were approximately 8,000 males' (Vansittart 1993: 173). This was almost certainly an underestimate. Furthermore, migration, not only on a seasonal basis and for trade[31], but also for employment in Darjeeling and elsewhere in India, appears to have increased in the last decades of the 19th century; some of these migrants did not return but settled in India. Vansittart remarks that 'the numbers of 'Gurkhas' (Nepalese) in India are becoming considerable'.

The first attempt to undertake a census in India was in the years 1867-1872, but it was not until the fourth census of 1911, that a reasonably reliable result was achieved. One of the striking features of the Indian 1911 census was the importance of immigration from Nepal in specific regions, notably Assam, which experienced a 60 per cent population increase between 1872 and 1911, and where the tea plantations are mentioned as a major attraction for Nepali migrant labour, and Sikkim, which after 1889 permitted immigration from Nepal, and was inundated as cultivators from that state flocked in; as a result of which there was a 94 per cent increase in population between 1891 and 1901.

---

31. Fitzpatrick notes that in his village in Taplejung, villagers used to travel southeast to Darjeeling, mainly to trade, taking items like butter, chickens, and *chiraita* (a local medicinal herb), to bring back goods that were locally unavailable, such as metal for tool-making, nails, cloth, sugar, salt and spices (2011: 210). One of the oldest villagers remembers his first trading visit to Darjeeling in 1942. It took nine days to reach Darjeeling via Sikkim carrying loads of 40 kg to 60 kg. This man made visits once-yearly from 1942 until 1961, by which point the construction of a road to Ilam made the journey shorter and market goods had made their appearance in his village.

While a significant proportion of immigrants settled permanently, it was estimated that in the five years before 1911, roughly 51,000 labourers and their dependants went each year to the tea-gardens, as migrant labourers (Gait 1906: 119). The tea garden population was estimated in 1911 at 700,000, the bulk of which was 'of foreign origin'. It was estimated that the tea gardens as a whole had given Assam 'at least one sixth of its total population'. However, when they left employment in the tea gardens, many 'coolies' cleared land and settled as farmers, while other 'ex-coolies' found employment 'as carters, hucksters and general labourers'.

❀ ❀ ❀

CHAPTER 20

World War I: Mobilisation

On 28 July 1914, Austria-Hungary declared war on Serbia. Within a week, Russia, Belgium, France, Great Britain and Serbia had lined up against Austria-Hungary and Germany, and the Great War had begun. Germany attacked Luxembourg on 2 August and on 3 August declared war on France.

Even before the outbreak of war, as the storm clouds gathered, Chandra Shumshere Rana made it clear that he would place 'the whole military resources of Nepal' at His Majesty's disposal (Rathaur 1995: 92). According to W. Brook Northey and C. J. Morris, three days before he had heard of the outbreak of hostilities, and a day before war was actually declared, Chandra Shumshere Rana 'called on the British Envoy'[32], asking him 'to inform His Excellency the Viceroy and through him the King Emperor that the whole military resources of Nepal are at His Majesty's disposal', adding that he was speaking 'in a double capacity; firstly, as Marshal of the Gurkhas, and secondly as a Major General in His Majesty's Army'.

Pandit Hem Raj Sharma[33] reports that on 3 August 1914, a letter was handed over to the British Resident, to be communicated to the Viceroy. It said, specifically:

32. This was the British Resident in Kathmandu. Three individuals held the position during the period leading up to and including the Great War: John Manners Smith VC CIECVO, who served from 1905 to 1916, Steuart Farquharson Bayley, from 1916 to 1918, and Sir William Frederick Travers O'Connor, between 1918 and 1923.

33. Pandit Hem Raj Sharma was put in charge of war preparations by Chandra Shumshere Rana. His memoir was published in Nepali as *Pratham Bishwayuddhako Varnan (Description of the First World (Great)War)* in December 2018 by Shree Press in Kathmandu at the instigation of his grandson, Prakash Raj Sharma. I had it translated into English during 2019 by Anish Subedi and other members of Square Services Pvt. and rely heavily on the English version (Sharma 2019)in this chapter.

'The war cloud looks very threatening. In the event of a continental war Great Britain will in all probability be involved. I have come to request you to inform His Majesty the King Emperor that the entire military resources of Nepal are at His Majesty's disposal. We shall be proud if we can be of any service, however little that may be. Though far from the scene of the actual conflict, we yield to none in our devotion and friendship to His Majesty's person and Empire. We have spoken of our friendship on many occasions. Should time allow, we hope to speak in deeds'.

On 4 August, after Belgium refused to permit German troops to cross its borders into France, Germany declared war on Belgium as well, and its troops entered Belgium. This was accompanied by the general military mobilization of Austria-Hungary. Britain declared war on Germany at 7 pm on 4 August 1914, following an 'unsatisfactory reply' to its ultimatum that Belgium must be kept neutral. At once, all of the forces of the British Empire were mobilized in support of Britain in its 'hour of need', including the Indian Army.

Several recruiting centres on the Nepal-Indian border were opened and recruiting agents allowed for the first time into the previously prohibited hinterland inside Nepal (Onta 1994: 26). Six recruiting centres were immediately opened: two in the east, in Ilam and Dhankuta where the majority of recruits were Rais and Limbus; three in the west, in Pokhara, Palpa and Syanja, where the majority were Gurungs and Magars, and one in the far west, in Doti. This number was increased to ten in subsequent years. The Kathmandu Valley and adjoining districts, where recruitment was normally prohibited, was opened up, and a temporary recruitment depot was opened in Kathmandu itself.

Officers were instructed to take special precautions in recruiting fit and willing soldiers (according to Rathaur 1995: 93), although there are some doubts as to the extent to which these 'precautions' were always applied. Onta, for example, suggests that 'there seems to have been considerable forced recruitment. Incentives of various kinds were given both to recruiters and to those being recruited' (Onta 1994: 26). It seems that there was a mixture of 'stick and carrot'.

Chandra Shumshere sent special messengers to each village to make clear the urgency of the situation. He threatened that those who fail to answer the call to arms would be dealt with strictly. No recruitment was to be delayed because of any on-going legal proceedings, whether for non-payment of taxes or because of family problems. Village headmen were offered rewards for their assistance, and other locals who recruited potential soldiers were also rewarded. In the eastern hills, in Indreni cluster in Ilam District, after the first two men from the region were enlisted in the Gurkhas prior to the First World War, military service came to be seen for the first time to be a viable means of earning income lost as a result of land mortgaging. Eleven men from Indreni were accepted into the army 'during the First World War, when recruiting was intensified and standards of induction relaxed' (Caplan 1970: 114).

Volunteers were provided with a substantial allowance to meet the cost of the journey and other expenses (Rathaur 1995: 93). But if there were clear advantages and benefits for those joining up, many, including parents, spouses and siblings, and particularly mothers and sisters, were often unconvinced. They were reluctant to see their sons depart, not just for war but 'overseas' – something largely unheard of until now. Those who were to serve overseas, across the 'dark water' (*kalo pani*), would be granted *patiya* – permission by a Brahmin priest to travel overseas and on their return to be accepted back into Hindu society without any religious penalty, after performing a specific religious ceremony, absolving them of sin associated with the breaking of caste rules. But even so, this was a major, and for most unprecedented, act.

However, many young men (and boys) apparently enlisted without their parents' permission. Shrabani Basu comments that 'young Gurkha boys from remote villages, eager for an adventure and hoping to make some money, managed to enlist as followers by increasing their age' (2016: 22). Often this would have been despite their parent's disapproval or even eithout their knowledge. Bernard Pignède reports, of the village he studied in the western hills not far from Pokhara in the 1950s, that 'one informant, an old retired Captain, calculated that 85 per cent of the boys from Mohoria left without their father's consent' (Pignède 1993: 253).

In fact, many of these 'boys' who left home to join the army were technically under age, but were nevertheless employed; 'many, some as young as ten, managed to lie about their age and board the ships to Europe as kitchen hands and syces (grooms for horses)' (Basu 2016: xxiv). Walter Lawrence, who was appointed as commissioner for the sick and wounded Indian soldiers in France and England, discovered and 'noted with dismay that young boys had been brought to England and France to work as followers. At the Lady Hardinge Hospital in Brockenhurst he found two boys, twelve years of age, who had been brought out as syces (grooms)'. At Marseilles he had seen a young boy, Ilihi Baksh, fifteen, kneading dough, and a child of ten in a hospital who had arrived as a bellow blower' (Basu 2016: 102).

In August 1914, some 26,000 men from Nepal were already serving in the 10 Gurkha Regiments of the Indian Army; the number of recruits required annually to keep up this strength was 1,500 – something easily achieved in 'normal times'. With the outbreak of war, however, the government of Nepal 'intimated that the demand for recruits was expected to be high, and the Maharaja took immediate steps to evolve an organization which would prove capable of being able to cope with the situation at once, abnormal and unprecedented as it was' (Brook Northey & Morris, 1928: 265).

The scale of recruitment for the War was unprecedented. As already indicated, prior to 1914, the number of recruits required annually to maintain this strength was about 1,500 men. Now tens of thousands were being called up. The number of Gurkha battalions was increased to thirty-three with the addition of 55,000 new recruits, and placed at the disposal of the British high command for service on all fronts. Many Nepali volunteers served in non-combatant roles, serving in units such as the Army Bearer Corps and the labour battalions, but there were also large numbers that served in combat in France, Turkey, Palestine, and Mesopotamia: some 200,000 in all - 50,000 in the 10 regular Gurkha infantry regiments, and others in labour battalions, bearer corps and other types of service, as cooks, cleaners and other menials. Addditonally, Nepal sent almost 17,000 men from its own army to act as a home guard oritecting India.

The total population of Nepal at this time was around five and a half million, suggesting that about 20 per cent of the adult male population of fighting age was recruited for the war effort; Farwell comments that 'Nepal was nearly denuded of its able young men' (1985: 85). 'When the war was over', wrote Francis Tucker, 'Nepal had bared herself to the bone to send her men to Britain's aid. In the fields were only the women, the children and the old men: her youth had flowed out along the mountain ways into the depots in India and away overe the wide seas' (quoted in Pahari 1991: 9).

As soon as war was declared, Chandra immediately established a 'war office' to manage Nepal's support to the British in India. The person charged with overall responsibility for this monumental task, was one of Chandra Shumshere's most eminent and trusted advisers, the royal priest, Pandit Hem Raj Sharma, whose account of the process is to be found in his personal memoir on the Great War, on which this discussion draws heavily. A workforce of more than 50 military personnel and civilians was recruited; then (on BS 71 Magh 29), as the demand increased, the war office was relocated to Singha Durbar and the workforce further reinforced. Eventually, the numbers involved amounted to hundreds, and the 'war office' became one of the largest government departments.

This 'war office' was generally responsible for the logistical aspects of deployment of all 10 units sent to India in 1914 and 1915, including the transport of arms and ammunition by horse-back, trail[34] and rail, as well as arrangements for accommodation for the troops, the management of hospitals, and postal services. Among other things, it was responsible for 1) drawing up a complete listing of all available army and other personnel, 2) establishing who else were available for military deployment to India (including those who had served previously and were now civilians) and who would remain at home in Nepal as reservists, as well as who were available to serve as 'camp followers'.

It is not clear to what extent women were formally recruited by the 'war office' but there can be little doubt that they were involved informally as camp followers and accompanied the troops, constituting an important element of the forces deployed in India – but not, as far I can determine, overseas.

Before World War I, the Indian Army was deployed maintaining internal security and defending the North West Frontier against incursions from Afghanistan. These tasks did not end with the declaration of war. The divisions deployed along the frontier were the existing 1st Peshawar Division, the 2nd Rawalpindi Division, the 4th Quetta Division. The only new division to serve in India was the 16th Division, formed in 1916; it was also stationed on the North West Frontier. All these divisions were still in place and took part in the Third Afghan War at the end of World War I.

In 1914, India had the largest army in the world, with a total military strength of between 150,000 and 200,000 and more than 45,000 non-combatants (cooks, grooms and tailors etc.). The Indian Army constituted nearly 17 per cent of the total 'British' forces available. It was now divided into two main elements: the field force that would remain in India as a 'home guard', and the forces that were to be deployed overseas, in Europe on the Western Front, and in North Africa and the Middle East. The field force that remained in India was regularly

---

34. There were no motorable roads in Nepal until after the Great War: legend has it that the first motor car driven in Nepal was carried in by porter in 1922 and then driven only in the Valley.

called upon to deal with incursions and raids on the North West Frontier and to provide garrison forces for the British Empire in Egypt, Singapore and China.

Based in Delhi, this field force was divided into two armies: the Northern Army, covering the region from the North-West Frontier to Bengal with five divisions and three brigades, and the Southern Army, which stretched from Baluchistan to southern India and had four Divisions, with further formations outside the subcontinent. The Bannu Brigade, the Derajat Brigade and the Kohat Brigade were all part of the Northern Army and were deployed along the North West Frontier. The two armies comprised 39 cavalry regiments, 138 infantry battalions – of which 20 were Gurkha battalions in 10 regiments (the Gurkha Rifles) - a Corps of Guides, three sapper regiments and 12 mountain artillery batteries.

The nine Divisions each consisted of one cavalry and three infantry brigades; each division had about 13,000 men on strength. The infantry brigades consisted of one British and three Indian battalions. Indian Army battalions were smaller than British battalions; they were often segregated, with companies of different tribes, castes or religions. The Gurkha regiments and battalions were separate and distinct, and manned almost entirely by Nepalis, apart from the officers, who were mainly British[35]. In addition to this, tens of thousands men served the Empire as soldiers in the Nepal Army, which was deployed by the government 'war office' across northern India to ensure that the peace was secured in India itself. In India, a country larger than Europe, the British garrison was reduced to 15,000 men.

The Government of India therefore gratefully accepted the offer made by Nepal's prime minister, which consisted of, 'firstly, the loan of a contingent of Nepalese troops; secondly, assistance rendered in connection with the special recruiting measures necessary for the maintenance of the existing Gurkha regiments and the provision of additional battalions; lastly, gifts of war material which were provided from Nepal's natural resources' (Brook Northey and

---

35. In addition to the regular Indian Army, the armies of the Princely States and regiments of the Auxiliary Force (European volunteers) could also be called upon to assist in an emergency. The Princely States formed the Imperial Service Brigades and, in 1914, had 22,613 men in 20 cavalry regiments and 14 infantry battalions. By the end of the war, 26,000 men from these units had served overseas. The Auxiliary force could field another 40,000 men in 11 regiments of horse and 42 volunteer infantry battalions. Also available were the Frontier Militia and the Military Police which could field 34,000 men between them.

Morris 1928: 263). In 1915, 340 mechanics from the Nepalese government armoury were offered to repair broken equipment in India; and seventy one were accepted.

A British request in February 1915, for 6,000 Nepali troops for garrison duties in India, was immediately met, and in March, some 7,500 men were sent to India under General Babar Shumshere for this purpose. A second contingent was sent in December under General Tej Shumshere; a third was sent subsequently, under General Kaiser Shumshere; and a fourth, under Major General Sher Shumshere, the prime minister Chandra's half brother. Altogether, over 16,000 Nepali troops were deployed on operations in the North West Frontier and as garrison battalions to replace British Army troops who had gone to fight overseas. According to *Wikipedia*, 'The Nepalese Army participated in World War I with The First Rifle, Kalibox, Sumsher Dal, Jabbar Jung, Pashupati Prasad, Bhairab Nath, Second Rifle, Bhairung and Srinath Battalions'. It is likely that these units were accompanied by a substantial baggage train and a mass of camp followers.

The men deployed to India saw action as the 'home guard' during the Great War, particularly in the North West Frontier region, and, even later, in 1919, in Waziristan and Afghanistan; and also suffered serious casualties. Little is known of how many men died in battle and of sickness, although often the numbers of the latter were greater than that of the former; little is known, either, of what happened to those who suffered disabling injuries. Virtually nothing is known about the fate of the camp followers in these campaigns, although, if those cases where we have a more detailed picture of what happened to them, in the Afghan Wars, for example, they often suffered heavy losses.

The troops and the camp followers, however, were – like those on the Western Front, North Africa and the Middle East - far from home and they found it hard to keep in touch with their loved ones, even though a postal service for these *lahures* was one of the first institutions to be put in place by the government of Nepal. A dedicated postal service was established in 1914-15 (under the Ministry of Foreign Affairs and the Central Postal Service) by the 'war office', so that the troops could send and receive letters and parcels free of charge while in service abroad. This was to prove a life-line, connecting those serving in the army in India and those back home through the four long years of the war – and even longer for some of the troops. These letters made it possible for the first time for those at home to hear the thoughts and feelings of their absent family members.

A similar service was set up by the British and the French on the Western Front, as we shall see shortly, and this also provided a facility much valued, not only by the troops and the camp followers, but also by those left at home who were able, by this mechanism, to hear directly from their loved ones half way across the world, and to speak to them. As we shall see, thousands of letters were written, many of them sent half way across the world between Nepal and Europe; and read at the other end. Basu also refers to the importance of 'letters home from the frontline' for all the soldiers from India serving overseas (Basu 2016: 31).

They were, arguably, even more important for those at home. It was also possible, at last, for those at home to send letters to their menfolk in India and France and elsewhere. For, even if the majority of Nepalis abroad were illiterate, and certainly most of the family members back at home could not themselves read or write, there were often people on hand who could help as scribes and as interpreters and translators. As Shrestha and Conway comment, with respect to Sita, in their discussion of 'the shadow life of a migrant's wife', over 60 years later, letters were an important link between the absent husband and the stay-at-home wife even if she could not read or write and had to rely on someone in the village to read her husband's letters to her. But these were less a means of communicating on a personal level, than 'a means of transmitting generally perfunctory information about health and well-being, seasonal changes in weather patterns, village news and social events, and farming and friends' (Shrestha & Conway 2001: 167).

The Indian Army began mobilisation and deployment to the Western Front and to the Middle East, and within India itself, as soon as news arrived that war had been declared.

Division	Theatres	Arrival in first theatre
1st (Peshawar)	-	Remained in India
2nd (Rawalpindi)	-	Remained in India
3rd (Lahore)	France & Flanders, Mesopotamia	October 1914
4th (Quetta)	-	Remained in India
5th (Mhow)	-	Remained in India
6th (Poona)	Mesopotamia	From November 1914
7th (Meerut)	France & Flanders, Mesopotamia	October 1914
8th (Lucknow)	-	Remained in India
9th (Secunderabad)	-	Remained in India

10th	Egypt	Formed in Egypt 1914
11th	Egypt	Formed in Egypt 1914
12th	Mesopotamia	Formed in Mesopotamia 1915
13th	-	Not formed
14th	Mesopotamia	Formed in Mesopotamia 1916
15th	Mesopotamia	Formed in Mesopotamia 1916
16th	-	Remained in India
17th	Mesopotamia	Formed in Mesopotamia 1917
18th	Mesopotamia	Formed in Mesopotamia 1917
Burma Division	-	Remained in India
1st Indian Cavalry	France & Flanders	November 1914. Renamed 4th Cavalry Division in November 1916
2nd Indian Cavalry	France & Flanders	December 1914. Renamed 5th Cavalry Division in November 1916

Thomas Bell, in his book *Kathmandu,* suggests that 'between 1914 and 1918, 55,000 Nepali villagers were sent to fight for Britain. Chandra even sent the prisoners from his jails. In 1920, he was rewarded for his 'unswerving loyalty' with an annual pension of one million rupees' (2014: 228). He provides no source for the number given of those who went to fight for Britain; but it coincides with the number of recruits who brought up the total of the Gurkha battalions up to thirty three (see below). Other sources generally suggest a larger number, up to 200,000 – a figure that Bell gives as the total number of those who fought for Britain in the Second World War (2014: 229).

Seven Indian 'expeditionary' forces served overseas during World War I

❖ Indian Expeditionary Force A - served on the European Western Front

❖ Indian Expeditionary Force B - served in the East African Campaign

❖ Indian Expeditionary Force C (composed of the Imperial Service Infantry Brigade) - served in British East Africa

❖ Indian Expeditionary Force D - served in the Mesopotamia Campaign

❖ Indian Expeditionary Force E - served in the Sinai and Palestine Campaign

❖ Indian Expeditionary Force F - served in the First Suez Offensive

❖ Indian Expeditionary Force G - served in the Gallipoli Campaign

The normal annual recruitment for the Indian army was 15,000 men; but during the course of the war over 800,000 men volunteered for military service and more than 400,000 volunteered for non-combatant roles. Recruitment continued throughout the war, with those who died or were wounded being replaced by others. In total almost 1.3 million men had volunteered by 1918. One source (*The Indian Army at Gallipoli 1915*) suggests that 1,440,437 men were recruited in all, of which 1,381,050 were sent for service overseas. According to Edwin Montagu's speech in November 1918, India sent 1,215,338 men overseas and suffered 101,439 casualties. The Government of India bore these enormous expenses and even contributed an extra £100 million for the British empire's war, increasing India's national debt by thirty per cent. The people of Nepal and India – the relatives of the men who died or returned disabled - bore the brunt, however, of these casualties

Over the period of just four years it is estimated that some 200,000 men from Nepal were deployed in the various theatres of the War. This compares with approximately 150,000 over the whole of the previous century (roughly 15,000 a year). They suffered serious losses (dead and missing)[36] and many more of those returning home were badly disabled, without medical or remedial facilities, and often unable to enjoy their 'retirement'. They were not the only ones, of course, for the 'soldiers of the Crown' came from the length and breadth of British India, 'from the Punjab, Garhwal, the North West Frontier, Rajasthan and Nepal, to Madras and Burma, and represented different religions, ethic and linguistic backgrounds' (Basu 2016: xxii). Basu refers to one small village, Dulmial in Chakwal, in the Punjab, which sent 460 men to fight in the First World War, leaving no young men there for four long years.

We cannot be sure how their families, and particularly their grand mothers, mothers, sisters, and daughters, regarded this massive call to arms generally and how they looked on the departure of their menfolk. Whatever the men leaving felt, there will have been at least mixed feelings among those who were to be left behind. The soldiers would be asked to cross the *kala pani* (black waters), for most of them for the first time; strictly forbidden to orthodox Hindus, which involved a significant proportion of the troops leaving home (although many

36. The Gurkha Voice (www.gurkhavoice.com/top-news/faqa-on-gurkhas/) suggests 22,000 - although it is rarely clear whether this number refers only to those killed or missing in action or to the total number of those killed and injured – and it is quite likely that even this is a serious underestimate. Shrabani Basu suggests 'the dead and missing were nearly 72,000, with may more wounded' (Basu 2016: xxi).

were Buddhists or even Muslims), this would mean a loss of caste, something that could only be restored by an elaborate purification ceremony on their return. We know little also of the impact on those families of the numerous casualties incurred during the War.

The mobilisation was, however, widely supported by the government of Nepal, as we have seen; and also across India, even by the nationalists. As Shrabani Basu remarks, 'Indian leaders addressed meetings all over the country expressing their support for the King Emperor' (Basu 2016: 12); and, as Indians rallied to support Britain and the Empire, King George sent them a message from Buckingham Palace, concluding with the assurance that 'in this hour of trial, the destinies of Great Britain and India are indissolubly linked' (Basu 2016: 19).

Over the next few weeks, the British regiments and the 'native' regiments of what would be the Indian Expeditionary Force mobilised and travelled from their 'stations' to the ports of Mumbai and Karachi. Some units were able to mobilise almost at once. Basu relates, for example, how 'at 6.00 am on 8 August, Major Harry Hill of the Jullunder Brigade received a telegram at the station in Dalhousie ordering the mobilization of the 3rd Lahore Divisional Headquarters. By 8.45 am he had issued the order to his units. By 9.00 am 15th Sikhs were directed to proceed to Karachi. With seasoned military discipline, troops from the different regimental centres began to fall in' (Basu 2016:20).

'The Gurkhas, however, had left on furlough for their homes in Nepal and the surrounding Himalayan region. It would take nearly two to three weeks to reach them. Men were sent off to the remote mountain areas to track them down' (Basu 2016: 21). The same applied to regions like the North West Frontier areas, to Rajasthan and to the Central Provinces. But eventually 'the Gurkhas, Dogras, the Baluchis, the Garhwalis, the Sikhs and the Frontier Forces assembled at the centres for kits and final orders' (2016: 21).

Basu tells us that the 39th Garhwal Rifles regiment was relatively quick to mobilise despite having to recall many of their soldiers from remote hill areas. The 1st battalion marched out of the regimental centre at Lansdowne on 20th August, and the 2nd battalion on the 21st. They marched to Dugadda where the camp was flooded by the monsoon rains; but they were able to borrow tents from the 8th Gurkha Rifles. They were delayed by the rains and the 1st battalion did not get to Karachi until 2 September. Already many were suffering from ill-health (malaria); the 2nd battalion arrived in Karachi on 16 September.

Once the thirty or so ships were prepared, embarkation began. The weapons and heavy kit, the horses and mules, the supplies and the mass of support personnel ('followers' - the equivalent of 'camp followers') including grooms for the animals, bearers or porters, cooks and other artisans went on board first, the troops were last. The first to depart was the 6th Poona Division, which sailed to the Persian Gulf and Mesopotamia; then the 3rd Lahore Division and finally a month later, on 21 September 1914, the Meerut Division, both of which were headed to Europe. Each Division consisted of four brigades, each of which comprised several regiments; each brigade had a British regiment attached to it. Of these, some 50,000 men were in the 10 regular Gurkha infantry regiments (www.army.mod.uk/brigade_of_gurkhas/history/index.htm).

Many Nepali volunteers served in the Army Bearer Corps and the labour battalions, as cooks, cleaners and other menials; but the majority served in combat. These comprised only males, with no women involved at all – in any capacity - as far as we can determine. A significant minority, however, as we have seen, were very young – sometimes as young as ten years old. In her study of Indian soldiers on the Western Front, Shrabani Basu has a photograph of 'Pim, a sixteen year old Gurkha boy, convalescing in the Brighton hospital' (2016: 100-101).

The First World War was the first time that such large numbers of Nepali troops were transported overseas to fight – although there had been several smaller deployments overseas earlier, during the Perak War in 1875, for example, and when a battalion of the 2nd Gurkhas undertook a tour of duty at the Malta Garrison and in Cyprus, which had come under British occupation in June 1879 (Parker 2000: 87). It also led to some of the longest absences from home and from the regimental 'homes'; and involved the largest numbers of Nepali men employed in the British army at one time since the beginning of recruitment into the Gurkhas a hundred years before.

It is estimated that roughly 200,000 Nepalis in all served the British throughout the War, suggesting that some 20 per cent on average of the adult male population of Nepal was recruited into the war effort, given that the total population of the country was about five and a half million at this time. And this does not take into consideration the tens of thousands who were deployed to serve in India to help keep the peace. This compares interestingly with the estimated 150,000-200,000 or so men deployed in the service of the British in India over the entire previous century[37].

---

37. Based on an estimated 1,500 men needed to make up the five Gurkha regiments each year for most of the 19th century, and 3,000 men from when each of these was increased to two battalions each.

The India Corps took a little while, even at 'full-speed', to mobilise such an un-precedently large military force. The Lahore Division was ready to sail by the third week of August, but the Meerut Division did not depart until nearly a month later, on 21 September 1914. Ships leaving from Karachi coordinated with those from Bombay and the convoy steamed towards the Suez Canal escorted by ships of the Royal Navy and the Royal India Marine. Later, they were joined by ships of the French Navy. There were also hospital ships in the convoy.

Among the hospital ships in service during the war, a number had Indian as well as British and other Allied medical staff, and these treated and transported mainly Indian Army casualties. These included: the *Glengorm Castle, Syria, Sicilia, Loyalty, Syria, Goorkha, Gascon, Marama,* and *Vasna.* A few of these – *Loyalty, Goorkha* and *Marama* - had only Indian Army medical staff and predominantly 'native' staff (including ward orderlies). The aptly named *Goorkha,* for example, was commissioned as a hospital ship on 20 October 1914; she had 408 beds and was stationed, together with the *Guildford Castle,* in the stream at Southampton (Basu 2016: 101). We do not know if any of these 'native' staff were Nepalis. Some of the nursing staff, however, were women; but they were predominantly 'Europeans'.

During the First World War it is estimated that more than 100,000 women served in the uniformed services (some estimates are double that), with around 50 per cent connected with nursing and very few (officially at least) anywhere near combat. One of the most highly regarded of nursing organisations was the Queen Alexandra's Imperial Military Nursing Service (QAIMNS), which was established in 1902, and had its origins in the Indian Army. In 1914, there were around 300 nurses in the QAIMNS with 2,223 in the Reserve; by the end of the war there were 10,404 members of the QAIMNS and QAIMNS(R).

These Army nurses eventually served in Flanders, the Mediterranean, the Balkans, the Middle East and on board hospital ships. Of the 200 plus army nurses who died on active service, a few, it seems, were 'Indians'. We know little about these 'Indian' nurses; but it seems likely that few, if any, of these, were Nepalis. Also, as far as we know, no Nepali women accompanied the Gurkha troops in any capacity during their overseas service.

Although there are many references, in descriptions of the Indian Army serving overseas during the First World War, to 'followers', it is clear that these were not the usual mixed body of men, women and children that accompanied the troops on their campaigns in India, as camp followers, but rather medical orderlies, cooks, cleaners, bearers, grooms, and other menials, all of whom were male – even if some were seriously under age and many were *dalits*. By contrast, the troops deployed in India, as a 'home guard' during the war, were often accompanied in their campaigns, by the traditional camp followers, which included men, women and children.

The voyage overseas was uneventful, if novel, for all those Indian and Nepali men who had never before seen the sea, let alone sail on it. The first fleet, with the Lahore Division, arrived at Marseilles on 26 September 1914. The troops disembarked and the Indian troops and their followers marched to their camps just outside the city. On 30 September, they left for Orleans. The Meerut Division arrived in Marseilles on 13 October. The weather had begun to turn cold and it was raining. They also left by train for Orleans, arriving on 21 October.

When the Indian Army was ordered to mobilise in August 1914, there had been no clear plan for their deployment. Now, although it had been decided that many would serve on the Western Front, provision of suitable clothing was not organized and now they found that their thin cotton khaki drill and jumpers did not protect them adequately from the wind, sleet and rain of October and November in central and northern France. Equally, if not more serious, the India Corps lacked artillery and, even more serious still, there was a lack of organization. As Basu remarks, 'in the confusion of the early weeks of the war, cavalrymen would be made to disembark and fight as infantry and battalions would be split up and used to plugs gaps in the British lines, often under officers they did not know and who did not speak their language. Used to working as a team, the units were confused and demoralised' (Basu 2016: 38). It was not a good start.

❀ ❀ ❀

CHAPTER 21

Caring for Casualties

The Indian Corps arrived on the Western Front, in Belgium, in the second week of October 1914. Several Gurkha battalions saw action at La Bassée, the first engagement of the India Corps on the Western Front, which began on 12 October 1914. Most of the Gurkha battalions involved were to remain on the Western Front for more than a year, until the Indian Corps as a whole was eventually withdrawn in 1915, to be deployed elsewhere, mainly to North Africa and the Middle East, where the enemy forces were those of the Ottoman Turks, supported by German units, after it was recognised that they were ill-prepared for the conditions they encountered in Western Europe.

In Egypt, their initial task was to protect the Suez Canal; in Mesopotamia, it was to protect British-controlled oil installations and other interests in the region. The Gurkhas were also among the forces deployed in 1915 to take Gallipoli in the Dardanelles, in a disastrous attempt to assault the Turks in their heartland. They fought in Egypt, in the Sinai and Palestine and in Mesopotamia from 1914 through to 1918. By the end of the war, Nepali Gurkhas had served overseas in all of the main theatres of the Great War, with a total of some 200,000 men involved. They enjoyed victories and received medals for bravery, but they also experienced terrible pain and suffering (*dukha*), high casualty rates and some devastating defeats. The Garhwalis and the Gurkhas shared four of the eleven VCs awarded during the War. The estimated number of those killed and wounded is usually put at about 20,000; but Shrabani Basu suggests 'the dead and missing were nearly 72,000, with many more wounded' (Basu 2016: xxi).

In the early days of the war, the female nurses on the Western Front were mainly Belgian and French, but very soon they were joined by British, Canadian and Australian nurses. Although some complained at the number of 'untrained' nurses involved, it was also the case that there were insufficient numbers at the front throughout the first year of fighting, and that soldiers were dying for lack of care from suitably trained nurses, and also for lack of suitable transport – existing transport was described as 'outdated, crude and makeshift'. As Yvonne McEwen makes clear, the organisation, management and delivery of nursing care on the Western Front was, at least initially, woefully inadequate. Furthermore, 'official information regarding the care and number of casualties was practically non-existent, in part because of censorship (McEwen 2014: chapter 2).

By the end of October 1914, when the troops on the Western Front included the first cohorts of the Indian Army, Boulogne had become the major centre of medical activity, and all the large hotels and casinos had been commandeered for use as hospitals. The total capacity for the care of 'the sick and wounded' in Boulogne was 2,310 hospital beds. Hospitals were also opened at Rouen, Le Havre, Etretat, Le Touquet, Calais, Le Tréport, St Omer and Abbeville. Most of the hospitals were filled to capacity and, due to the shortage of beds, stretchers were placed between occupied beds, in corridors and on balconies, and men were also nursed on trestles and on the floor. There was a dearth of all the necessities for the care and comfort of the sick and wounded (McEwen 2014: Chapter 2, passim).

In December 1914, the King of England, George V, accompanied by the Maharajah Sir Pertab Singh and the Maharajah of Bikaner, paid a visit to France and expressed a desire to visit some of the British and Indian sick and wounded. On the last day of his visit, he was to present the VC to 33-year-old Naik Darwan Sing Nevi of the 39th Garhwal Rifles. But many of the 'Indian' casualties were housed in woefully inadequate accommodation in a badly-ruined Jesuit College in Boulogne, and some were 'housed, against orders in tents, pending the construction of huts'. In advance of the King's visit, ambulances were provided to re-locate these men to hospital ships, but when the ambulances reached the quay, no hospital ships were available, and were put into sheds until the official inspection was over (McEwen 2014: 75).

This reveals that the Indian Army casualties were generally treated less well than their British, French and other European counterparts. They also suffered from the climate and the weather: 'the first winter of the War was severe, and the continual exposure of the troops to cold, wet and damp weather produced illnesses such as bronchitis, pneumonia, rheumatic fever, trench fever and nephritis, as well as trench foot and frostbite' (McEwen 2014: 77). The Indian

Army troops, whose equipment, including their footwear, was less than adequate for such conditions, suffered badly.

Eventually, according to Corrigan's *Sepoy in the Trenches* there were six Indian Military Hospitals established on the south coast of England. These were largely staffed by RAMC and all-male VAD personnel, '..it being considered that females would be out of place in an Indian unit'. Most did, however, employ women in other capacities. The Kitchener Hospital in Brighton, however, which was equipped to accommodate over 2,000 patients, was run by officers of the Indian Medical Service, with a staff of male assistant surgeons and sub-assistant surgeons belonging to the Indian Subordinate Medical Department, and a staff of about 400, comprising Indian male nursing orderlies, storekeepers, writers, cooks, water carriers, conservancy sweepers, and other 'followers'. Among hospitals in England it was unique in the total absence of female assistance, with even the laundry work being done by Indian washer- men specially brought in for this purpose.

It is interesting, however, that on 22 January 2006, Major General Jonathan Saunders wondered (in comments on the www.greatwarforum.org/topic/45561-indian-women-in-the-first-and-second-world-wars/) whether, in view of the fact that in 1914 there was a large Indian population in London and possibly other British cities, and that some of the Indian women were midwives (ie with some experience in nursing, albeit of a specific kind) 'whether any of these Indian women, as individuals, would have worked in the abundance of official and unofficial military hospitals that were set up post-August 1914, to nurse wounded soldiers'. In a detailed response to this (on the same day), Sergeant Major Sue Light stated that she had

> never seen any mention of Indian women working as nurses in British military hospitals - not in Britain, or India or places like Mesopotamia or Egypt. The hospitals were staffed totally by British female trained nurses, and male orderlies, both British and 'Indian'. During WW1 there were several hospitals for 'Indian' troops in England, with Indian staff, and there was a lot of unrest about British women being used in these hospitals - it was thought inappropriate that they should make themselves 'subservient to native troops.' This situation ended in November 1915, when the hospitals in England closed, and from then on all 'Indian' troops were nursed elsewhere - mainly in 'Indian' hospitals in France.

It has been widely thought that even in the hospitals set up specifically for casualties from the Indian Army in France (at Boulogne, Rouen, Abbeville,

Montreuil and Hardelot), and in Britain (at Brighton and Brockenhurst, at Barton-on-Sea and at Netley), women did not, generally, directly nurse the wounded 'Indians'. There were, however, exceptions, one of whom was Hilda Beatrice Hand, who was born 16 November 1876 in Acton, Middlesex and completed her nurse's training at St Olaves' Infirmary from November 1897 until July 1901. She then had fifteen years of nursing practice both in Britain and in India.

In January 1915, Hilda started work at the Lady Hardinge Hospital for Wounded Indian Soldiers in Brockenhurst, named after Lady Hardinge, the wife of the then Viceroy of India, Baron Charles Hardinge, who had recently established a medical college for women in Delhi, as she recognized that the lack of such a college made it impossible for Indian women to study medicine. The foundation stone was laid by Lady Hardinge on 17 March 1914 and the college was initially named the Queen Mary College & Hospital to commemorate the visit by Queen Mary in 1911-12. The college was inaugurated on 7 February 1916 by Baron Hardinge in the Imperial Delhi Enclave area. On the suggestion of Queen Mary, the college and the hospital was named after Lady Hardinge to perpetuate the memory of its founder.

Its namesake, the Lady Hardinge Hospital for Wounded Indian Soldiers in Brockenhurst, where Hilda Hand nursed the Indian and Nepali patients, was part of an enormous hospital complex at Brockenhurst in the New Forest, involving over three main buildings and several newly erected tin huts and tents. The wounded arrived from the battlefields and clearing stations via the rail connection from Southampton and its port. Over the course of nearly two years it would nurse over 3,000 Indian Army soldiers, including Gurkhas. Once they arrived at Lady Hardinge's Hospital the patients were housed in the tin huts where the nursing took place.

Here it was not only British but also Indian nurses too; in fact, an extract from a poem in Hilda's notebook alluded to the difference in skin tone of the nurses: 'U. for the uniform which we all wear, it suits most be she dark maid or fair'. Food was a big part of the daily routine in Brockenhurst. Officials were careful to observe the different religious practices of the soldiers. They utilised coloured disks on the end of every bed to mark the different dietary needs. There was also a distinction in the food prepared for Hindus and Muslims with separate staff and food preparation for the different religious culinary requirements.

We actually know of at least one Indian woman who volunteered as a nurse at the Lady Hardinge's Hospital. Shrabani Basu refers to 'Princess Sophia Duleep Singh, who worked in Brockenhurst Hospital where 'Indian' soldiers were treated' (personal communication). Princess Sophia was a Sikh, the daughter of the last Maharajah of independent Punjab and a god-daughter of Queen Victoria. She was a well-known socialite in London and a prominent suffragette, joining the Women's Social and Political Union and leading the Women's Tax Resistance League to fight for women's right to vote.

During the First World War, she worked as a volunteer with the Red Cross and as a Voluntary Aid Detachment (VAD) nurse for sixteen months at the Percy House Auxiliary Hospital in Isleworth, caring for sick and wounded soldiers. She also visited 'Indian' soldiers convalescing in Brighton and organised Flag Days to raise money for the wounded. Some sources suggest that her involvement was even greater and that she actually tended personally to the 'Indian' troops at the Brockenhurst Hospital complex. The main section was formally known as 'The Lady Hardinge Hospital', but the complex as a whole was also known to the locals as 'Tin Town' - a 500-bed tented and galvanised accommodation hospital complex – with the two minor sections at the commandeered Balmer Lawn and Forest Park Hotels, known collectively as the 'Meerut General Hospital'.

The hospitals treated soldiers of the 3rd (Lahore) and 7th (Meerut) Divisions from the Indian Army Corps. Almost 3,000 'Indian' wounded were treated here before the Corps was posted to Egypt in November 1915. According to the Brockenhurst official website, the hospitals recruited villagers as support staff. Villagers also actively engaged in fundraising events for the war while 'the ladies made surgical dressings, some using Sphagnum moss collected from the Forest by children.

It seems, however, that, despite the undoubted involvement of at least some Indian women in nursing at the Lady Hardinge Hospital in the Brockenhurst complex, even Indian male personnel were not readily available to look after the 'Indian' wounded in the British hospitals. William Lawrence, who was in charge of the overall hospital service for 'Indian' soldiers, complained that 'there is no Indian personnel available... it is remarkable that no sweepers have arrived. We do not want *bhistis*, barbers, tailors, etc. we only want sweepers and cooks for the convalescents' (Basu 2016: 99).

Men were engaged from the Asiatic Home on West India Dock Road in the East End of London; but even so, it seems that there was a shortage of sweepers and cooks and, as the demand for beds increased, a further supply of men from the Indian Volunteer Corps was requested to act as dressers, food distributors and interpreters (Basu 2016:100). Indian students were also drafted in. The shortage of cooks seems to have been a particular problem, for it had been decided that separate kitchens were required to provide for different food preferences and taboos – ordinary Hindus, Brahmins, Muslims and Sikhs were all to be cooked for separately, avoiding the meat that was forbidden and ensuring that ritual purity was maintained. Cook houses were constructed, as were abattoirs, so that sheep could be slaughtered according to religious requirements. Crematoria were also built to fulfil religious requirements.

Visitors were strictly vetted. Basu tells us that the rules issued for the hospitals for Indian Army patients in England indicated that, 'officers of the Indian Army were welcome to visit (but) women would be admitted only if they were related to the men in the hospital' (2016: 96-97) – a tantalising phrase suggesting that it was envisaged that some of the 'Indian' patients in these hospitals might have female relatives who could visit them.

In 1916, Lady Hardinge's closed and the site became a hospital for New Zealand soldiers. With the Indian and Nepali sepoys gone, Hilda's skills in Hindustani were no longer required and in June 1916, she started at King George Hospital, London, which had opened in the previous year, as one of the largest military hospitals in Britain. Her first official military posting was to the No. 8 General Hospital, Rouen, France, in 1917. She nursed throughout the war, and later became a Sister with the Queen Alexandra's Imperial Military Nursing Reserve (QAIMNSR).

At the time of the outbreak of the war, there were two permanent British Army hospitals in Egypt – one at the Citadel in Cairo, and a smaller one at Ras-el-Tin, overlooking the harbour of Alexandria. These, however, were equipped only on a peace-time footing, with 250 and 120 beds respectively. The arrival of the Indian troops sent to guard the Suez Canal and reinforce the garrison in Egypt (including a brigade from the 3rd Indian Division of Indian Expeditionary Force A as well as the 10th and 11th Indian Infantry Divisions) added all of their field ambulances and two complete General Hospitals, which were stationed one at Cairo and one at Alexandria. The Anglo-American Hospital immediately placed its wards at the disposal of the British Army Medical Service. Later, a hospital was opened at Choubra for infectious cases.

The New Zealand Imperial Force with its field medical contingent arrived in Egypt about the same time, and towards the end of the year the First Division of the Australian Imperial Force reached Alexandria, bringing with it five complete units of the Australian Army Medical Corps fully equipped. In the meanwhile, the permanent Military Hospital at the Citadel had its bed accommodation doubled, the number of beds eventually reaching 775. By the end of 1914, around 300 Australian Army Nursing Service (AANS) nurses had left Australia for Egypt. On arrival, they were posted either to the 1st Australian General Hospital (1AGH) in the grand Heliopolis Palace Hotel in Cairo, or to 2AGH in Mena House, a former royal hunting lodge. 1AGH initially had only 200 beds, but it subsequently expanded to 1,000. With the influx of sick and wounded, additional buildings in the neighbourhood were pressed into the hospital service, until over 6,000 beds were available.

The Egyptian Government lent its civilian hospitals in Kasr-el-Aini and the Army hospital at Pont de Koubbeh. The Saidieh Government School building was also handed over, and within a few weeks had been opened as a hospital by the Red Cross Society with a complement of 200 beds which was rapidly increased. The No. 5 Canadian Stationary Hospital was established in the Cavalry Barracks at Abbassieh; and the Egyptian Government Primary School, known as Nasrieh School, became a British Military Hospital (BMH) with 584 beds, and the Palace, or rather group of mansions, at Montazah near Alexandria had been lent by the Sultan of Egypt and a convalescent depot created, where mainly Australian patients could be housed; this alone took over a thousand patients. The El Hayat Hotel at Helouan had also been converted into a convalescent depot.

In addition there was No. 5 Indian General Hospital at Alexandria, which was expanded to 950 beds; and No. 8 Indian General Hospital, which was installed at the Citadel Bijou Palace in Cairo and contained up to 900 beds. These hospital facilities were specifically dedicated to the wounded from the Indian and Nepali troops now stationed in Egypt. There was also a permanent hospital at Ismailia used for The Egyptian Labour Corps and the Camel Transport Corps which had been placed under British command, with British officers. If local hospitals were unable to deal adequately with the wounded, there was always the possibility of their being shipped off back home in hospital ships. The British and Allied troops were supported by a number of hospital ships.

J. H. Paterson's memoirs specifically mention the well-named hospital ship *Gorkha*, which was in operation during 1914-15 transporting the sick and wounded from Egypt to England. He was very impressed:

> 'I was put on board the hospital ship *Gorkha*, which I found very comfortable, with excellent food and a most excellent medical staff, a colonel, three majors, and a captain, all of the Indian Medical Service; and I thought what a pity it was that some of these able and experienced officers could not be utilized to take charge of such hospitals as Ras-el-Tin, where they could guide the junior staff into the way they should go. It is just another example of not utilizing in the right way the wealth of talent which we possess in skilled and able men. I do not for a moment mean to suggest that the talents of these Indian Medical Service officers were wasted on the Gurkhas. What I do mean is that one or two of the senior men would have been ample on the ship, with a couple of younger men as assistants, and the other senior men could then have been released for similar work among some of the ill-staffed hospitals in Egypt or Mesopotamia'.

In April and May 1915, the use of gas as a weapon on the Western Front added to the tribulations of the troops and the demands on the medical and nursing staff. In the same period, a new front opened up in the Mediterranean, and British, French, Australian, New Zealand and 'Indian' troops were soon on their way to the Dardanelles, which Winston Churchill saw as a key to defeating the Turks, who were now actively aiding the Germans. When the campaign in the Dardanelles was launched, many of the larger hospital ships were re-deployed to provide support for the troops at Gallipoli.

The landings at Gallipoli were supported by a number of hospital ships, some of which – known as 'black ships' - were no more than converted troop transporters, whose facilities were considerably inferior to the better equipped hospital ships - and were not even recognised and protected under the Geneva Convention. These were serviced by 'lighters' - small flat-bottomed boats usually capable of ferrying twelve stretcher cases per trip - available to take the wounded off the beaches and out to the hospital ships which would take them to the nearby Greek islands of Lemnos and Imbros, or further afield to the main hospital base at Alexandria.

Within hours of their landing on 25 April 1915, New Zealand soldiers were falling in distressing numbers. Already by the evening of 25 April, 557 wounded had been taken on board one ship alone, the *Gascon*, lying off Anzac Cove. Sister

Ella Tucker of the AANS remembered how wounded men were ferried out to the *Gascon* (Ella Tucker, in Barker, *Nightingales in the Mud*, p.30; Ella Tucker, in Bassett, *Guns and Brooches*, p.44).

'The wounded came in an endless stream, day and night, some barely able to walk, others on stretchers, shivering or unconscious through loss of blood. Medical supplies were limited and there was a desperate lack of fresh water. Despite the constant threat of Turkish shelling or torpedoes, the exhausted nurses cleaned, bandaged, warmed, and comforted their patients, many of whom had ghastly wounds or were suffering from the effects of gangrene and disease'.

Ella Tucker stayed with the *Gascon* for the next nine months as it ferried over 8,000 wounded and sick soldiers between the Gallipoli Peninsula and land-based tent hospitals on Imbros, Lemnos and Salonika. From that first day onwards, for nearly nine months, medical staff and nurses, including female nurses from different nursing services, including the Australian Army Nursing Service (AANS), treated and cared for hundreds of casualties in the hospital and transport ships anchored off-shore, or else sent to tent-hospitals on Lemnos or Lesbos or at Salonika, or shipped back to better facilities in Malta, Egypt, or even England, Australia and New Zealand.

Most of the wounded were evacuated first to the nearby Greek islands of Lemnos or Imbros by hospital ship or 'black ship', where they might be treated or alternatively sent on to Malta, or to Egypt, over 1,000 kms away (Tyquin 1993: Appendix V, page 218). The 'black ships' in particular were poorly equipped with even the most basic items in short supply; the sanitary facilities were appalling. There was also a serious lack of medical and nursing personnel; and the nursing staff were often called upon to make decisions and undertake procedures that would normally be the prerogative of a doctor.

With the rapid influx of patients from Gallipoli in April and May 1915, the facilities were soon overcrowded, and equipment and supplies inadequate. Nursing staff worked around the clock. Within three months 1 AGH, which was operating as a 1,500-bed hospital, was overwhelmed. On 10 May when the newly appointed Matron-in-Chief of the Mediterranean Expeditionary Force arrived in Egypt, she found that 'there were no more than a handful of nurses at the Base in Egypt and these were already fully employed... No fewer than 16,000 cases were landed and distributed among the hospitals ashore in the first ten days' (McEwen 2014: 99). Within three weeks, according to one of the doctors, 'nearly twenty thousand wounded were brought back to the base at Alexandria, and hundreds still arrive daily' (McEwen 2014: 97)

But, in any case, this facility was hundeds of miles away, and most of the casualties were ferried first at least by hospital ships to tent hospitals on Lemnos and Imbros, and to Salonika. Among the tent hospitals on Lemnos was No 3 Australian General Hospital (3AGH), where Matron Grace Wilson and her staff of AANS nurses tended Australian and other Allied wounded. 3AGH had been landed at the beginning of August on a bare and treeless hillside on the island of Lemnos. The tents and equipment were delayed for three weeks, water was in short supply, and there was no sanitation. When their tents and equipment failed to turn up, medical staff of 3AGH had to sleep rough. When Matron Grace Wilson and 80 nurses arrived, they were closely followed by more than 150 patients from Gallipoli. Sister Pratt described the scene in her diary:

> Things were in rather a state of chaos when the wounded began to arrive. Their dressings which had been applied on the hospital ships were saturated and covered in flies. Dysentery was a scourge on the island ... many of the wounded fell prey to the disease ... the cold weather brought frost-bitten patients. It was pitiable to see gangrene feet.

In her diary, Matron Grace Wilson also described the steady flow of new patients during the August 1915 offensive on Gallipoli and the effect that lack of proper equipment and supplies had on the care of the wounded (Grace Wilson, in Bassett, *Guns and Brooches*, p.46)

> The tent hospital presented new challenges for the nurses. They had to learn how to mend tears, re-hook walls, and manage guy ropes. And they were constantly at the mercy of the weather, with tents regularly blowing over. The tent wards were draughty and hard to keep clean. But, leading by example, Grace Wilson set about bringing order out of chaos at the tent hospital. Despite their own discomfort and the huge workload, the nurses persevered and within a month were treating over 900 patients. Sister Frances Selwyn-Smith wrote of Wilson's leadership: "At times we could not have carried on without her. She was not only a capable Matron, but what is more, a woman of understanding."

Whatever the dedication of most of the doctors and nurses, the overall management of the wounded was poor and indeed subject to criticism from many quarters. Questions were even asked in the House of Commons regarding the evacuation and treatment of the wounded at Gallipoli. In June 1915, Mr

Roch MP raised the issue after the fighting in early May (Part of Hansard, Consolidate Fund (no. 3) Bill, HC Deb., 23 June 1915 vol 72 cc. 1276-303) and described arrangements as 'totally and absolutely inadequate and insufficient'. A similar criticism was voiced by F. H. Cripps, a Yeomanry Officer in the Royal Bucks Hussars, wounded on 21st Aug 1915 and then evacuated in a transport ship converted to take the wounded, where he complains of the conditions on board and the poor medical treatment, and refers to there being only two doctors and two nurses for some 800 patients.

Earlier, in April 1915, the 29th Indian Infantry Brigade of the 10th Indian Division had been ordered to re-deploy from Egypt to Gallipoli. As originally constituted in October 1914, the brigade consisted of the 14th King George's Own Ferozepore Sikhs, the 69th Punjabis, the 89th Punjabis and the 1/6th Gurkha rifles. It had sailed from Karachi for Egypt on 2 November 1914 under the command of Brigadier General H. V. Cox. For the next six months it was engaged in the defence of the Suez Canal. Now the 29th, consisting of three battalions of Gurkhas (including the 6th and 10th Gurkhas) and one of Sikhs (the 14th Sikhs), was to be dispatched from Egypt and attached to the British 29th Division, which had been decimated in earlier battles; in this way, they were to became part of the 'British' forces at Gallipoli.

Little did they know what was in store for them. On 24 April 1915, they embarked at Port Said on SS *Dunluce Castle* for the Dardanelles. The ship anchored off Sedd-al-Bahr at 12.30 on April the 30th and the troops landed in Cape Helles in early May, five or six days after the invasion of the peninsula had begun. As Farwell remarks, 'it was not until five days after (the) initial landings that the first Gurkhas, the 1/6th, commanded by the Honourable Charles Bruce, arrived a Gallipoli, landing in the Cape Helles sector' (1985: 97). They were placed in immediate reserve but within a few hours suffered their first casualties. Although the casualties were heavy among all of the troops, on both sides of the conflict, the 'Indian Army' took the brunt of them.

In its first five weeks at Gallipoli, the 2/10th Gurkhas lost 70 per cent of its British officers and nearly 40 per cent of its other ranks; in the attempt to take Achi Baba, the 1/5th lost 7 British officers and 129 other ranks; and the 1/6th took 95 casualties (Parker 2000: 118). From then onwards, casualties from the 29th Indian Infantry Brigade were as heavy as those experienced by the British and ANZAC regiments. It is not clear, however, to what extent the quality of care they received was similar; nor whether they were treated literally along-side each other, once they reached the hospital ships and the land-based hospitals. They tended to be treated in separate facilities and were cared for, for the most part, by male orderlies, usually also 'Indians'.

For excample, while the bulk of all casualties were evacuated to Lemnos (only 50 miles from the fighting, whereas the hospitals in Egypt were over 650 miles away, a journey of 1½ days), the 1st and 3rd Canadian Stationary Hospitals, the 3rd Australian General Hospital and other medical units were stationed on both sides of Mudros bay and a considerable Egyptian Labour Corps detachment was employed to support them. It is not clear where the Indian Brigade casualties were treated; nor is it clear that they benefited from direct nursing by AANS female nurses, but seem to have been tended largely by male medical and nursing staff, for the most part by orderlies.

By July, the Indian Brigade had been reduced to a skeleton force and was moved wholesale to Imbros for rest and recuperation. The 1/5th and 1/6th Gurkhas had been temporarily amalgamated because of their losses, and the 14th Sikhs were by now so depleted in numbers – they had only one British officer, 1 VCO and 117 other ranks – that they were attached to the 2/10th Gurkhas for rations and maintenance. Like the 14th Sikhs, the 1/5th Gurkhas had only one surviving British officer, with only eight in the 5th Gurkhas as a whole, including the staff officers, and every unit was severely reduced in numbers. However, it seems that the 'shortage' of British officers was the primary reason for withdrawing the brigade from the front.

During its stay in Imbros, the Indian Brigade was once again brought up to strength by the arrivals of drafts from linked battalions and from depots in India. On 21 July, the Indian troops with the Mediterranean Expeditionary Force were designated the Indian Expeditionary Force (IEF) 'G'). Commanding Officer of the 1/6th Gurkhas, Colonel the Hon Charles G. Bruce, who had been badly wounded, was temporarily replaced by Major Cecil J. L. Allanson. After less than a month in reserve, the battalion returned with the rest of the Brigade to Gallipoli, now with the addition of the 2/10th from France, this time landing at Anzac Cove. Brought up to strength by its 20,000 or so reinforcements, Force 'G' took to the field again as part of the August offensive on the Anzac front, and fought side by side with the ANZACs until the final evacuation from the peninsula in late December 1915.

The Mesoptamian campaign began effectively with the capture of Basra, followed by the occupation of Kurna, and the establishment of a presence in the

Tigris Delta. This took place during 1915. Throughout the year, injured soldiers were for the most part cared for by male medical and nursing staff, orderlies for the most part, not only in the field but even in the larger hospitals where the more seriously wounded were sent. If the situation as regards the treatment of casualties was bad on the Western Front at Gallipoli, it was even worse in Mesopotamia.

By the end of September 1915, the British and Indian Army forces had taken the town of Kut, 120 miles south of Baghdad, and attempted to move deeper into Ottoman held territory. But, they were pushed back and had already suffered over 4,000 casualties when they fell back on Kut and were besieged there by the Ottoman forces. The withdrawal was a gruelling experience, particularly for the wounded. Those who could not walk were carried back to Lejj, 30 miles back, in unsprung carts, jolting over the rough ground. Having been transferred there to boats, they made their way – with constant upsets mainly caused by grounding in the shallow waters – all the 13 day journey to Basra.

Townsend hoped to defend Kut as stoutly as he had Chitral on the North West Frontier in 1895, an action for which he had been created a Companion of the Bath (CB). He had one month's rations for the British troops and two months for the 'Indians', as well as plenty of ammunition – sufficient if reinforcements reached him within two months. Casualties were dealt with by a number of hospitals, including the British General Hospital in Kut Bazaar, the Indian General Hospital, and four smaller hospitals or Field Ambulances where minor injuries and cases of dysentery and other problems were dealt with. All were overcrowded and hygiene was difficult to maintain; also all of them also came regularly under fire.

It was not until November 1915 that a 200-bed No. 3 British General Hospital was established in Basra. The new hospital was a converted liquorice factory which consisted of corrugated-iron sheds, wholly unsuitable for casualty care and effective nursing. If they survived that, they were taken by hospital ship to India. It was generally recognised that the medical arrangements, both for evacuation and for treatment were scandalously inadequate. It was not until January 1916 that a mere six nursing sisters from the Queen Alexandra's Imperial Nursing Service for India (QAIMNSI) were assigned to the Mesopotamia Campaign.

An attempt in January 1916 to relieve the siege of Kut was made, but failed. The relief force experienced significant casualties and Major T. C. Catty of the

69th Punjabis was Deputy Assistant Adjutant General at the headquarters of the 3rd Indian Division wrote in his diary on 14 January that

'the tales of the wounded.... are really awful & if one wasn't on the spot they would be unbelievable. There were no MOs to dress them properly and not 20 % of the proper number of stretcher bearers. Men were left out for 2-3 days before being picked up & we had won the battle. Some poor devils with fractured legs crawled in 4 or 5 miles. ...The arrangements for taking down the wounded to Basra & Amara are just as bad. There are no hosp'tl ships equipped as such – boats bring troops up river, sick & wounded are shoved on board under a MO & a few personnel & back it starts on its downward journey. There are no beds or bedding, no conservancy, and no cooking arrangements. Men with fractured thighs are shoved alongside dysentery cases & there they lie till they get to Basra. They're lucky if their wounds are dressed once during the voyage. It is a wicked shame as river transport on a river like the Tigris is the easiest form known. Half a dozen steamers properly equipped & all would be simple. I fear that many poor devils will die – of wounds officially – really of neglect' (cited in Carver 2004: 139-140).

In the meanwhile, the British and Indian forces cut off in Kut were suffering increasingly difficult conditions, with dwindling food supplies, near starvation rations and appalling medical facilities, with little or no equipment or supplies to care for the sick and wounded (McEwen 2014: 111). There was another major confrontation with the Ottoman forces at the beginning of March. The defenders had the superior numbers and the advantage of strong defensive positions. The 1st/2nd Gurkhas, fighting their first action in Mesopotamia, lost 80 all ranks killed and 100 wounded, while the 1st/9th also suffered heavily, losing a number of their officers, including the colonel and subedar major. Total losses were around 4,000 men. The next day, exhausted and very short of water, the British and Indian Army forces withdrew eighteen miles, with the wounded suffering considerably through the long, hot day.

In March 1916, the Conservative MP for Nottingham South, Lord Henry Cavendish Bentinck expressed his disgust at the inadequate management and treatment of the sick and wounded in both the Dardanelles and the Mesopotamia campaigns. He declared that it was

'really lamentable to see the experience of Gallipoli being repeated in the Mesopotamia Expedition. We hear of a shortage of hospitals, and we hear of a shortage of nurses, doctors, medical dressings, anaesthetics and antiseptics.

We hear of men being shipped down the Tigris with only one blanket for three men in these bitter cold nights' (McEwen 2014: 113). He was not the only critic of the army's arrangements for the treatment and care of the sick and wounded'.

In the meanwhile, in Kut, rations had to be further reduced. Draught animals (like oxen) were the first to go; then the transport animals (donkeys, mules, horses and camels). Many of the Indian troops refused to eat the meat, on religious and cultural grounds; but the Gurkhas, like the British troops, were quite prepared to do so. Eventually, the defending forces were obliged to eat even dogs, cats, starlings and hedgehogs. The lack of food and general conditions in Kut led to the serious debilitation of the troops, particularly the Indians, and of the townsfolk; morale was also flagging as various attempts to raise the siege proved futile.

Sisir Sarbadhikari and his fellow volunteers of the Bengal Ambulance Corps were among those ministering to the sick and wounded. His diary of the siege as it continued through March and April is reproduced in a posting on 27 August 2012 by Amitav Ghosh – amitavghosh.com/blog/?p=4525) is a major record of historical interest. At the end of March 1916, a further deployment of 26 nurses and a matron departed from Suez and arrived at Basra on 9 April. Shortly after arrival, the nursing staff were split up, with 11 sisters despatched for duty on hospital ships and eight stationed at the no 32 General Hospital. The matron and remaining sisters were deployed to the Rawal Pindi Hospital, Amara. All of this, however, was of little use to the besieged garrison at Kut.

The final relief attempt involved a series of encounters that took place over a couple of weeks, beginning on 5 April 1916. The British allied forces deployed numbered about 30,000 soldiers, roughly equal to the Ottomans, and at first they made significant progress, approaching to within 20 miles of Kut. The final effort was made on 22 April; in this 'advance', the Gurkha units played their full part, with the 1st/9th leading the assault and the 1st/8th being among the first of the British forces to reach the first line of the Ottoman trenches. But they were unable to break through the Ottoman cordon around the besieged town and losses had been very heavy. The 'relief' forces had suffered over 21,000 casualties in the vain attempt to save the garrison of around 10,000 and a civilian population of some 6,500.

This was the last attempt by ground forces to break the blockade and relieve the siege of Kut. In the meanwhile, the garrison in Kut was now starving. A truce was eventually agreed so that the many wounded on both sides could be evacuated, the Ottomans under the Red Crescent and the British under the Red Cross. Sisir Sarbadhikari wrote, in his diary, on April 27th: 'from today there is a three-day Armistice. We hear that Townshend is holding discussions with Khalil Pasha regarding our surrender. Some say that we will all be paroled and sent back to India; some say that only the medical units will be released'. On April 28th he reported: 'there's not a grain left of our rations'. On 29 April, Townshend finally surrendered.

After the surrender of Kut, many of the sick and injured were evacuated; the men arriving at the main hospital in Basra were described by one of the senior sisters as being in 'a pitiable state' - which was not surprising as it took weeks for the wounded and sick to be transported from Kut to Basra or Amara, and they received very little, if any, medical attention along the way. When they arrived, most were half-starved, infection-ridden and emotionally disturbed, as well as physically injured. The corrugated-iron huts of no 32 GH, where many were housed, were described as 'insufferable' and they were clearly unsuited for casualty care and effective nursing. Generally, there was a scarcity of suitable tentage, rations and medical supplies, and drinking water. The situation for the nursing staff, many of whom also suffered from sickness and emotional trauma, was also extremely difficult.

In Kut, however, by the time Townshend surrendered, conditions were – as Malise Ruthven comments, in his review of Justin Marozzi's *Baghdad: city of peace, city of blood* in the *London Review of Books* (23 October 2014) – 'apocalyptic'. 'Never can I forget the cats, starved of course, eating dead Turks and feeding out of their skeletons', wrote one British doctor, according to Marozzi. The surrender itself, after the longest siege that British troops had ever experienced, was clearly a disaster. Townshend's force – which had now surrendered in its entirety - consisted of 13,309 men, 3,248 of these being 'Indian' non-combatants.

Some 2,600 British and 9,300 'Indian' other ranks were rounded up and marched away. Some were marched to captivity elsewhere in Mesopotamia; others all the way to Turkey. About 1,750 men died from wounds or disease during the siege. The majority (1,136) of the 1,456 who were sick or wounded were exchanged and sent down to Basra by boat; the rest (345) went by boat to Baghdad, from where they were sent to Basra by boat three months later. All the rest had to march to Baghdad. The historian and war poet Geoffrey Elton was a junior officer at Kut and saw the rank-and-file being marched away, officerless, 'none of them fit to march five miles ... full of dysentery, beri-beri, scurvy, malaria and enteritis; they had no doctors, no medical stores and no transport; the hot weather, just beginning, would have meant much sickness and many deaths, even among troops who were fit, well-cared for and well supplied'.

From Baghdad, these prisoners of war faced a grim journey all the way to central Anatolia, where they were to suffer two and a half years of cruelty and neglect in disgraceful conditions as prisoners of war (Carver 2004: 155). Cruttwell said: 'the men were herded like animals across the desert, flogged, kicked, raped, tortured, and murdered'. Two-thirds of the British and about a seventh of the Indians never saw their homes again.

The War Office in London was immediately informed and issued a statement which shocked the nation, and caused great dismay throughout the Empire, especially in India and Nepal. In July 1916, the woefully inadequate, arguably criminally negligent state of affairs with regards to the care and treatment of the sick and wounded in the Gallipoli and Mesopotamia campaigns was addressed, belatedly, in the Special Commissions (Dardanelles and Mesopotamia) Bill, following a debate in the House of Commons. For tens of thousands of men, fighting on different fronts, in different campaigns and in different battles - including those on the Western Front, which continued to result in the largest number of casualties (including at Verdun and on the Somme) - the commissions of enquiry envisaged in this Bill came too late to be of any significance.

Furthermore, despite improvements in the quality and quantity or scale of medical equipment and personnel, medicines, treatment and care of the sick and wounded, there were still serious shortages in the autumn of 1916, in all theatres of the war, including on the Western Front, and especially shortages of trained nurses. The demand was exemplified by an assessment which estimated that the total number of casualties resulting from the Somme offensive amounted to not far short of 1.3 million (McEwen 2014: 133). The winter of 1916-1917 was particularly bad and meant that a significant proportion of those requiring treatment and care were suffering from problems other than those caused directly by the conflict.

The publication of the report of the findings of the Mesopotamia Commission in 1917 proved utterly damning; 'the revelations could hardly have been worse, barring the Black Ships at Gallipoli' (McEwen 2014: 163).

The findings of the Dardanelles Commission were equally critical. At the end of 1917, *The Times* stopped publishing complete casualty lists; previously they had published figures for all kinds of casualties – the number never fell below 1,000 a day, and were often as many as 5,000. The 1917 campaigns at Arras, Messines, Passchendaele and Cambrai had cost the British and Allied forces dearly: the total casualties for France and Flanders amounted to nearly 1.8 million, higher even than in the Somme offensive. And still the war was not over; not until 11 November 1918.

❀ ❀ ❀

CHAPTER 22

Campaigns and Communications

While the majority of Nepali *lahures* involved in the First World War fought overseas, on the Western Front, in North Africa, the Eastern Mediterranean and the Middle East, those who remained behind were also involved in active service. Several localised actions along the north west frontier took place over the four years of the war, and included Operations in the Tochi (1914–15), Operations against the Mohmands, Bunerwals and Swatis (1915), the Kalat Operations (1915–16), the Mohmand Blockade (1916–17), as well as Operations against the Mahsuds (the Waziristan Campaign) (1917) and Operations against the Marri and Khetran tribes (1918).

Gurkha contingents were involved in many of these campaigns, while in the actions again the Mahsuds (the Waziristan Campaign), three regiments of the Nepalese Contingent – referred to in one bulletin 'as our gallant allies' - also participated under General Sir Babar Shamshere Jang Bahadur Rana, in his capacity as representative of the Nepalese Army and liaison officer. According to Prakash Raj Sharma, an account of the Waziristan Campaign, *General Babar Shamsher's Journey to Waziristan* was written in verse and published by Yog Bikram Rana in 1919 in Bombay, India. The 53 page booklet was full of praises for Babar Shamshere, as it was written by someone in his entourage to Waziristan. It deals with the rationale for sending the Nepalese Army to British India and an account of his travels as well as of the actions that eventually crushed the insurgency by the Mahsud tribesmen.

According to this source, eight thousand Nepal Army troops had been sent to India in February 2015 to provide support to the Indian Army. One brigade was stationed in Dehra Dun under the command of Tej Shamsher Rana; a second was sent, under the command of Padma Shamshere Rana, and was stationed in Kakul near Abbotabad in what is now Pakistan; and a third was sent, under the command of Sher Shamshere. A separate unit was sent in May 1917 under the command of Babar Shamshere Rana, second son of the Rana Prime Minister Chandra Shamshere, and this was deployed to help quell the rebellion by the Mahsud tribes in Waziristan.

There is no specific mention of camp followers in any of the accounts of these campaigns, although baggage trains of camels and mules were clearly relied upon to carry the necessary supplies. One account, by Private Parker of the London regiment, states that 'on the whole campaign we had 4 killed & 13 wounded, 6 have so far died of disease & half the battalion went into hospital & were sent out of the country. There is hardly a man but what was sick at some time or the other'. Parker refers to the injured being 'sent back to hospitals' away from the Frontier, but there is little detail as regards these. He makes no reference to *lahure* women of any kind, even though there were several Gurkha units involved, and also several regiments of the Nepalese Army, which almost certainly had their own baggage train and camp followers, some of whom are may well have been women.

Altogether, some 16,000 Nepali troops were deployed on operations on the North West Frontier and as garrison battalions, to replace troops that had gone overseas to fight on the Western Front or in the Middle East. The 2nd Battalion saw service in the North-West Frontier of India, gaining the Battle Honour 'North-West Frontier 1915–17' in the process. In 1917, a 3rd Battalion was raised for home service in India. Furthermore, even after the war, as the European armies demobilised in 1919, all ten Gurkha regiments were engaged on the North West Frontier of India, as were three battalions of the 11th, which, raised for the war did not long survive it. In 1919, the 1st and 2nd Battalions saw service during the brief Third Afghan War for which they gained the Theatre Honour 'Afghanistan 1919'. In 1921, the 3rd Battalion was disbanded. After this the Regiment participated in a number of campaigns on the North-West Frontier, serving mainly in Waziristan.

The *lahure* woman's task during the First World War – wherever their menfolk were deployed - was, for the most part, to remain at home in the village or in the 'lines' at the regimental 'homes', waiting for news of their husbands, sons, brothers and fathers, fighting in India or across the black sea (*kalo pani*) and keeping 'the home fires burning'. Shrabani Basu writes, movingly, for example, about one young Garhwali child bride of 13, Satoori Devi, from a small village in Chamba District, whose husband Gabar Singh Negi was a rifleman in the Garhwal Regiment, having enlisted in 1913. Exceptionally, we are able to follow her and her husband through his first year on the Western Front, up to and after his death on 10 March 1915 at Neuve Chapelle.

Gabar Singh was one of several soldiers in the Indian Army to be awarded the Victoria Cross posthumously, so we know something very personal about this star-crossed young couple (Basu 2016: 1, 21, 78, 109, 112-13, 191-92). Still only 14 years old, Satoori Devi, Gabar Singh's widow, pinned the medal to her sari and wore it all the time, even during her mundane daily tasks, for the rest of her life. Until an artist painted a portrait of her husband, she did not even have a photo of him; but after the Memorial to Gabar Singh was built in 1925 in the main square in Chamba, she organised an annual Chamba *mela* (fair) on his birthday, and every year until her death in 1981, she stood and received the salute on his behalf.

While the Nepali men in the Brigade of Gurkhas fought in Europe, the Eastern Mediterranean and the Middle East, their women-folk also, for the most part, like the Garhwalis, stayed behind. Few received any recognition for the anxieties, the absences and the losses that they suffered, often over many years. Some had to wait a very long time for the return of their men folk, or for the devastating news that they would not return. Active service kept men away for months, even years. The 1st/10th, for example, did not leave its depot at Maymyo until mid-August 1915, a year after war was declared, but it did not return for four and a half years, after fighting Turks, Arabs and Kurds in the Middle East. The 2nd/5th left its 'home' in Abbottabad in December 1915 and did not return until June 1919. They had only one day at 'home' before they marched out to take part in the Third Afghan War.

But, while most *lahure* women remained at home, we can be sure that at least some of those who served as soldiers in the Indian 'home guard' during the First World War were accompanied by their women folk, as they had been for a century or so. Equally, we can presume that some Nepali women migrated independently to India to provide services of various kinds to the Nepali soldiers serving there, and to contribute to the economic and social life of the settlements and small towns that had already grown up around recruitment centres, army barracks and regimental homes.

While most women spent months and even years without their menfolk, some were able to keep in contact by letter as special postal services were established early on both for those Nepalis involved in the 'defence' of India and for the Gurkhas fighting with the 'Indian Army' overseas. There had been a postal service in Nepal, which had been in existence since around 1875, but the bulk of items carried by this service comprised official government memoranda and other documents. In 1911, the postal service was re-organised with the establishment of the Hulak Goswara (Post Office), which then worked largely as a clearing house and centre of distribution for all government documents.

However, as we have seen, the 'war office' established a dedicated postal service for those serving in India during the First World War, and this continued throughout the period that Nepali soldiers were posted abroad. A postal registration service for private civilian individuals did not begin until 1922, on the initiative of the Indian Embassy; the service was confined, in any case, to the Rana notability and members of their families. As regards contact by telephone, the first trunk line between Kathmandu and Raxaul was established until 1914 while the Telephone Office was created and a basic telephone network set up to connect the major government offices and the palaces of the senior Ranas in 1915.

It was not until 1934, however, that telephone communication lines linking all government offices in Narayanhitti Durbar and Singha Durbar were established; and not until the mid-1930s that an automatic telephone exchange with 25 lines was installed, in the royal Palace. Very few people had access to or owned a 'wireless' – indeed it was not until after the Second World War (in 1946) that a government ban imposed much earlier on keeping wireless sets at home was lifted – and so, in the early decades of the 20th century, and throughout the First World War, communications with the outside world were still extremely limited, and for the most part it was still by 'word of mouth' that news travelled inside and outside the country. Even second-hand news from abroad was limited, although for a tiny minority the Indian press provided a source of information.

The first Nepali newspaper – *Sudha Sagar* - was published in 1898. But the history of journalism and the press did not really start until the publication of *Gorkhapatra*, as a weekly newspaper, in 1901. The circulation of the very few publications being produced remained extremely small over the next few decades, as few among the Nepalese population were able to read, or write. In fact, the level of development of communications and the media generally was very low.

In the meanwhile, postal services were also established for the troops fighting on the Western Front. There was considerable concern, however, on the part of the British High Command, that seditious literature produced by Indian nationalists, like the Paris Indian Society, might be distributed to the troops; there was also concern that letters sent home by soldiers at the front or recovering from injuries in hospital might reveal information of use to the enemy or likely to discourage further recruitment in India and Nepal. So, by arrangement with the French authorities, all suspects domiciled in France were kept under observation, and all of the letters produced by the Indian troops were submitted to the British Censorship authorities. Where they were written – as they tended to be – in anything other than English, they were translated first, copied and then censored.

The troops were told that they were not allowed to mention any war-time locations or operational details in their letters; but they were quick to work out that their letters were read in any case, and soon they invented code words and phrases to disguise the meaning of passages they felt the censors might otherwise censor. The censors, in turn, did not take long to decipher most of these codes words and phrases. The censors submitted a weekly report along with a series of extracts from letters to and from India and Nepal. It gave them an insight into how the troops were feeling; also, any dissent could be quickly spotted.

By the first winter of the war, the censors noted that the mood of the troops from the Indian sub-continent were changing from optimism to widespread pessimism and even despair. One of the reasons for this was that men who had been hospitalised and recovered were being sent back to the front line, and the soldiers were demoralised by this as they felt that anyone who had fought and been seriously injured had 'done their bit' and should be sent home. But morale was low for many other reasons also – the heavy casualties experienced, the fact that they were often led by officers from other units, the artillery bombardment on a scale never before encountered, and above all perhaps the mud and the wet and the cold.

Also, as Basu remarks, 'they were missing their families and longed to return' (2016: 72); one indication of this was the volume of letters now being written and sent home. Copies of these letters are now housed in the British Library; Shrabani Basu has made good use of them in her book *For King and Another Country: Indian soldiers on the Western Front 1914 to 1918* (Basu 2016). Basu reports that 'by January 1915, the postal censorship department was working at full pace, as a large volume of correspondence was passing through the Indian base. (The officer in charge of censorship), had to request three more readers.

The Indians were pouring out their thoughts and experiences in the West to their family and friends. Two more officers were appointed... the former to look after the correspondence in Hindi. The latter would look at the letters in Marathi and other languages from Bombay Presidency' (Basu 2016: 53).

One Sikh soldier wrote to his friend in India on 20 January 1915, that

'...In the trench, the snow rises from the feet to the neck, and the feet and hands are frostbitten.... It rains and snows day and night. The sun is never seen. On all sides, men were fighting with swords and bayonets. Corpses lay at every step and the blood ran in little rivers. Since we arrived, the Lahore and Meerut Divisions have been constantly fighting. They came 72,000 strong. Of these, 42,000 have been killed or wounded. The commander of the Lahore Division says that until both Divisions are killed the third Division will not join in' (Basu 2016: 81).

The censors were concerned at letters like these; less because of any sympathy they might have felt for these soldiers, than because they feared that demoralisation might lead to disloyal sentiments and even action. General Willcocks, the officer in overall command, was also concerned. According to Willcocks, in a memo at the end of the year to the Viceroy in India, 'the Sikhs had done well, but the Gurkhas had disappointed'; the British generals of the Indian Army had also performed poorly, in his estimation; many of them, like many of the rank and file, were reservists whom he considered 'too old' and 'quite useless' (Basu 2016: 89).

Following the General's complaints, the Secretary of State wrote to the Viceroy, saying that 30 per cent of the reinforcements were declared unfit for service by the British officer commanding the base depot at Marseilles while the Medical Board had pronounced 68 soldiers unfit for service in Europe on medical grounds, 32 temporarily unfit due to old age and weakness. It was decided that the despatch to Europe of reservists of over 15 years of service should be prohibited. This would affect thousands of older men and their families who would no longer be involved directly in the war. But the campaign for recruitment would continue and some of those in service were sent back to the villages to bring in fresh recruits (Basu 2016: 90); and whatever their fathers, mothers, wives and families thought about more of their menfolk going to the killing fields of the Western Front, men continued to sign-up.

In fact, there was a continuing supply of recruits: the Indian Corps was getting an average of over 8,000 recruits a month, whereas the normal intake was usually 15,000 in a whole year. More soldiers came in February 1915, arriving as before at Marseilles and being transported by train to the front. Of the 130,000 'Indians' who served in France and Belgium, almost 9,000 died and many more were injured. The generally low morale of the Indian Army on the Western Front resulted in many being re-deployed after October 1915 for the rest of the war to other theatres, where they, together with other elements of the Indian Army, continued to face often appalling conditions and severe injuries and losses – in the disastrous assault on Turkish positions at Gallipoli during 1915 and in the equally disastrous defence of Kut in Mesopotamia, for example, in April 1916.

Eventually, however, Germany and its Allies were defeated, an armistice was signed on 11 November 1918, First World War came to an end, and the troops – or at least most of them - went home. The de-mobilisation took many months, however, and some soldiers were not, as we have seen, united with their families until well into 1919, and some did not return home until even later, as their continuing army service led to their involvement in other campaigns, in India and elsewhere. Many also, decided to settle in India and either continued in army service from there or left the army and started other livelihoods.

❀ ❀ ❀

CHAPTER 23

The Impact of the War

The absence of so many men overseas for so long had a substantial impact on the local economy and society, not to mention on those left behind. The pain (*dukha*) and the cost of the war were very considerable both for those directly involved and for those indirectly affected. Many men never returned home; others returned seriously disabled and/or traumatised. According to most sources, some 200,000 men from Nepal took part in the First World War, but it is not clear if this includes those deployed in various parts of India or further afield in Afghanistan or in Burma, for example. It is also estimated that some 10 per cent were killed or injured, although this may well be an underestimate.

Not all those who survived the war returned home. Some found reason to remain and settle in Europe; a few in the Middle East; and many in India. Of the 10,932 men discharged from service at the end of the war, only one third (3,838) returned to Nepal, according to Mojumdar (1975: 73, cited in Seddon 1987: 25). 'Many of them stayed back in India to work either as watchmen or even to work in the police under the government, or in other positions available to them. For many Indian merchants had good faith in the Gurkhas as honest and loyal servants' (Kansakar 184: 52). Brook Northey and Morris observed in 1927 (1927: xxvii) that

'ever since the war there has been a greater difficulty than ever before in getting discharged soldiers to return to their homes. Looked at in a broad way, this is, no doubt, due very much to the isolation of the country, although the isolation may have been health from the point of view of keeping the people primitive and simple in their habits. Yet, once they began to mix freely with the outside world, it was bound to produce difficulties. Men found that they could earn quadruple the amount by taking positions as watchmen, and so forth, in India, that they lived in greater comfort than was possible in their own country, although in greater heat, and, therefore, there was a great diminution in the number of men who returned to their homes.'

But, if some decided to remain in India, or to settle there, after being de-mobilised, and either kept their families with them or brought them from villages 'back home', the majority of the survivors returned home to be re-united there with their families and the re-start a new life. For some that was still in the British Army; for others it meant a renewed involvement in agriculture or some other civilian livelihood back in the village.

In the early anthropological studies of village Nepal, however, there is surprisingly little information about the impact of the Great War overall on village economy and society. In his study of the Magars of 'Banyan Hill' (in PanderaThum), where he undertook fieldwork ten days' walk to the northwest of Pokhara in the mid-1950s, John Hitchcock remarks that 'the most important non-local source of income in Banyan Hill is army service, a source that is part of a long-standing hill tradition. Ever since 1815, Magars, together with Gurungs, Limbus and Rais, formed the backbone of the British Gurkha Brigade. In the two World Wars, half the Nepalese holders of the Victoria Cross, Britain's highest decoration for bravery, were Magars, one of whom came from a village adjacent to Pandera Thum' (Hitchcock 1966: 17).

Hitchcock discusses the importance of this additional income, in the form of remittances and pensions, for the local economy and society at the time of his study, but does not explore the subject of the overall impact and implications of army service over time in any depth, nor does he indicate whether any of those receiving pensions at the time he was there had fought in the Great War, even though anyone over the age of 60 might well have done. It seems, however, that there were only sixteen men in the village who were 40 years older or more, so perhaps memories of the impact of the War had already faded. There is no mention of anyone disabled through injuries suffered during army service, or of women widowed during either of the two Wars.

Bernard Pignède, author of *Les Gurungs,* who spent nine months in a predominantly Gurung village not far from Pokhara in 1958, comments that 'according to Northey and Morris, 55,000 recruits fought alongside the British troops from 1914 to 1918. Landon reckons that 200,000 Gurkhas served in India during the First World War' (Pignède 1993: 19). Actually, what Brook Northey and Morris do say is that 'during the war, no less than 200,000 Gurkhas joined our service, and 55,000 of these were enlisted in the regular Gurkha battalions of the Indian Army. Nepal suffered some 20,000 casualties on our behalf, and its men fought in almost every theatre of war...' (1927: 263).

Pignède does remark that 'at the time of the first World War, many young men enlisted. One informant, an old retired Captain, calculated that 85 per cent of the boys from Mohoriya left without their father's consent' (1993: 253). This 'old man' was 52 when he talked to Pignède. Other soldiers whose biographical outlines Pignède provides were all younger. He also mentions, with specific regard to the village in which he lived and undertook his research, that 'many men had served in the Gurkha troops under the command of British officers whom they held in high esteem. A good number of these soldiers had been through Europe during the two World Wars' (1993: xl).

He suggests that 'men between 40 and 50 years are a little less numerous than those between 50 and 60, which is explained by the drop in births occasioned by the massive exodus of Gurungs fighting for the British during the First World War' (1993: 35). He makes no comment about the relevance of deaths of men fighting in the First World War during 1914-1918, some 40 years previously, but there were very few men alive in his village from that period in any case.

Pignède talks interestingly of the factors that caused those enlisted as soldiers to return home before their service was completed. While he was referring to the situation in the 1950s, many of the same factors would have applied in earlier times as well, at least to some extent.

Some of those who quit early, did so because they found the discipline and the rigours of army life too much to take; others because they saw others promoted over them, even after as many as 9 or 12 years of service. More, however, left army service because of family reasons, including the need to secure an inheritance on the death of a father, or because of a wife's demands. Sometimes, the responsibility of the house is too much for the wife who has children; and she demands her husband's return. Pignède suggests that 'usually the latter gives in to her reasoning to avoid the break up of the marriage' (1993: 258).

Another factor on which he comments was the absent husband's fear of adultery on the part of the wife. Long periods of absence put great strain on marriages, and among the Gurungs, Pignède suggests, adultery and divorce are matters essentially for the parties involved, and 'no appreciable social pressure is brought to bear' (1993: 226). He remarks that 'sexual relations between spouses are... hindered by the absence of a husband who is a soldier'; but on the other hand, he reports that 'adultery is very rare on the part of women whose husbands are away'. He also suggests that 'the husband ... also seems to avoid having extra-marital relations' and that 'soldiers billeted abroad have little sexual contact with the women whom they associate with there' (1993: 252).

He adds, however, that 'officers of the Gurkha troops have indicated that several cases of adultery followed by divorce have happened in the cantonments and were mostly due, it seemed, to the idleness of the wives'; furthermore, 'when a young woman is alone in the village, it occasionally happens that she goes back to her parents and does not return' (1993: 273). It does also happen that a partner who discovers that her husband or his wife has had extra-marital sexual relations asks for a divorce. Adultery was rarely given, it is suggested, as grounds for an actual divorce, though it is possible, as Macfarlane suggests, that 'with so many males away so much of the time it is not uncommon' (Macfarlane 1976: 227). Morris (1935: 150) certainly thought that this was the case.

Pignède comments that, 'even though recruitment has been particularly extensive for about the last thirty years, it does not seem that the number of divorces has significantly increased'. He makes no direct reference, however, to the incidence of adultery in Mohoriya before then, or during the First World War, presumably because there was little or no information on the subject. Also, he does not refer to the issue of sexually transmitted diseases (STDs) being brought back by men who had spent a good deal of time abroad, even if, as we have seen, the incidence of STDs among soldiers in the Indian Army (particularly British soldiers) was a matter of concern to the military hierarchy and medical personnel. Macfarlane does consider this issue, but suggests that 'there is little evidence that such disease is at all widespread among the Gurungs among whom I lived' (1976: 236).

As regards the eastern hills, Lionel Caplan has referred to the involvement of the Limbus of the Indreni Cluster in Ilam District in the First World War, mentioning in particular the recruitment of soldiers from the area and deaths that occurred during the war itself, including one man – the first in his family to enlist – who, he says, died at Gallipoli (1970: 155; 1995: 40). In 1915, the second battalion of the 7th GR took part in the Dardanelles Campaign as part of the 29th Indian Brigade. The Brigade landed at Cape Helles in early May and the 2nd Battalion took part in the Battle of Gully Ravine which began on 28 June. The brigade as a whole was moved to Anzac Cove in August where it took part in the August Offensive. The 2nd Battalion as a whole suffered heavy casualties during its participation in the Gallipoli campaign.

The two regiments in which Limbus were mainly enlisted were the 7th and the 10th Gurkha Rifles. The first battalion of the 7th GR, which had historical links with Burma remained there on the outbreak of the First World War as a training unit, providing reinforcements and replacements to the 2nd Battalion which was on active service until 1916. At least five drafts were supplied. The third draft was sunk at sea by an Austrian submarine in the Aegean Sea with the loss of 187 men. The second battalion went to the Suez Canal and from there to Mesopotamia, where they were taken at the fall of Kut, but received the honour of marching out under arms. A newly raised replacement battalion took part in the re-capture of Kut. The 2nd/7th received battle honours for the Suez Canal, Egypt, Megiddo, Sharon, Palestine, Shaiba, Kut al Amara, Ctesiphon, the Defence of Kut al Amara, Baghdad and Sharqat.

On 15 August 1916, the 1st Battalion embarked from Rangoon for the Middle East after a farewell ceremony given by the Governor of Burma. It fought in Mesopotamia from 1916. Much of the regiment's involvement in the war was relatively quiet but it did take part in a number of engagements including the offensive against Baghdad in 1917 and the last battle of the Mesopotamian campaign in late October 1918 at Sharqat. The 1st Battalion remained in Mesopotamia upon the conclusion of the war. It saw service during the revolt of Southern Kurdistan in 1919. The 2nd Battalion took part in the Third Afghan War in 1919 and in operations on the North West Frontier.

As regards the impact of army employment generally, Caplan suggests that 'it was the most depressed sections of the population which first turned to Gurkha service. These were mainly members of lineages and households without traditional rights to *kipat* land'. He gives the example of one man, Bhage Sur, whose father had come to the Indreni cluster to marry the sister of a resident, and was given a small plot to cultivate. The two sons of the marriage found the plot too small to divide, so Bhage Sur joined the Gurkhas, and died in the First World War. His son and grandson both spent a period in the army' (Caplan 1995: 40, see also Caplan 1970: 115). It is evident from this and other examples that, among the Limbus at least, and probably also among other groups, there were 'army' families, in which it had become a 'tradition' to serve in the Gurkhas.

Caplan remarks that he was never told by a serving or former Gurkha soldier that he had joined because he wanted to follow his father into a regiment, although several of them did in fact do so' (1995: 40). He suggests that this was in part because there were only two regiments – the 7th and the 10th Gurkhas – that enlisted men from the east of Nepal, so the chances of serving in the same regiment as a close forebear were comparatively high. Furthermore, he says, 'the induction centre, learning that a new recruit had family links to a regiment would likely have placed the young man in that regiment' (ibid).

According to Caplan, one Indreni Limbu family, with a long record in the Gurkhas, served as follows: the first man to enlist was in the 2/10th GR and was killed at Gallipoli. Two of his sons saw service in the same battalion of the regiment, although both transferred to an Indian unit (11th GR) when the Gurkha regiments were divided between the British and Indian armies at the time of India's independence in 1947. A third son was in a different battalion (3/10th GR), raised during the war. In the succeeding generation, only one man joined the army, but it was also the 2/10th GR that he joined, and two of his sons were serving in the mid-1990s in the 7th GR. So, at least in this family, a tradition that began in the First World War was evidently continued over the next 80 years.

Interestingly, it seems that in Thak, a Gurung village studied by Alan Macfarlane in the late 1960s, 'the wealthier landholders of the 1920s did not send their sons into the army; there was plenty for them to do at home. But the poorer families who were recruited then have now profited and increased their wealth' (Macfarlane 1976: 194). Macfarlane also notes that 'now it is becoming more and more obvious that the wealthy persons in the village are those who own land' (ibid 197). Historically, then, it seems, one of the long term effects of involvement in army service has been the re-investment of army salaries and pensions in the acquisition of land and the accumulation of wealth. Those who came back without serious injury or disability from the First World War almost certainly increased their investment in land and were thereby able to improve their relative economic situation back home.

The investment in land was almost certainly associated with an intensification of farming – involving the gradual decline of shifting agriculture in favour of settled agriculture on established fields both for irrigated and dry cereal cultivation and a reduction in reliance on livestock: 'the main trend in the last hundred years would seem to be away from a predominantly pastoral but many-sided economy to one heavily dependent on two types of work, arable farming and the army' (Macfarlane 1976: 30). This process was slow, but he remarks that, although it was said, by Morris (1933), that the Gurungs could be described as 'chiefly a pastoral people', this was 'probably out of date by the 1930s' (Macfarlane 1976: 30, n 13, 340). This suggests that the mass return of soldiers from the First World War might have accelerated the intensification of farming to which he refers.

The implications of this process for the growth of inequality in village economy and society, and for an increasing involvement of women in agriculture, even when they were not allowed to plough – which was generally the case. Women's work in the village was always hard, involving as it did both domestic and agricultural work, and also the collection of wood for fuel, leaves and grasses for animal fodder, and water. The decline in pastoralism is likely to have increased the burden of work on women, in so far as they were obliged now to take on greater responsibility for farm-yard livestock production and domestic activities but also for inputs into crop production and processing.

Increasingly, also there were tendencies towards the development of a more clearly delineated agrarian class structure in which landowners increasingly employed wage labourers as ploughmen and agricultural workers, thereby contributing to the erosion of 'traditional' caste relations (involving *jajmani*) and relations of mutual labour exchange (*parma*), but not necessarily diminishing the social discrimination against low caste *dalits*.

❀ ❀ ❀

CHAPTER 24

The Inter War Years: the 1920s

The number of Nepalis living and working in India after the end of the First World War was already considerable and Nepalis accounted for not far short of half of all those born outside India. According to the 1921 Indian Census (published by the Superintendent Government Printing, Calcutta in 1924), 'the number of persons resident in India who were born outside the Indian Empire is 603,526, and of these 274,000 were born in Nepal' (1924: 95). The majority of Nepalis were males, but there was also a significant female Nepali population - 161,119 were males and 118,818 were females. The numbers in this regard were not very different from the situation recorded in the census of India of 1911 (160,974 and 119,274).

The largest number of Nepalis was in Bengal, with Assam a close second. But whereas Bengal showed a marked decline in comparison with 1911, Assam showed the largest population increase – by a long way - between 1911 and 1921 of all Indian provinces or states. This was largely because of substantial immigration, to work in the tea gardens and to settle in the hitherto largely uncultivated Brahmaputra Valley, mainly from elsewhere in India, and to a smaller extent from Nepal and Sikkim. Some 16 per cent of the total population was recorded as having been born outside the province, and the proportion of women among the immigrant population was higher than anywhere else. Many Nepalis, however, were attracted by the possibilities of livestock production (Census 1921: 86).

The census states that 'the Nepali settlers in Assam were originally mostly old Gurkhas who had settled down with their families, or temporary or periodic visitors, for the most part buffalo graziers. There has, however, been a large influx of late of more permanent settlers, the majority of whom are cattle-owners and graziers. Basing his estimate on the number of persons who speak Naipali or some kindred language, Mr. Lloyd calculates that there must be at least 104,000 persons of Nepali race in Assam at present, the number having doubled since 1911 (Census 1921: 96).

Bengal, however, also recorded a significant increase in population, in large part because of immigration from elsewhere in India and to a lesser extent (5 per cent) from Nepal. The most important streams of immigration included those involving 'immigrants into the Darjeeling and Jalpaiguri tea gardens from Nepal and Chota Nagpur' (Census 1921: 87). Not all of the immigrants, and not all of the Nepali immigrants, however, were employed in agriculture. In Darjeeling itself in the 1920s, there were menials of all kinds, including both men and women, to transport the tourists and other visitors to the hill station, and their goods, and to serve them in various capacities.

According to a 1922 handbook: 'on arrival at Darjeeling the men mount ponies and the ladies and children get into dandies and rickshaws.. which carry them away to the several hotels and boarding establishments, to be followed shortly afterwards by female porters...' (cited in Neale 2002: 29). But, if women, many of them Nepalis by origin, were working in a variety of capacities, usually in menials jobs, it seems that few, if any, were able to join the mountain expeditions which were beginning to become a major source of employment.

United Provinces came third in terms of total population of Nepali origin in the 1921 Indian census. Here, the majority of Nepalis were thought to be Gurkhas or ex-Gurkhas who either remained in the army and lived in the numerous army barracks or cantonments with their wives and families or else had left the army and settled in India to take up other sources of income. We have already noted that, after the First World War, many Gurkhas and ex-Gurkhas decided to stay in India rather than return to their village. Of the 10,932 discharged from service at the end of the war, only one third (3,838) returned to Nepal, according to Mojumdar (1975: 73). Some married locally; others brought their wives or sweethearts to live with them in India.

Kansakar comments that 'many of them stayed back in India to work either as watchmen or even to work in the police under the government, or in other positions available to them. For many Indian merchants had good faith in the Gurkhas as honest and loyal servants' (Kansakar 1984: 52). Brook Northey and Morris also observed at the time that 'ever since the war there has been a greater difficulty than ever before in getting discharged soldiers to return to their homes.... Men found they could earn quadruple the amount by taking positions as watchmen, and so forth, in India, that they lived in greater comfort than was possible in their own country, although in greater heat, and therefore there was a great diminution in the number of men who returned to their homes'(Brook Northey & Morris 1927: xxvii).

Other provinces or states with significant numbers of Nepalis recorded were Bihar and Orissa, Sikkim and Burma. In the first two of these, unlike in any of the other provinces or states, women of Nepali origin were in the majority among all those of Nepali origin – as had also been the case in 1911. But, whereas in 1911 they had accounted for two thirds of all those born in Nepal, in 1921 they accounted for an even greater proportion (22,151 females to 8,303 males). The reasons for this are not entirely clear. The census explains it largely as the result of 'wives brought over the Nepal border and married to members of the lower castes' (1921: 96). What is not clear, however, is why the proportion of women among those Nepalis living in Bihar and Orissa increased between 1911 and 1921.

We have already referred to the fact that many soldiers and even ex-soldiers from Nepal did not return home, but either remained or settled in India. The majority of these were serving soldiers. The number of Gurkhas actually serving in India at the time of the 1921 census was 21,365, consisting of 497 officers and 21,138 of other ranks' (1921: 96). It does not, however, state the number of Nepali women in total accompanying these Gurkhas. The majority of the Gurkhas, however, were in the United Provinces: 'the majority of the Nepalese enumerated in the United Provinces consist of soldiers in the Gurkha regiments and their families, and of a substantial number of settlers, mostly old soldiers. There were Gurkha regiments also stationed in the Punjab, the North West frontier Province and Burma' (1921: 95). So, in all these areas there were *lahures* and *lahure* wives.

The 1921 census of India comments, when considering immigration into the United Provinces, that 'the foreigners in cantonments are drawn from overseas and from the various recruiting grounds of the military forces in India, the number from Nepal including a considerable proportion of ex-service settlers as well as men on the active lists' (1921: 92). The 'foreigners from overseas' were mainly British, the others were Indians and Nepalis. Many of these last were now more critical of living conditions and the authoritarian regime that had ruled over Nepal for nearly a century than perhaps they had been earlier. Uprety suggests that some at least of the war veterans, especially those who remained in India, expressed these feelings openly: 'Jamadar Keshang Jang Gurung even sent an open letter to Chandra Shumshere Rana, demanding the establishment in Nepal of parliamentary democracy under the leadership of a constitutional monarch' (Uprety 1992: 37).

Nepali intellectuals living in Benares, Darjeeling and other cities in India where the Nepali expatriate community was significant were also beginning to voice criticism of the Rana regime and its failure to promote economic and social development. Dharanidar Koirala, for example, wrote a poem, Awake, Awake, Now Awake (*jaga, jaga, aba jaga*), which called on the Nepali elite to rouse themselves from their comfortable way of life and intellectual slumbers to work for the progress and development of their country. For intellectuals like Koirala, foreign labour migration was a reflection of the unsatisfactory states of affairs, whereby employment was not being created for Nepalis within Nepal, and they were obliged as a result to migrate abroad. This was considered shameful. Koirala also wrote a poem or song, directed at Nepali workers abroad, called What a Shame it is to go to Foreign Lands and Work as Coolies (*bidesh ma janchcha kulli kam garcha kasto lajmarnu ni!*).

The 1923 'friendship treaty', which recognised Nepal's full sovereignty and independence had the double effect of consolidating the repressive political system of Rana rule while at the same time opening up the economy even more to Indian commerce and imported goods (Landon 1928; Blaikie, Cameron & Seddon 1980: 38). Nepal had little to offer in exchange, except rice and timber, mainly from the *terai*, and of course labour, mainly from the hills. This arguably 'semi-colonial' relationship encouraged the deepening of Nepal's peripheral position vis-a-vis British India, and certainly promoted increasing labour migration as well as migration for re-settlement. It also led to increasing criticism of this relationship.

In 1926, at a meeting held in Darjeeling, Shukra Raj, leader of the Nepali Arya Samaj movement, bitterly criticised the high caste Nepalis in particular, for having forgotten the sacred scriptures and for either living as cooks in India or at home cheating the masses' (Uprety 1992). In his essay, The Present Condition of our Race and Nation (*hamro desh au jati ko varttaman awasta*), published in 1929, Khadga Bahadur Chettri, a Nepali domiciled in India, argued that the rulers of Nepal, unresponsive to the needs of the people, had 'closed the gates' to the development of the country; the result was that 'the poor and the destitute of the unfortunate motherland were travelling from door to door in foreign lands in search of food and livelihood there. Here, in search of a few hateful pieces of silver they underwent humiliation and indignity' (Uprety 1992: 38).

But none of this criticism prevented a growing exodus from Nepal, as men and women chose to leave their villages to find economic opportunities not just in the urban areas of Nepal but abroad, mainly in India. Timelines recorded during research project on rural livelihoods in 1996 in villages near Pokhara in the western hills indicated that locals began to seek civilian employment in north and north west India in increasing numbers during the 1920s and thereafter. Further east, Brook Northey and Morris observed that migration to Assam and Darjeeling also continued, with an increased impetus, from the hills and from the mountain areas, and not only to find employment in agriculture, tea gardens and other sectors of the economy, but also in other, new emerging occupations, where they were regarded as unusually 'capable and industrious' (1927: 97).

For example, some 50 'Bhotias' - all men – from Darjeeling were employed by the British in their first attempt on Mt. Everest in 1921, following the opening up of the Tibetan border. The distinctions between the Nepalis, Sherpas, Tibetans, Sikkimese and Bhutanese were lost on the Britsh, who referred to them all, generically at this time, as 'Bhotias'. Soon, however, this term was replaced by that of 'Sherpas', as men from this group came to dominate the mountain portering scene. Sherpas from Darjeeling were recruited to support the second and third British expeditions in 1922 and 1924.

The 1924 expedition, in which Edward Norton came to within 900 feet of the summit, and George Mallory and Andrew Irvine met their deaths near to (or perhaps even after having reached) the peak, also employed numbers of Sherpas as well as non-Sherpa, Nepali porters. Sherpa men were always on the lookout for the possibility of employment by a climbing expedition, even if that involved not only hard work but danger and hardship (*dukha*). Mountain expeditions at this period were launched from Darjeeling, outside Nepal itself, and approached the Himalayas through Sikkim. From early on, Sherpas – or those thought to be 'Sherpas' - were employed as high level porters.

Most of those recruited in this early period as porters would have been from the lower classes (the 'small people') in Sherpa society, and from among those who had already migrated from Solu Khumbu to Darjeeling district, the expatriate population of urban porters, rickshaw pullers and manual labourers. As Ortner puts it, '... 'big people' never carried. Middling people, ordinary Sherpas, carried their own loads, but it was something of a point of pride not to carry for others, except as a favour, or in a reciprocal arrangement. On the other hand, the 'small people' - the tenants, the servants, the hired laborers – carried not only for themselves but for the big people' (Ortner 2000: 66). No women are mentioned in any of the expedition records at this time, as porters, or even as 'followers'.

Not all of the 'Sherpas' employed as high level porters, however, were in fact Sherpas from Solukhumbu. Many were Gurkhas from other ethnic groups. The Gurkhas were first engaged in mountain exploration in 1889. when they traversed several till-then unknown glaciers in the Karakoram, The most interesting early Gurkha exploits were by Amar Singh Thapa and Karbir Burathoki, who together with some alpine guides crossed 39 passes and climbed 21 peaks in 86 days of Alpine traverse. A.F. Mummery's 1895 attempt on Nanga Parbat (8125m) involved two Gurkhas. The three never returned, and were believed to have been perished in an avalanche. Gurkhas were also members of the successive expeditions on Chomolongma from 1921 onwards. In 1922, for example, Naik Tejbir Buda of the 3rd Gurkhas - spent two nights at 7772m on the mountain. In 1927, he received an Olympic medal from the President of France for his high altitude resilience.

❀ ❀ ❀

CHAPTER 25

The Interwar Years: the 1930s

Throughout the 1930s, migration from Nepal to India continued, and increased. Subedi argues that 'the lack of required skilled and semi-skilled local manpower for industries in the *terai* provided employment opportunities to migrants from North India. But on the other hand, for Nepali non-agricultural emigrants, the availability of low-level jobs such as hotel boys, *durbans*, watchmen, etc. in the Indian towns provided employment opportunities there' (Subedi 1991: 86). Tanhang Thakalis from the western mountain region were beginning to migrate south to take advantage of growing trade links with India. Already in 1924, the first of these had begun to migrate to Butwal on the edge of the west central *terai,* and thereafter they established themselves in Bhairahawa on the Indian border and in Nepalgunj further to the west in the *terai,* bringing their families with them in many cases (von der Heide 2001: 79).

The 1931 Indian Census showed the highest level of immigration in the country as a whole to be in Assam, with 121,648 (or 10.5 per cent of the total population) born outside the province. With a population of a nine and quarter million, the province showed an overall increase in population since 1921 of 15.7 per cent, much of this from immigration. The volume of Nepali immigrants, however, showed an overall decline and the number of Nepalis in Assam had fallen from 89 to 36 per cent of the total population. Bengal's immigrants, however, included some 250,000 Nepalis, more than twice as many as the total immigrant population in Assam. The total population of Bengal was now just over 50 million – including some 110,000 Sikkimese - accounting for more than one sixth of the total for the whole of British India.

One Indian town towards which there was significant migration, as there had been during the 19th century, was Darjeeling. According to the Census of 1901, tea garden labourers and their dependents constituted 2/3rd of the total

population in the District; in 1931, they formed 42.25 per cent. In the three sub-
divisions, they formed 31.5 per cent of the total population. In 1934, Darjeeling
town had a population of 30,000, of whom several hundred at least were Sherpas
and Sherpini, and many more were men, women and children of other Nepali
ethnic groups and castes, mainly from the eastern hill areas, notably the Khambu
Rais, who constituted one of the most numerous groups.

Mountain climbing was now one of the main sources of income – apart from
farming and employment in agriculture – and successive mountain expeditions
in the Himalayas and in Kashmir between 1930 and 1939 all employed Sherpas
from the Solu Khumbu area and/or from Darjeeling district as high altitude
porters (Ortner 1999: 50). Hugh Ruttledge wrote, of the Sherpas he employed
for the 1933 expeditions: 'many of them come to Darjeeling, ten days' march,
seeking work in tea plantations, or as porters or rickshaw coolies' (Ruttledge
1936: 57). One of those recruited for the 1933 expedition was Lhakpa Chedi,
'the best of the 'tigers' of 1924', who 'had been for some years a very efficient
head waiter in a Darjeeling restaurant' (Ruttledge 1936: 59). But access to
employment as high altitude porters, and even as regular porters remained
largely an all-male prerogative.

As Ortner remarks, 'it is ... difficult to find traces in the pre-war period
of Sherpa women climbing, beyond 'local portering'; that is carrying loads to
the base of the mountain' (Ortner 2000: 219). However, in Hugh Ruttledge's
account of the Everest 1933 expedition, when it reached the lower 'glacier'
camps, 'arrangements had been made... to employ local Tibetan labour up to
Camp II; and Nima Dorje had been sent from Shekar Dzong to Solu Kumbu
to collect more Sherpas' and 'soon, men and women began to assemble from
distant villages' (1936: 113).

These were engaged as porters, not just for the 'local portering'; but first up
to Camp I at 17,000 feet, and then to Camp II at about 19,800 feet. In Hugh
Ruttledge's account of the Everest 1933 expedition, when it reached the lower
'glacier' camps, 'arrangements had been made... to employ local Tibetan labour up
to Camp II; and Nima Dorje had been sent from Shekar Dzong to Solu Kumbu
to collect more Sherpas' and 'soon, men and women began to assemble from
distant villages' (1936: 113). These were engaged as porters, first up to Camp I
at 17,000 feet, and then to Camp II at about 19,800. At this point, Ruttledge
explains, 'the regular porter corps finally takes over from the local labour for the
more difficult carries to Camp II and above' (1936:121).

Gradually, the local porters (whom he refers to as 'local Tibetans') dwindled in numbers as the ploughing season arrived demanding their presence at home. At this point, Ruttledge explains, 'the regular porter corps finally takes over from the local labour for the more difficult carries to Camp II and above (1936:121). In other words, it should be noted, these 'local porters', some of whom were women, carried up to 19,800 feet. Ruttledge seems not to consider these women as 'high level' porters. But Jennifer Bourdillon refers to at least one high-level woman porter, known as 'Eskimo Nell', attached to this 1933 expedition.

'I had heard tremendous stories of her efforts as a porter to Everest in 1933, when she had been the driving force among the Sherpas and her caustic tongue had spurred the others on to carry to even greater heights' (1956: 2023). Ortner states that 'it is known that.. (she)... was the wife of one of the male porters on the 1933 expedition' (2000: 220).

More recently, Emily Cheung has written about this legendary Sherpa woman (2012). Cheung's 'project' was 'to bring to light the role of Nepalese women in adventure sports; a phenomenon that has existed in Nepal for the past few decades but has been widely unappreciated, if not unnoticed' (Abstract). She notes that, during the 1920s and 1930s, Nepali men, particularly Sherpas,

'began to make their living working for foreigners as porters and guides, and were paid heftily compared to their previous earnings as farmers and traders. Some went on to be part of great expeditions; their successes were celebrated, and failures were mourned. Their stories spread, but the story of the Nepali women was usually omitted. Back at home, women were left alone waiting with uncertainty for their husbands and sons to return from the mountains'.

She also notes that examples of Nepali women in the mountains during this time period are rare; but underlines the fact that they existed, even if they remained effectively invisible to the authors of the accounts of mountain expeditions.

If tourism and mountaineering was to draw men and women from Nepal into an attractive emerging sector of the economy in the inter-war period, many were obliged to seek economic opportunities abroad because of the difficulty of life in the hills of Nepal at this time. Morris notes that while he was recruiting officer for the British Army in the 1930s, he was 'able to observe many thousands of Gurkhas of all sorts, and most of them were under-nourished' (Morris 1963: 135). He adds that before the Second World War, 'life in a Gurkha village is harsh and unrewarding: a matter of unremitting toil'. But if life back in the village was harsh, soldiering was often even more difficult, although the attraction of regular payment and social status back home meant that there was no difficulty in finding recruits.

Brook Northey and Morris were concerned, however, about the widespread practice of illegal recruitment in Nepal by intermediaries, despite the official ban on this by the government of Nepal and official disapproval by the British Army itself: 'the enlistment of men in Nepal is under the strictest regulations, agreed to mutually by the Nepalese Government and our own. Safeguards of all kinds are required and given, both for the purposes of recruiting and for the well-being of the recruits. But now, entirely due to the high wages prevailing in India, and the like, illegal recruiting has become a great nuisance, and those who carry it on for their own benefit are doing an ill service, both to the British Empire and to the Kingdom of Nepal'. They added to this that they could 'only hope that the excellent conditions under which Gurkhas now serve in the Indian Army may partially help to counteract this tendency, by keeping recruitment on legitimate lines and by supplying an annual influx of wealth into the country' (Brook Northey & Morris 1927: xxviii).

Once recruited, each battalion took care of its own as best it could. The care of families when the soldiers were away became, with the establishment of the regimental 'homes', the responsibility of the battalion, and a depot commander was always left behind to look after them. Families grieved when the men marched out, but usually the soldiers' wives kept their grief and their anxieties to themselves. Any public expression was unusual, and when the 5th Royal Gurkha Rifles (Frontier Force) moved out at short notice to quell rioting in Peshawar in April 1930, men were startled and a little shaken, according to Farwell, to hear 'a high pitched keening from the married lines as the march began which, though quickly suppressed, was a weird and unique experience' (Farwell 1985: 146).

Before 1935, arrangements – even in the married lines of these settlements – included only the barest essentials. There was just a room and a kitchen for each family. There was no separate family hospital, just a family welfare room, where care or treatment would take place in the case of illness or a birth. There was no dedicated nurse, so the wives would have to get together and help one another. Gurkha Major Rakansingh Rai of the 1st/10th Gurkhas, reminiscing about his childhood in the married lines at Maymyo, recalled that 'in order to make the first in the cooking place, husband and wife had to go out into the forest and cut firewood. The women sat at home all day, knitting stockings or scarves. Their chief responsibility was cleaning the house, caring for the children, and helping their husbands prepare the curry and rice' (cited in Farwell 1985: 149).

After 1935, there was usually a regimental health centre for the soldiers' families, with a Nepali nurse and midwife at least. When Khemkala, the midwife of the 1st/6th Gurkhas died in 1967, she had served the battalion for 26 years. Sobha Kumari Chhetri served as a midwife for the 10th Gurkhas for 34 years, from 1938 until 1972. Her son was a major in the Gurkha Transport Regiment and her son-in-law a Gurkha captain.

In the mid-1930s, the British Army was still fighting in the North West Frontier region. The Waziristan campaign (1936–1939) comprised a number of operations conducted in the area by British and Indian Army forces against the fiercely independent tribesmen who inhabited this region, and particularly again the followers of the Pashtun nationalist Mirzali Khan. Also known by the British as the 'Faqir of Ipi', Mirzali Khan was a religious and political militant who was spreading anti-British sentiment and effectively undermining the government in Waziristan. One Nepali *lahure* recalls, laconically, that 'from 1934 to 1937, we were in Waziristan, chiefly at Damdil. It was a bad place' (cited in Cross & Gurung 2002: 114).

Another comments, more fully, that 'in about 1936, we were on the North West Frontier, in Waziristan. We were posted to Bannu, Razmak, Malakand and other places. One was Damdil, where a battalion from Abbottabad suffered heavy casualties, a company being destroyed by Pathans' (Cross & Gurung 2002: 66).

In fact, according to the military records, 2nd/5th Gurkha Rifles lost a British officer and five other ranks killed and 14 men wounded, 1st/6th GR lost a British officer, two Gurkha officers, and 24 men killed and one British officer, one Gurkha officer and 27 men wounded at Damdil. In 1938, 1st/6th GR returned to Abbottabad and on to Malakand for peace time duties and to relieve the 1st/4th. But in 1940, the 1st/6th was back in Waziristan again (Cross & Gurung 2002: 114).

A portrait of 'the *lahure*' is to be found, Michael Hutt explains (Hutt 1989), in one of the finest Nepali short stories, Sipahi, written just before the Second

World War (*The Soldier*, 1938) by B. P. Koirala, a writer and politician who later became Nepal's first elected prime minister. The story's protagonist is a young student returning on foot to his home in Ilam. On the way, he meets up with a soldier, stationed at Quetta but returning to Nepal to select new recruits. They walk for a day together, and the soldier tells the student all about his life. The student is nervous of him at first, but gradually warms to him because of his entertaining conversation. The main characteristic which Koirala attributes to the soldier is his complete freedom from responsibility: this, he seems to imply, is something to be envied. But is it to be admired?

> 'I'm stationed at Quetta. I've been there for a long time. I do have a wife, but she's sickly and good-for-nothing. But we've had two children, all the same. I haven't been home for ages, and I don't want to go either. She'll have gone off with someone else by now, and my sons will have turned into rogues. Well, the little one seemed bright enough and I really hoped to educate him. But who could be bothered? My father didn't have me educated, and I'm content. I found myself a wife in Quetta too. Wherever you go you should have what you want'. (Koirala 1938: 95).

Hutt remarks that 'the serious young student is mildly shocked by his friend's attitudes, and particularly by the fact that the soldier claims to enjoy himself in battle'. What he does not discuss is the fact that the soldier has a wife at home, whom he suspects will have 'gone off with someone else', because he has not been home 'for ages', and also that he found himself a wife in Quetta too. The soldier fears the adultery of his wife and the misbehaviour of his sons, for whom he had high hopes; but he himself has committed adultery, justifying it by his sense of entitlement.

The student, however, finds the soldier appealing, particularly when he teases all the young women who pass them on the path. Hutt suggests that 'the most telling passage comes at the end of the story, when the pair part company after a night in a lodging-house' and the soldier walks off, apparently 'care-free' but actually caring for no-one. His bravado seems to be taken at face value; his denigration of his family is not questioned. But it could be argued that Koirala actually intended him to be a tragic figure, making light of his own pain to others, hiding his real feelings of loss and isolation.

Within a few years after the publication of this short story, tens of thousands of Nepalis would be sent overseas to fight for Britain in the Second World War, and spend years in many cases away from their wives and families, half-way across the world in different 'theatres' of the war. Most of them would, once again, suffer the *dukha* of modern warfare and trauma of separation from their loved ones. Their families would also suffer long separation and anxiety about the fate of their menfolk.

In the meanwhile, as the Gurkhas continued to fight on the North West Frontier for the British, Nepalis from the eastern hills were migrating to Sikkim to settle and to work in agriculture to help develop farming in that region. Balicki notes that 'in the year 1938, a group of a dozen Limbus from eastern Nepal were granted permission by Sir Tashi Namgyal to settle and open fields within the Phodong Estate at Mangshila [in Sikkim], working as labourers for the Tingchim Lhopos (the Bhutia or Sikkimese) and teaching them (sic) how to practise permanent irrigated agriculture' (Balicki 2008: 53). But the transfer of agricultural knowledge and technology evidently worked both ways. For Fitzpatrick reports that, in 1949, two locals from northern Taplejung, a Chhetri from Mamangkhe and a Limbu from Yempang, travelled to Sikkim looking for work' (2011: 210).

This Chhetri worked on cardamom plantations for six years and finally returned having accumulated Nrs 2,500. He used this money to buy a large amount of land in the ward from which he came and in parts of another ward, including high altitude grazing land. Later he sold this land to another Chhetri from Yampang, and migrated to Jhapa in the *terai*. After this became known, other villagers began to migrate to Sikkim.

Migration to Darjeeling continued to be of great significance. In 1901, Nepalis had constituted more than half the total population with some 134,000 (L.S.S. O'Malley, Bengal District Gazetteer: Darjeeling, 1907. rept., Logos Press, New Delhi. pp 41). Forty years later, in 1941, the number of Nepalis had virtually doubled and now constituted nearly 255,000 (254,608) or 68 per cent of the total population. Lepcha was the official language of Darjeeling District until 1911 – and indeed, when Darjeeling was granted as a gift to British East India Company, the deed was written in English, Hindustani and Lepcha - but increasingly Lepchas and Bhotias and others spoke Nepali as the lingua franca, increasingly forsaking their own languages.

These figures indicate the cumulative growth of the Nepali population in Darjeeling over a period of more than half a century. It is interesting to compare them with the data provided by the 1941 census of Nepal, which recorded only about 82,000 (81,817) or 1.7 per cent of the total enumerated population of Nepal as being 'away from home for more than six months' at the time of the survey. The number recorded ten years later, after the Second World War, in 1952-54, was significantly larger, nearly 200,000 (198,120) or 2.3 per cent of the total population of Nepal (figures cited in Gurung 2001:14).

❀ ❀ ❀

CHAPTER 26

The Second World War

Nepal was involved once again in a major international conflict when the Second World War broke out in Europe in 1939, largely through the deployment of the Gurkhas, yet again as part of the Indian Army. Once again, however, as in the First World War, the government of Nepal provided direct support of various kinds, including many personal gestures on the part of the Prime Minister and the Court of Nepal, in a spirit of friendship.

Firstly, following the German invasion of Poland, the Kingdom of Nepal declared war on Germany on 4 September 1939. Then, the whole of the Nepali Army was once again placed at the disposal of the British Crown. The final agreement between Nepal and India relating to the loan of the Nepali contingent to India was finalized and signed in Calcutta on 4 December, 1939. The signatory from the Indian side was General Lead E. Le Burgh, while Nepali side was represented by the General Bahadur Shumsher who signed on the behalf of the Nepal Government.

When permission was sought to recruit an additional twenty battalions for the Gurkha Brigade and for Gurkha troops to be allowed to serve in any part of the world, after the fall of France in 1940, when Britain stood alone, this was readily granted by the Prime Minister who remarked to the British Resident in Kathmandu: 'Does a friend desert a friend in time of need? If you win, we win with you. If you lose we lose with you'.

Eight regiments were sent from Nepal to India, as they had been during the First World War for internal security duties and for operations on the North-West Frontier; and when Japan entered the conflict in December 1941, sixteen battalions of the Royal Nepalese Army were deployed to fight on the Burmese Front under the Allied Command. The Nepali units that took part were the Sri Nath, Kalibox, Surya Dal, Naya Gorakh, Barda Bahadur, Kali Bahadur, Mahindra

Dal, Second Rifle, Bhairung, Jabbar Jung, Shumsher Dal, Sher, Devi Dutta, Bhairab Nath, Jagannath and Purano Gorakh Battalions. Nepalese battalions – Mahindra Dal, Sher, Kali Bahadur and Jagannath. The Jagannath Battalion took part as engineers in order to construct tracks, bridges, water points, etc. Aside from that, there were many high-ranking Nepalese in the joint Army HQ and Commander-in–Chief Kiran Shamsher Rana and Field Marshal Nir Shumsher Rana were liaison officers from the Royal Nepalese Army.

In addition to military support, Nepal contributed guns, equipment as well as hundreds of thousands of pounds of tea, sugar and raw materials such as timber to the Allied war effort. Large sums of money for the purchase of weapons and equipment, including many for the provision of fighter aircraft during the Battle of Britain, were presented as gifts from Nepal. Considerable sums of money were also donated to the Lord Mayor of London during the Blitz for the relief of victims in the Dockland area. An equally generous response was made to a variety of appeals for aid – all this from a country which was then, and still is by western standards, desperately poor. As Bolt remarked, 'once again Nepal denuded her rice fields and maize terraces, her high villages and mountain pastures to send forth her best. In all, some 160,000 men streamed down to the recruiting centres' (Bolt 1967: 98). Once again, hundreds of thousands of women were left behind, to bear the main burden of maintaining the family and the household.

In all, the Indian Army provided some 250,000 men; and, according to Cross and Gurung, '114,971 Gurkhas were recruited from 168,294 volunteers' (Cross and Gurung 2002: 31). They served in 43 Gurkha battalions - third and fourth battalions were raised for all ten regiments, with 1st GR, 2nd GR and 9th GR having fifth battalions - as well as in parachute, garrison and training units, in Syria and the Western Desert, in Italy and Greece, and also in Malaya, Singapore and Burma - for this was a war fought in the East as well as in the West. A total of 250,280 Gurkhas joined the army. They experienced some 24,000 fatalities and over 40,000 soldiers were incapacitated (according to Bolt 1967; Husain 1970; *Himal* 1991)[38]. Many served several years overseas without returning on leave. The Gurkhas earned 2,734 awards for bravery.

Pignède, writing about the Gurung village in the western hills near Pokhara that he studied in the late 1950s comments that 'the second world war marked

---

38. Cross and Hurung refer to '23,655 casualties' (2002: 31) and suggest that this was 'slightly more than there had been in World War I.

the high point in the history of the Gurkha soldiers. The fighting force of each regiment was tripled, quadrupled and even quintupled. The troops were mainly used on the Assam frontier and in Burma, and formed 8 per cent of the total fighting force of the Indian Army at the end of the war' (1993: 19). He adds that 'important contingents took part in the Italian campaign (Monte Cassino)'. He comments that, in his village, whereas perhaps 85 per cent of young men signed up without their father's consent in the First World War, the percentage fell to 45 per cent in the Second – suggesting greater support from the older generation than before.

In the eastern hills, Limbus and Rais joined the two Gurkha regiments which recruited in that area, but they were by no means the only source of fighting men. In the case of the 7th Gurkha Rifles at least, the official history notes that 'Gurkha officers and soldiers have come predominantly from the Rai and Limbu clans but the roll records many names from the less numerous Sunwar, Tamang and Eastern Gurung clans, men from the Sherpa families of mountaineering fame and a sprinkling from Western Nepal and India as well'.

In December 1941 the Japanese entered the war when it launched a surprise attack on the US base at Pearl Harbour and launched a number of swift invasions of British and other countries territories. During the course of the war the 7th Gurkha rifles raised a further three battalions, the 3rd in 1940, the 4th in 1941 and the 5th in 1942. The Regiment saw ferocious fighting during the Japanese invasion of Malaya; the 2nd Battalion, part of the 28th Brigade, was involved in heavy fighting at Jitra where it was forced to hastily retreat after taking part in the initial resistance on the Asun and being isolated and confronted by overwhelming Japanese forces which included tanks. The 2nd Battalion was in action a few weeks later at Kampar where they successfully held off superior forces. Within a few days they were again in action but were out-numbered and sustained heavy casualties during the engagement at the Slim River Bridge on 7 January 1942.

The Allies had withdrawn from Malaya to Singapore by the end of January 1942. The Japanese subsequently launched an invasion of Singapore and bitter fighting ensued; Singapore, which had once been perceived as impregnable, fell on 15 February 1942 with 130,000 British, Australian and Empire troops, including men of the 2nd Battalion, taken prisoner by the Japanese. In Burma, a similar situation occurred. The Allies—having come under intense attacks from the Japanese who had begun their offensive in December—were forced to retreat to India during the period from February to May 1942.

In all, 23 Battalions of Gurkha soldiers (as well as garrison, training and parachute units) fought in Malaya and Burma, remaining steadfast during early losses against the advancing Japanese assaults and proving instrumental in the fightback down into Burma, after the halting of the Japanese advances towards India at the battles of Kohima and Imphal in 1944. Gurkha troops from various regiments formed a key part of the two Long-Range Penetration 'Chindit' Operations in 1943 and 1944, harassing and tying down Japanese troops from behind their lines deep in the jungles of northern Burma.

Later, the Gurkhas saw heavy fighting in 1944 in the Arakan campaign and during the Japanese offensive against north-east India where two important battles, Kohima and Imphal. Imphal was besieged by the Japanese until the Allies achieved a decisive victory at Kohima in June and the Japanese fled back into Burma. The Gurkhas subsequently took part in the successful Allied offensive into Burma and, on 3 May 1945, the Burmese capital Rangoon was liberated by British forces. There were still Japanese forces present in Burma but the fight against the Japanese was now ostensibly a mopping up operation.

Gurkhas also fought as part of the British 8th Army in North Africa, against Italian and German troops, suffering heavy losses at battles such as Tobruk, where the 2nd Battalion of the 7th Gurkha Rifles was captured. After the final defeat of Italian and German forces in North Africa in 1943, Gurkha troops remained a key component of the Allied forces deployed in the liberation of Italy from 1943 until 1945. The 43rd Gurkha Lorried Brigade, composed of the 2nd Battalions of the 6th, 8th and 10th Gurkha Rifles, fought alongside the 4th, 8th and 10th Indian Infantry Divisions. During the Battle of Monte Cassino in 1944, the 1st Battalion of the 9th Gurkha Rifles managed to reach the walls of the Monte Cassino Monastery itself, holding out nearby for 9 days before being forced to withdraw due to lack of supplies.

Twelve Victoria Crosses (of which five were posthumous) were awarded to Gurkha soldiers and British officers within Gurkha Regiments during the Second World War. In total, however, as we have seen, some 40 per cent of those recruited from Nepal suffered casualties in the Second World War. As in the First World War, most of the casualties in the field were treated, nursed and otherwise looked after by male medical personnel and male orderlies; but, unlike the First World War, there was also now a much more organised system of recruitment and training for female nurses. Also attitudes had changed considerably during the inter-war years, not only in Britain but in many of the other countries in the Western Alliance.

In Britain, in theory, any young woman wishing to train as a nurse at this time could apply to a nursing school attached to a hospital and work on the wards as an apprentice. Recruits were generally between 21 and 30 years old (at 21 a girl was considered able to cope with the naked bodies of strangers), and the ideal candidate was mature and reliable, someone who would fit easily into the hospital – an educated middle-class girl perhaps, or a girl with the manners of a superior domestic servant.

The nursing profession was all female at this time and no training existed for male nurses until some time after the war. Most of the more serious casualties were treated first in the field at casualty centres by members of the Royal Army Medical Corps (RAMC), aided for the most part by male orderlies and then shipped back to Britain or to a local or regional hospital centre (British Military Hospital) in whichever theatre was concerned. The Second World War, however, brought about major change for women in the services: in December 1941 the government passed the National Service Act (No 2), which made provision for the conscription of women. At first, only childless widows and single women 20 to 30 years old were called up, but later the age limit was expanded to 19 to 43 (50 for WWI veterans).

A great many of the British nurses served during the Second World War in hospitals in Britain, caring for and nursing injured soldiers sent back 'home' from the various 'fronts', particularly those in North Africa, the Middle East and Europe. One nurse, Mary Goodhand, recalls (in a BBC archive 'WW2 People's War – Recollections of a nurse during WW2') that

'Morale throughout the country had been at its lowest ebb during 1941 and also early 1942 with disastrous news from the North African campaign. However when 'Monty' was appointed commander of the 8th Army and arrived in the desert, the North African campaign took a new turn. In early October there was a great Allied victory with Rommel's troops being routed, and Tobruk taken. This news was a great boost to the country, but the hospital was told to prepare to receive many casualties. It was feared that there would be many cases of gangrene due to the slow and tedious journey required to bring the injured back to England.... Most were suffering from severe and complicated leg wounds, which had been treated by casualty clearing stations at the front.

Nevertheless, there were also hundreds of female nurses who served in the field as well as in hospitals across all theatres of war, including France, Gibraltar, Italy, Malaya, Palestine, Singapore, and Africa, often under the auspices of the Queen Alexandra's Imperial Military Nursing Service (QAIMNS) - which was renamed the Queen Alexandra's Royal Army Nursing Corps (QARANC) in 1949. The majority of British military nurses in both the First and Second World Wars worked in these services. One such as Marjorie Allen, from Cannock, who served during the Second World War as a Lieutenant in the QAIMNS, spending time in North Africa and Italy before coming back home to continue her service. But there were also those nurses who were caught up in the War in an involuntary fashion.

Pamela de Neumann (née Thane), for example, was born in Malaya. Her father was a rubber Plantation Estate Manager in Nilai Seremban, in the state of Negri Sembilan. She left Malaya to go to a boarding-school in Sydney, Australia when she was seven, but when she left School she returned to Malaya with her parents. As she was interested in nursing, she started training in the St Johns Ambulance Brigade and earned their Medale, which was worn on the lapel of the uniform. They first called it the Voluntary Aid Detachment (VAD), then the Women's Medical Auxiliary Service. This was distinct from the Auxiliary Territorial Service (ATS) which was the women's branch of the British Army during the Second World War and was formed on 9 September 1938, initially as a women's voluntary service. When the war started she and her mother were evacuated to Singapore; her father followed later. Her mother was a trained nurse too, and staff were needed desperately at the St Andrews Hospital at Singapore. There they both nursed wounded members of the armed forces as they came to the hospital from the north of Malaya. They worked up until a few days before the fall of Singapore, which was on 15 February 1942. On 12 February, she and her mother left on the steamship Mata Hari, leaving her father as a local volunteer. They were stopped on 15 February and taken prisoner. Civilians were sent first to the Island of Banka, Muntok then to a camp on Palembang in Sumatra; anyone in the military was sent to Burma.

They spent three and half years on these two islands, sleeping on concrete slabs. She carried on nursing as best she could but the Japanese confiscated the medicines from the Red Cross parcels. It was worse than terrible; many thousands died, including her mother who was only about fifty when she died in May 1945, just before the war finished. Pamela had to dig her grave in the camp and then bury her: Roman Catholic nurses put her in a box which sheI had to carry with rod supports and other prisoners-of-war from the camp.

When she finally left the internment camp she was extremely ill, with ulcers all over her legs and arms, and had severe malnutrition - weighing approximately 4 1/2 stone (63lbs). When she arrived back in Singapore she needed two weeks in hospital. She met her father, who had not been sent to Burma as he was not in the army, but had been in Changi Jail. They decided to go back to Australia, and left Singapore in September 1945 on a ship bound for Sydney. This is where she stayed, but her father went back to Malaya to manage a rubber plant estate and lived in Serembang in a bungalow until he died in 1973.

Malaya had been by far the most common destination for British colonial nurses from the 1910s onwards. During the 1930s, Malaya had double the number of nurses of any other British colony; in 1939, for example, there were 183 colonial nurses working in Malaya (compared to 60 in Nigeria and 40 in Kenya). The second most common destination was Shanghai; and Hong Kong also consistently received a large number. Many of those who served as civilians joined up when the Second World War broke out, and served within the military.

Members of the US Army Nurse Corps also took care of the sick and wounded throughout the world, often in dangerous and difficult conditions. Nurses from Australia, New Zealand and Canada (ANZAC) also served in various theatres where ANZAC troops were deployed. There were also local nurses, some of whom did more than treat and nurse sick and injured patients. For example, Sybil Kathigasu secretly supplied medicine and treated patients during the Japanese occupation of Malaya - now known as Malaysia - during the war. She also shared information with resistance fighters obtained by listening to BBC on a short-wave radio, before being arrested in 1943. She was freed when Malaya was liberated by allied forces in 1945 and was awarded the George Medal for bravery, one of the UK and Commonwealth's most significant rewards for gallantry.

Generally, however, the Indian and Nepali soldiers of the Indian Army were looked after by male medical and nursing personnel. After the 'liberation' of Malaya and Burma from the Japanese, many were taken on board hospital ships or conveyed to hospitals in Hong Kong. In Nepal, in the meanwhile, in the last three decades, there had been a significant expansion in the medical facilities available. The Chandra Lok Hospital had been established in Bhaktapur, Prithvi-

Chandra Hospitals in Palpa, Palhi (Parasi), Doti, and Ilam and Tribhuvan-Chandra Hospitals in Dhankuta, Bhadrapur, Sarlahi, and Rangeli, all in the first two decades of the 20th century. In 1925, the Tri-Chandra Military Hospital had been established in Kathmandu.

Between 1929 and 1932 under Prime Minister Bhim Shamsher, Tri-Bhim Hospitals were set up in Bhairahawa, Butwal and Bahadurganj, in addition to the Ramghat dispensary inaugurated at Pashupati in 1929. Under Juddha Shamsher (1932 to 1945), Tri-Juddha hospitals set up, in 1931 in Dharan and in 1940 in Bhimphedi, Bardiya, and Kailali. In addition to the Tri-Chandra Military Hospital, there were facilities available for ex-servicemen in most of these hospitals.

The medical staff and orderlies were, however, still all male, for the training of nurses did not officially begin in Nepal until 1956. In India, courses of nursing for Indian women had begun in 1946 in Delhi and in Vellore in 1947. Outside the hospitals, though, there was little support for ex-servicemen and their families until 1969, when the Gurkha Welfare Trust was established for ex-British Gurkhas 'when it was realised that a great many elderly Gurkha soldiers and their dependants or widows were living in destitution in Nepal. Many had served in the Second World War; however, they had not served the 15 years needed to qualify for an army pension' (Gurkha Welfare Trust).

In India, the 28th Indian Infantry Brigade was formed in March 1941, at Secundarabad in India and assigned to the 6th Infantry Division. In September 1941, the brigade was sent to Malaya and came under command III, the Indian Corps, and specifically the 11th Indian Infantry Division. It included, among other units, the second battalions of the 1st, 2nd and 9th Gurkha Rifles. The 11th Indian Division was defeated by the Japanese at the Battle of Jitra and suffered some of its worst casualties during the retreat from Jitra and at the Battle of Gurun.

At the Battle of Kampar (30 December 1941 – 2 January 1942), where heavy casualties were inflicted on the Japanese, the 28th Indian Infantry Brigade, though intact, was low in strength and morale; its three Gurkha battalions had suffered heavy casualties in earlier fighting around Jitra, Kroh, Gurun and at Ipoh. It was almost completely destroyed, however, at the Battle of Slim River in January 1942. The division was reformed in Singapore with the remains of the 9th Indian Division.

In the Second World War, as in the First, it seems that there were no *lahure* women accompanying the troops overseas; their role was, yet again, as it had been down the decades and over the centuries, to 'keep the home fires burning', always anxious to have news from 'the front' and to keep up their hopes that their menfolk would return home eventually without serious wounds and injuries. Some, however, were not prepared just to wait, and there were always some cases of adultery. But, for the most part, it seems, wives were faithful and were prepared to immerse themselves in domestic and farm work, bearing the double burden of their menfolk's absence, until they returned.

Pignède notes that, in the Gurung village he studied in the late 1950s, the age pyramid showed a definite lack of young persons in the age group from 10 to 20, and explains that by the fact that, during the Second World War, 'a great number of men were engaged in the British Army and did not return to their village for the duration of the war. ...The number of births fell and the consequences of this are now felt in the 15 to 20 age group' (1993: 34). He goes on the suggest that 'the fact is less obvious among the women, as the 15 to 20 age group is mainly made up of young wives who have come from neighbouring villages to compensate for the lack of young women of the same age born in Mohoriya. This was possible because a certain number of villages in the valley were less affected by recruitment than Mohoriya and did not suffer a fall in births of the same magnitude' (1993: 34).

He does not mention any impact from the small proportion of villagers leaving to work in the private sector in India, presumably because this was relatively unimportant, certainly as compared with the absence of men as soldiers during the War. This was probably generally the case across the country, for estimates of the number of foreign migrant workers (the 'absentee population') in 1941-42 suggested that only around 88,000 were living and working outside the country at that time, roughly 1.4 per cent of the total population. By the time of the census of 1952-54, the number of migrant workers had more than doubled and was recorded as around 198,000, roughly 2.3 per cent of the total population. The vast majority of these were from the hills, and just over 12 per cent of all migrants were women (Adhikari & Gurung 2009: 39).

❀ ❀ ❀

CHAPTER 27

The Gurkhas Divided and Re-Deployed

In August 1947, on the eve of Indian independence, a Tripartite Agreement was signed between the British and Nepalese governments and the Indian nationalists, which divided the 10 existing Gurkha regiments between the British and Indian armies with four going to Britain and six remaining in India, under the control of the newly independent Indian government. Following the division of the Gurkha regiments between India and Britain, the British decided that joining would be entirely voluntary for the Gorkha soldiers and decided to hold a referendum. Large numbers of men from the 7th Gurkha Rifles and the 10th Gurkha Rifles, which were recruited predominantly from eastern Nepal, decided not to join their regiments as part of the British Army. In order to retain a contingent from this area of Nepal, the Indian Army made the decision to raise a new unit to be called the 11th Gorkha Rifles.

The other regiments that joined the Indian Army were the 1ˢᵗ Gorkha Rifles (previously 1st King George V's Own Gurkha Rifles (The Malaun Regiment), the 3ʳᵈ Gorkha Rifles (previously the 3rd Queen Alexandra's Own Gurkha Rifles), the 4ᵗʰ Gorkha Rifles (previously 4th Prince of Wales's Own Gurkha Rifles), the 5ᵗʰ Gorkha Rifles (Frontier Force) (previously 5th Royal Gurkha Rifles (Frontier Force), the 8ᵗʰ Gorkha Rifles (the First Battalion was converted into a Mechanised Infantry Regiment) and the 9ᵗʰ Gorkha Rifles. In 1949, the spelling of 'Gurkha' in the Indian Army was changed to the historic 'Gorkha'.

Regimental Centres of the Indian Gorkha Regiments were established in several major Indian cities; these also host four training centres: 11th Gorkha Rifles Regimental Centre (11 GRRC) located in Lucknow, Uttar Pradesh; 14th Gorkha Training Centre (14 GTC) located in Sabathu, Himachal Pradesh; 39th Gorkha Training Centre (39 GTC) located in Varanasi, Uttar Pradesh; 58th Gorkha Training Centre (58 GTC) located in Happy Valley, Shillong,

Meghalaya. Apart from this the Gorkhas are mainly recruited from GRD (Gorkha Recruiting Depot) Kunraghat, Gorakhpur, Uttar Pradesh, which is less than 60 miles from Nautanwa (a former Gurkha base and recruiting centre) on the border with Nepal. All of these regimental centres have barracks for recruits; all have some facilities for army wives.

A large number of Nepalis have served in the Indian Gorkhas since Indian independence, and the Gorkhas have fought in every major campaign involving the Indian Army. In the 1950s, far more Nepalis were employed in the Indian Army than in the British Gurkhas, and the differential has only increased since then. In addition, thousands of Nepalis were employed in the Indian Police and other public sector services, as well as millions in the private sector.

There has always been a lack of precise information on the number of Nepalis serving in the Indian armed forces at any given time, however; and also about those who have retired from Indian military service. Considering only a few estimates that have appeared in the recent past in Indian sources, it is clear that there is a fair amount of variance, with the number of active Gorkhas today given by one source as being 'anywhere from 25,000 to 40,000' (Sharma & Thapa 2013: 8), and by another as 'near a half a million' (Adhikari & Gurung 2009: 29 footnote 15).

On 1 January 1948, four Gurkha regiments became an integral part of the British Army, forming the Brigade of Gurkhas. Those involved included: the 2nd King Edward VII's Own Gurkha Rifles (the former Sirmoor Rifles), the 6th Gurkha Rifles (later the Queen Elizabeth's Own), the 7th Gurkha Rifles (later the Duke of Edinburgh's Own), and the 10th Gurkha Rifles (later the Queen Mary's Own). The following Gurkha units were also raised in 1948: the Gurkha Engineers (now the Queen's Gurkha Engineers), the Gurkha Signals (now the Queen's Gurkha Signals), the Gurkha Military Police and the Gurkha Transport Regiment (now the Queen's Own Gurkha Logistic Regiment). Under international law, according to Protocol 1 Additions to the Geneva Conventions of 1949, Gurkhas serving as regular uniformed soldiers are not mercenaries.

The British were granted permission by the Indian government to continue to recruit Gurkhas from new depots near the border with Nepal. Also, the Gurkha battalions that were deployed to Malaya after the British Indian Army ceased to exist, had an element of Indian-domiciled Gurkhas (Indoms). At the time of the battalions' move to Malaya, nothing was mentioned regarding these Gurkhas. But later, in February 1950, the Government of India issued instructions that

Indian labour exchanges were not to supply Indian domiciled Gurkhas for appointment in foreign armed forces except in 'the local area'; in March 1950, the War Office also issued orders for the cessation of such recruitment. Despite this, hundreds of these Indoms were illegally recruited at the recruiting depots at Jalapahar in Darjeeling and Lehra, about 40 miles north of Gorakhpur.

In 1953, the Indian Government withdrew these facilities and asked the British to carry out the enlistment and attestations of the Gurkhas on Nepalese soil with immediate effect. From 1953 onwards, therefore, recruiting took place at Simana near Jalapahar for Gurkhas from the eastern regions of Nepal and at Paklihawa near Lehra for Gurkhas from the western regions. Later, in 1956, Simana was closed and all recruiting was done at Paklihawa. From October 1960, recruiting from east Nepal was done at Dharan and from west Nepal at Paklihawa. Today, Pokhara is now the only recruitment centre for all British Gurkhas.

From the 1950s onwards, the old principle of recruiting mostly from the four main ethnic groups – the Limbus and Rais in the east and the Magars and Gurungs in the west – was effectively abandoned, and Nepalis from a wider range of ethnic and caste backgrounds were recruited. Von der Heide remarks, for example, that 'only after 1950 did Thakalis begin to be recruited as soldiers for service principally in Hong Kong, but also in England' (2001: 76).

The recruitment of the Indom Gurkhas continued throughout this period, however, on the sly. These men were supplied with various Nepali village addresses in Nepal and told to memorize them. Should there be any queries either by the Indian Government or the Nepalese authorities regarding their nationality, they were ordered to lie and say that they came from these Nepali villages. The reasons for this was that the British were in dire need of the service of educated men to run the administration of the Brigade after their arrival in Malaya. They considered that only the Indoms could provide this as the majority of recruits from Nepal were un-educated and inappropriate as administrators.

Initially, Indom Gurkhas with the necessary educational background were given direct entry to the rank of Sergeants and a special rate of pay. Later these facilities were withdrawn for no apparent reason. When the Gurkhas arrived in Malaya, these Indom Gurkhas again served as inter-links between the uneducated Gurkhas, the British officers and the local authorities. They visited the local government offices to learn the local customs and traditions and also translated the official rules and regulations and other information applicable to the Gurkhas. 'Roman Gorkhali' was the language of the day and these people were the ones who translated the orders and instructions of the white officers for dissemination to the Gurkhas.

The Indoms, like most of the Gurkhas deployed to Malaya, were often accompanied by their wives and children, who would also have been used to living in India, even though they would for the most part have been of Nepali origin. Eventually, the need for these Indom Gurkhas began to decline as recruits from Nepal began to acquire a better education; at the same time, the wives and children of recruits from Nepal would tend to have come directly from the villages of Nepal.

The deployment of the British Gurkhas began immediately after the signing of the TPA. In January 1948, the eight battalions of the 2nd, 6th, 7th and 10th Gurkha Rifles – all under-strength - left India for Malaya, where they were to play a significant part in countering the nationalist insurgency. At the start of 1948, and together with other units of the British Army already there, they were formed into a Division which, being largely Gurkhas, was designated the 17th Gurkha Infantry Division. When the soldiers moved, some were able to take their wives and children with them, and regimental 'homes' were set up in Malaya.

Furthermore, the Tripartite Agreement stated that 'on assurances that Gurkha families would go to Malaya on the same scale as presently obtained in the case of Gurkha units based in India, the Maharaja of Nepal agreed at Kathmandu to facilitate the recruitment of Gurkha (female) nurses to the British Army'. It is not clear, however, what measures were actually taken by the government of Nepal to facilitate the recruitment of female nurses from Nepal for the British Army, in Malaya or elsewhere, and there is considerable debate about the recruitment of 'Gurkha' (Nepali) women to QARANC (Queen Alexandra's Royal Army Nursing Corps), as we shall see below.

In 1950, an 18-bed ward was opened at British Medical Hospital at Kinrara, near Kuala Lumpur, to treat Gurkhas suffering from tuberculosis. A year later this was increased to 100 and reached a capacity of 146 beds. Those who needed thoracic surgery were flown to Britain to the Army Chest Centre at Connaught Hospital near Hindhead in Surrey. Another BMH was opened at Kamunting in Taiping. The British Military Hospital at Kluang was part of the Panang Hospitals in the Cameron Highlands which supported the Far Eastern Land Forces (FARELF) British Army in Malaya. The majority of nurses were young women - usually British QAs[39] or Indian and Chinese, recruited locally from 'Malay Other Ranks' (MORs).

Over 10,000 men in all were deployed throughout the Malayan 'emergency', from 1948 to 1960, but while no other unit was there for more than two or three years before moving on to another theatre, the Gurkha battalions served there for year after year; the wives and families remained there also. Many of those in Malaya were settled in the Burma Lines. Additionally, other units were raised for 'the Emergency': a Gurkha Military Police Unit (disbanded in 1964), a Gurkha Dog Company, and the Gurkha Parachute company. The Training Depot Brigade of Gurkhas was established on 15 August 1951 at Sungai Petani, Kedah, Malaya.

The campaign in Malaya was to prove long and arduous – longer than either of the 'World Wars' – particularly for the Gurkhas and their families. Malaya achieved independence eventually in 1957, but operations for the British Army did not end until 1962. During the campaign a total of 213 Nepali members of the Brigade of Gurkhas, and 13 British officers were killed, and 382 members and 10 British officers were wounded in action. Once again, as in all of their previous campaigns, the wives and children of the Gurkhas waited for the return of their menfolk from the field; over 200 families did not see them come back alive and nearly 400 experienced their return maimed and disabled, and suffering from various injuries both physical and psychological.

In his *Life Story,* Ram Bahadur Limbu – who received the VC in 1966 for 'his heroism, self-sacrifice and devotion to duty and to his men of the very highest order' during action in Malaya in 1965 – tells how he was recruited into the 10th Princess Mary's Own Gurkha Rifles in November 1957 and recounts his experiences in Malaysia thereafter (Limbu n.d.). This 'life' has surprisingly little to say, however, about his experiences of a fighting Gurkha in Malaya over the years, about the casualties and suffering of the troops, and about the privations and the anxieties experienced by their wives and families. Others, however, were more forthcoming.

Cross and Gurung interviewed some 22 Gurkhas from several different battalions who took part in the Malayan campaign, and their stories provide a

---

39. The Queen Alexandra's Royal Army Nursing Corps (QARANC) had served the nursing and medical needs of the British army, their allies, prisoners of war and local civilians since 1854. Though they were first known as the Army Nursing Service and then the Queen Alexandra's Imperial Military Nursing Service before becoming QA's and forming the corps of QARANC in 1949.

vivid tapestry of experiences. The focus is very much on the military action, but occasionally there are references to their families back home. Tul Bahadur Rai, for example, mentions, almost in passing, that 'I learned that my mother had died and the house had fallen down, so I could not concentrate properly' (Cross & Gurung 2002: 190). Kesar Pun admits that 'once in the army, I made new friends and only thought of my village and my family when talk turned to Nepal' (Cross & Gurung 2002: 239).

Illiterate and single when he joined up in December 1941, Tul Bahadur Rai was eventually promoted to lieutenant and sent to the UK on a mortar course, and was made Mortar Platoon commander. He then worked with the Australians in Borneo. He was promoted to captain and sent to the UK on another course. 'It was almost unbelievable that I, one time so poor I had no shoes and was illiterate, should find myself as QGOO'[40], he said. He was awarded the MVO and had his photograph taken together with Field Marshal Slim. When he returned home on a pension he converted to Christianity and was jailed for his beliefs. He died a few months after recording his experiences.

Bupi Serchan, one of Nepal's most popular poets, referred in his poem *'Sadhaim, Sadhaim Mero Sapnama'* (*'Always, Always in My Dreams'*), to the heavy casualties experienced by the Gurkhas during the 1950s (Hutt 1991: 123); and Onta recalls how Ramesh Bikal's short story, *'Bamko Chhirka'*, published in the late 1950s, tells of his mother's reaction to the news of her son's death in Malaya (Onta 1994: 29). He recounts how 'word arrives that the enemy's bomb has killed an elderly woman's son in Malaya. The woman does not cry, she is speechless, and her eyes are suddenly stilled. She dies of shock'. In Bikal's words: 'a splinter of a bomb that exploded in Malaya lodged itself in the chest of an old mother in one corner of remote Nepal'.

In the popular ballad *'Ama Ley Sodlin-ni Khoi Chhora Bhanlin'*, the Gaine (singer) Jalak Man Gandarva sings of the fallen soldier who tells his companion how to break the new of his death to each family member, including his mother back in his home village. Clearly the families of most of those serving in Malaya remained at home in Nepal; but there will have been wives, at least during the first few years of the Malayan campaign, who would have been waiting anxiously for news from the field in the cantonments out in Malaya, far from home and left behind. By now, however, postal and telegraph services made it possible for information and messages to be transferred relatively swiftly back to Nepal, if

40. Queen Gurkha Orderly Officer.

not immediately to the villages where families awaited news of their loved ones living and working far from home.

In addition to the major deployment of Gurkhas to Malaya, there was deployment to Hong Kong, Singapore and Brunei; for the most part, in the case of these overseas destinations, wives and families went to accompany their Gurkha husbands stationed over there. In Singapore they were settled in the Slim Lines.

The 26th Gurkha Brigade was the first batch of Nepali soldiers to arrive in Hong Kong; they were stationed from 1948 at Whitfield barracks (now Kowloon Park, which was handed over to the government in 1967). They were replaced by the 51st Infantry Brigade in 1950. This brigade was a curious mix of Scots and Gurkhas that saw action in Brunei and Borneo with the elite SAS. By 1962, it had returned to the UK where it became 51st Gurkha Brigade. The 48th Gurkha Infantry Brigade came to Hong Kong in 1957. It was renamed Gurkha Field Force in 1976, but returned to its old name in 1987 and stayed that way until 1994 and preparations were started for the handover of Hong Kong to China.

It was during the 1950s that Tamhang Thakalis from the western mountain regions began to be recruited for employment in the British Gurkhas for the first time. They served mainly in England and in Hong Kong. Some later entered the service of the Sultan of Brunei. They tended to be accompanied by their wives and families. Some of the Gurkhas were deployed to Brunei at the time of the 1962-63 rebellion. Suk Deo Pun of the 1st/2nd GR was badly wounded during this campaign and taken to hospital for an operation. He tells how 'after the operation my wife was brought to see me and wept. I told her not to weep as I was not dead and I could look after her even with a medical pension' (Cross & Gurung 2002: 228). He recovered and was promoted to Lieutenant.

Singa Bahadur Gurung served with the 1st/6th GR in Borneo, then with the Gurkha Independence Parachute Company (GIPC) and with 2nd/2nd GR as platoon commander. He was then promoted to captain and 'put in charge of the families' and says that it 'was a very big job'. He handed over the family lines to 10 GR aafter he had arranged for all the families to be returned from Borneo to Nepal (Cross & Gurung 2002: 245). Another man who served in Borneo was Hindupal Rai, who joined the army on 30 October 1953. His battalion, 1st/10th, went first to Malacca and then to Hong Kong for training. He was sent on a drill course at Sungei Patani and had only one night in his family quarters on his return before being transferred to Sarawak. Eventually, after being involved in several encounters he returned to Hong Kong and 'peacetime activities'. He was awarded a DCM and went to England to receive it. He retired on a pension in 1968, as his father was paralysed and his mother was dead.

Yet another who served in Borneo was Ram Bahadur Limbu of the 2nd/10th GR, who won a MVO and a VC. His father had been 'a war time soldier with four years' service' who had been wounded, and died when Ram Bahadur was eight years old. After he married, his mother told him he was 'on no account to be a soldier'. However, he enlisted on 21 November 1957 at the age of 22. He joined 2nd/10th in September 1958; by 1965 he was a lance corporal with significant years of service, and was entitled to have his wife with him in the family lines. He was then transferred to Borneo. He was badly wounded and returned, with his and small infant, to Singapore in January 1966. On 2 February, his wife became ill and was admitted to hospital. Four days later, she died. His son was six months old.

He asked for leave, to show his son to his wife's family. He was told he could go, 'but not quite yet'; and so his Major's wife arranged for his son to be looked after by a Chinese woman. A special parade was organised in which he was supposed to be involved; he did not realise until the ceremony began, and the Command-in-Chief announced that he had been awarded the Victoria Cross. He was so surprised. That night nobody slept at all and parties were held in all the messes and in the company lines. He was in two minds: he was very proud of his ward, but he mourned his wife and his dead comrades in his section (Cross & Gurung 2002: 253).

Although Gurkha units took turns to be stationed in Hong Kong from 1948, elements remained based in other countries until 1971, when the Brigade of Gurkhas – the term to describe all the different Nepalese units in the British Army – were headquartered in the territory. By that point, they numbered about 8,000. After the handover of Hong Kong to the People's Republic of China in 1997, and the Brigade was withdrawn, 'Gurkha' families were granted the right to remain; hence, the majority of the Nepali population of Hong Kong today are the children and grandchildren of Gurkha soldiers.

The Gurkha Contingent was formed in Singapore on 9 April 1949 in the wake of Indian independence, and replaced the Sikh unit stationed there (which then returned to the Indian Army). The Gurkhas were involved in December 1950 in the repression of (religious/race) riots which broke out between Malay Muslims and Dutch Catholics within a year or so after their deployment[41]. As a neutral force, they were also especially invaluable during the 1964 race riots. Formed with an original staff strength of only 142 men, the contingent has grown to more than 1,500-strong in the last 50 years. Currently, there are six Gurkha Guard companies commanded by Nepali Chief Inspectors. The Gurkhas also have their own Gurkha Band Contingent to provide the music for their parades and ceremonies.

❀ ❀ ❀

---

41. The riots were the result of a dispute over a court decision regarding the custody of Maria Hertogh, a Dutch girl of Eurasian extraction and Malay upbringing.

CHAPTER 28

Nepalis in India, Burma & Thailand

Historically, government policy was to restrict emigration and re-settlement abroad – even if it clearly was unsuccessful in preventing Nepalis from leaving to work and live abroad - and visas were even needed to travel from the Kathmandu Valley to the *terai*, and vice versa. With the overthrow of the Ranas in 1951, this system of visas was abolished (Kansakar 1996: 7). Even before that, however, in 1950, Nepal and India signed a Treaty of Peace and Friendship that provided free movement to Nepali and Indian nationals across the 1,400 km border and 'the same privileges in the matter of residence, ownership of property, participation in trade and commerce (Article 7, Appendix 8).

The border itself was not physically demarcated, except at the limited number (22) of official crossing points that were patrolled by the Indian and Nepali police and armies. Crossing the border was unimpeded by formalities, and tens of thousands of people crossed daily in both directions. Formal trade relations were established in 1951 with the signing of the Treaty of Trade, and commercial exchange grew rapidly thereafter.

Even the 1950 Treaty – the one document that is considered the bedrock of inter-state relations between the two countries - does not, however, explicitly mention the issue of labour migration although it does recognise the fact of cross-border human mobility. Various rules and regulations have been formulated to cover migration to non-Indian destinations and ensure the rights and welfare of labour migrants there, but, in the case of those going to India, there is still no legal framework to provide specific protection.

Data derived from the Indian censuses over the decades suggests, however, that the number of Nepalis living in India grew significantly in the decades after 1950, from around 280,000 in 1952-54 to around 500,000 in 1981, and

600,000 in 2001. Other sources, however, suggest that these figures are gross underestimates, with totals for the contemporary population ranging from 890,000 to 3 million (Adhikari, Gurung & Seddon 2001; Amatya 1987: 24, Baral 1992, Gurung 1998: 19 and Seddon 2006: 102-103).

Most Nepalis living and working in India were still men, but a minority, perhaps 10 per cent or so, were women, either accompanying their husbands and families, or working themselves in agriculture, industry or commerce. Usually, all of these Nepalis were working in the informal sector with low paid and insecure jobs. Nevertheless, clearly for thousands, the prospects were better than remaining at home.

The first official census in Nepal was undertaken in 1952-54, following the establishment of a Department of Statistics. It suggested that the total population of Nepal was 8.43 million. Eastern Nepal was more thickly populated than Western Nepal. It also suggested that population growth had been significant between 1941 and 1951, in part because of deforestation and encouragement of immigration from India into the *terai*, and in part because of the return of Nepali soldiers after the Second World War (and a baby boom as a result). Population density in the *terai*, however, remained low and population growth was mainly in the hill areas. There was a small surplus of males in the population of Nepal, which suggests that, whatever the scale of foreign migration from Nepal, emigration still had a limited impact on the overall gender balance of the population. According to the 1952-54 census of Nepal, there were just over 157,000 Nepalis living and working in India at that time.

Darjeeling was the main destination of those emigrating from Solu-Khumbu until the first half of the 1950s. After Indian independence, however, Darjeeling experienced a significant decline, as did the tea industry; and from 1951 onwards, the mountaineering industry also moved to a large extent to Kathmandu. 'After that, within the same decade, the migration pattern successively changed, and different destinations, namely Sikkim, Bhutan, Arunchal Pradesh and Assam became dominant. Among these, Assam took the lead, with up to 64 per cent of all emigrants within a single year going there' (Hoffmann 2001: 118).

There was also continuing migration to Assam from much further afield; for example, von der Heide remarks that 'already in 1940-45, ten to fifteen Tamhang Thakali families left Nepal to stay in Assam, where their descendants still live (2001: 76). A significant proportion of all these migrants from Nepal were women; and a significant proportion of the settled population in Darjeeling and Assam of Nepali origin were always women. In the 1950s, more than 90 per cent of the Nepalis living and working in India were to be found in northern India, with some 70 per cent in Assam, Darjeeling and Sikkim, Bihar, West Bengal and Uttar Pradesh (Seddon 2006: 103).

The Indian census of 1951 recorded a total of 125,320 Nepali speakers in Assam alone, and a total of just over 280,000 Nepalis in India as a whole. There had been around 255,000 Nepalis in India in the 1941 census; by 1961, the figure had increased to around 525,000, suggesting a rapid rate of increase during the 1950s. This was a result of both 'push' and 'pull' factors as economic opportunities, which remained very limited in Nepal, opened up in India during its first decade after independence. The northeast of India gradually replaced Darjeeling as the main destination for Nepali migrants in the 1950s, and, as Hoffman points out, 'the numerous building sites of the various infrastructural projects along the Himalayas in particular offered work and income to the Nepalese migrants' (Hoffman 2001: 121-122).

After Indian independence, the British started to leave. 'Darjeeling experienced a rapid decline. The usual summer guests did not come to Darjeeling any longer, so the recreation industry face enormous losses. After the departure of the British tea garden management, the tea industry of Darjeeling faced decline as well... Finally, Darjeeling began to lose its importance as the centre of Himalayan alpinism after the opening of Nepal to foreigners in 1951 and the growing importance of Kathmandu in the same field' (Hoffmann 2001: 121).

In Assam, the situation was different. The tea gardens continued to provide work for Nepali, as well as for Indian migrant workers. Hoffmann notes that 'among the Nepalese migrants to Assam, the Sherpas specialised in the illegal distillation of *rakshi*, local liquor, and sold it to the frequently alcohol-dependent tea-pickers' (2001: 123). But the mass immigration of Indian labourers from Bihar and Orissa led to a situation where further immigration of foreigners was discouraged, and there were increasing attacks on Nepali immigrants. Any Nepalis returned back to Nepal, as a consequence; and Nepalis, especially from the eastern hills, tended rather to migrate to Bhutan, Sikkim and Arunachal Pradesh. They also continued to migrate to Burma.

Ten years before Indian independence, in 1937, after decades being part an integral part of British India, Burma had finally become an autonomous colony of the British Empire with its own constitution and a parliament of its own. In 1942, the Japanese army invaded Burma as well as Malaya and Singapore. But eventually British forces, with the support of the Gurkhas, succeeded in regaining a good deal of the ground lost, and when Japan surrendered after the dropping of nuclear bombs on Hiroshima and Nagasaki, they re-occupied those former colonial territories.

Many of the 'Gurkhas' living in Burma today are descendants of migrants from Nepal who went there in the late 19th century when it first became part of the British Empire. Burma was strikingly similar in some ways to the *terai* of Nepal, with glistening paddy fields, lush jungles, and a heritage that had elements of both Buddhism and Hinduism. In the immediate post-War period, the earlier Nepali settlers were joined by many Gurkhas and their wives. In accordance with agreement reached at the Kandy Conference in September 1945, the British Burma Army and the Patriotic Burmese Forces (PBF) were re-integrated. The officer corps comprised ex-PBF officers and officers from British Burma Army and Army of Burma Reserve Organisation (ARBO). The British also decided to form what were known as 'Class Battalions' based on ethnicity.

Some ex-Gurkha soldiers, however, fought as allies alongside Burmese freedom fighters to achieve independence from the British, at which time they joined the infant Burmese army. After Burma's independence in 1948, Nepali ex-Gurkhas were granted full rights as Burmese citizens and many brought their wives and families to live with them in Burma. They were considered key assets for the military during the new republic's campaigns against ethnic insurgents. Many former Gurkhas served in the new republic's various campaigns against ethnic insurgents and the Kuomintang invasions in the late 1940s.

But after the military came to power in 1958, the Gurkhas were not classified in the new Constitution as one of the country's official ethnic groups, and as a result they faced restrictions that prevented them from retaining or applying for citizenship. On 23 June 2020, *The Nepali Times* carried a piece by Mukesh Pokhrel from Bhairahawa town, where many Nepalis with links to Burma still live - in 'Burma tol' in Bhairahawa and in surrounding villages in Rupandehi District, having returned from Burma in the 1960s, cleared land and settled there, and became known locally as 'Burmalis'. He reported on how

'Dhankala Pandey was married at age 12 to Reshmalal in Nepal, and migrated to Pungchang of Burma in 1952. They started a new life in a new land, building an 8-hectare farm with 300 cows, 50 water buffaloes and employed seven farmhands. "I used to milk 80 cows every morning all on my own," recalls Chudamani Pant, 80, a Nepali dairy farmer in Burma who carried two containers overflowing with milk to deliver in surrounding villages. "At that time, they used to have a saying in Burma: Bengalis in the courts, and Nepalis in the fields," says Pant, who remembers Burma as a melting pot of local groups as well as immigrants from the Subcontinent.

However, in 1962, Burma was plunged into chaos after the coup d'état by Gen Ne Win which overthrew Prime Minister U Nu. There followed a mass expulsion of Indians and Nepalis who had been living in Burma for generations and their property and businesses were nationalised. About 200,000 Nepalis fled from Burma, either returning to Nepal, fleeing to Thailand, or settling in Bengal and Assam. Many, however, remained in Burma, despite the difficulties.

'Dhankala Pandey still has her brother-in-law, sister-in-law and a cousin in Burma, and they visit every five years or so. Her husband Reshmalal died two years ago, and says he was troubled by what he left behind: "For him, Burma was home. The most beautiful place in the whole world. He loved it there, and he would constantly talked about going back."

There are about 310,000 ethnic Nepalis still living in Burma. Known locally as 'Gurkhas', these ethnic Nepalis live throughout Burma, particularly in Rangoon and Mandalay divisions. They form a large minority in Myitkyina as well as the hill station of Maymyo (Pyin Oo Lwin) in Mandalay Division. Most practice Hinduism or Buddhism. 'Gurkhas' continue to face discrimination today: they cannot form political parties or vote if they are not citizens, nor can they travel outside the country. And discrimination begins early, with Gurkha youths being turned away from schools if their citizenship applications are not approved.

There is a village in Thailand, created and settled by Nepalis after the end of World War II, that neither the Nepali nor Thai governments knew existed till recently. The tiny, isolated village of Pilok is situated, amidst the thick forested hills along the Burmese border, 261 km west from Bangkok, near where the legendary River Kwai railway prisoner-of-war camp was once located. Pilok is near the border town of Kanchanaburi, and the scenic mountains must have reminded the early Nepalis who settled here of home. The Nepalis were for the most part ex-Gurkhas previously serving with the British Army in Burma; they settled here with their families after 1945 to work in the tin mines. And some of them are still there – forgotten by the world.

Santa Raj Rai was born in Nepal, but he moved to Burma. He had a reputation for being an experienced miner. Legend has it he could detect tin and other underground minerals just by smelling the earth. Rai was certain that the jungles were rich in ore and settled down here. Once the word spread, the Thai government sent officials to look for Pilok, and asked Rai to work for the Thai state. As the mines grew, Pilok attracted more families from Burma and it became a proper Nepali town. But in the 1980's, the mines ran out of ore and closed down one by one. Most Nepalis moved to Bangkok and the tourist resort towns in Thailand in search of jobs, but because they did not have legal papers, they were treated as outsiders. Many opened tailoring shops, while the women worked as housemaids in Bangkok.

Today, there are 80,000 Thais of Nepali descent, and the Thai Nepali Association tries to preserve the language and culture through various programs. 'Although it has been several generations since we left Nepal, we have ensured that each generation of Nepalis here stay true to their culture and values', says David Khanal. Indeed, the Nepalis here value their heritage even if they are third or fourth generation Nepalis who have never been to Nepal. Says Maila Acharya: 'We always thought of ourselves as Nepali, no matter where we were situated. We will continue to live as Nepalis, wherever we are'. There are still some who remain in Pilok, clinging to what remains.

❀ ❀ ❀

CHAPTER 29

The View from the Village

In the meanwhile, back in Nepal, the overthrow of the Rana regime was followed by a decade during which various compromise political arrangements were tried and limited social and economic development took place. It was not until the intervention of King Mahendra in 1961, that a coherent strategy for development was implemented under a distinctive regime, known as the Panchayat Raj, in which political parties were banned but a form of 'managed democracy' was implemented for nearly three decades.

As we have already seen, Pignède's account of the economic and social life of Mohoriya, a village in the western hills just north of Pokhara provides a wealth of information and insight into the local hill economy and society and into the importance of foreign labour migration in the late 1950s. There is a tendency in his analysis to equate emigration with employment in the British or Indian army, although men from this village, and from the western hills more generally, were also working at this time in the private sector in India, sometimes after having left the army. Indeed, he states that 'a certain number of soldiers never return to the village, whether because they die during service (illness, injury) or because they have settled down in India, most often in Calcutta' (1993: 254).

Pignède draws attention, however, to what he calls 'the essential role which military life plays among the Gurungs'. Out of a male population (between the ages of 19 and 84) of 134, he reported that 93 (70 per cent) had been or still were employed in the army (Pignède 1993: 38). Of these, the majority had either served with the Gurkhas before Indian independence or were now employed by the Indian army. Those currently serving with the British Gurkhas were a minority (14). In 1958, 62 per cent of the active men were absent from the village; 53 per cent were serving with the British or Indian armies 9 per cent worked as civilians.

In addition, he reports that 10 women (12 per cent of females aged between 19 and 45) lived abroad with their husbands.

Gurung men from villages like Mohoriya employed in the British army overseas in the 1950s were stationed in Malaya, Singapore and Hong Kong. Active duty in Malaya was interrupted by periods of rest at Penang or Singapore, where garrison life was easier. Soldiers were sometimes accompanied by their wives, and these had the right to receive a family allowance at least as large as the overseas allowance (Pignède 1993: 23). There was an incentive, therefore, for men to take their wives. Many of those serving in the Indian Army were stationed in Kashmir or Assam, again often with their wives. Pignède suggests that it was easier for the men from Mohoriya and their wives to live in India than overseas, where cultural differences were more marked and life more confined to barracks and 'the lines' (Pignede 1993: 23).

The majority of those men of Mohoriya who completed their 15 years of service felt able to retire to the village, but those who left before their rights to a pension had been established were less secure, and many of these continued to work away from home, either in the *terai* or in India in civilian employment. This was particularly the case for those who had not become NCOs. Of the 35 ex-soldiers who had been *sipahi* (sepoys) or riflemen (privates), 13 had a pension and lived in the village; but of the 22 who left before serving the full 15 years or were discharged, 14 lived in the village, but eight (nearly a third) lived in India, or in the *terai*. Pignède says nothing, however, about women migrating alone to India, or indeed elsewhere. He also says little about the 14 *dalit* families and one Brahmin family. There is no indication that any of these non-Gurung households were involved in work outside the village, although he hardly discusses the economic life of these members of the village community in any detail.

Writing about his research in a Gurung village not far from Mohoriya in the late 1960s, Alan Macfarlane comments that 'from before the beginning of the present century, but more intensively since the First World War, the Gurungs have been a society based on migrant labour. Almost all those leaving the village have enlisted in the British or, since partition, Indian armies, and they serve between three and twenty-five years (normally between ten and fifteen) in India or the Far East'.... Of 109 Gurung men in Thak aged 21 or over , some 74 (69 per cent) are, or have been, in the army' (Macfarlane 1976: 288). The importance of labour migration could not be overestimated: it resulted in a situation where there were two females for every male in the village.

There can be no doubt that this meant an additional burden on the women who remained in the village. As we now know from detailed studies by anthropologists and others in more recent periods, women generally work longer hours than their menfolk, not only performing all of the main domestic tasks but also contributing crucially to agricultural activities and fetching water, wood and fodder from the forest. Acharya and Bennett estimated that in the 1970s, women accounted for 57 per cent of the adult input into subsistence agriculture and related activities and for half the household income (1983: 45). When so many men are away from home, often for long periods of time, the burden is clearly increased even more. This is underlined by the detailed example provided by Shrestha and Conway of Sita, who lived 'the shadow life of a migrant's wife' in Dura Danda, a village in Lamjung District, at the end of the 1970s (2001: 153-177).

But Macfarlane remarks, unlike some other commentators on the effects of substantial male emigration we have quoted (eg Shrestha & Conway 2001), that 'the women are cheerful and the men seem scarcely to be missed'. He thinks that 'one reason for this could well be that there has for long been a tradition of male labour migration... Thus wage labour in the army did not come as a new and sudden change; furthermore, the numbers recruited increased gradually over half a century' (Macfarlane 1976: 291).

This differs markedly from the experiences and feelings of Sita which Shrestha and Conway consider in some detail: her husband was away for long periods and had returned only twice since their marriage; he was not present for the birth of either of their two sons. Sita was also fearful that he might associate with prostitutes or even fall for an Indian woman. The first was the more likely; 'after all, she had heard many stories of Nepali workers in India falling prey to prostitutes and wasting their entire earnings. But there was little she could do about it except to wait for his safe arrival. And wait and wait!' (Shrestha & Conway 2001: 167-68).

In the eastern hills of Nepal, there were also villages in which employment abroad, either in the army or in civilian occupations, was an important part of the economy, with remittances and pensions playing a major role in supplementing the local farming economy. Caplan describes such a situation in his study of local Limbu and caste economy and society in the Indreni cluster in Ilam District in the 1960s. In Ilam, we know that there was 'an almost total lack of formal educational facilities in Ilam until the 1940s. Traditionally, young Brahmans were instructed by religious teachers individually, or attended informal 'schools' (*patshala*) organised by learned men in the area where, through the medium of Sanskrit, they became literate in the Devanagri script...Some of the wealthier men sent their sons to Benares, Darjeeling or Kathmandu for schooling' (Caplan 1970: 61-2). Very few, if any, girls were sent abroad for their education.

If some left the village for the purposes of education, more left for economic reasons, to secure employment or other sources of livelihood. Migration from the villages of eastern Nepal to Darjeeling, and the growth of the diaspora or expatriate Nepali population in Darjeeling, which we have discussed previously, were both important phenomena in the 1950s. Young Sherpa women as well as men continued to migrate from Solu Khumbu in Nepal to Darjeeling, attracted by the prospects for employment and a 'good life'. From the perspective of the village, for young women as well as young men, the 'bright lights' were increasingly attractive; also, there were sometimes other reasons why they were keen to leave home and substitute the town for the village.

Jonathan Neale interviewed Sherpa Galtzen who had worked as a climber and mountain porter in the 1950s, and then, later, made good money as a trader in Tibet; at the age of 84, the second oldest man in Namche and the richest, he recalled how his girlfriend persuaded him as a young man to run away to Darjeeling. She told him she was pregnant and reminded him that her father would demand a fine, asking him 'Where will you get the money for that?' 'I don't know', he replied. They went to Darjeeling for several years and returned with children. Her father had to accept the relationship then, and 'that was that' (Neale 2002).

Ortner confirms this example as being quite common among young Sherpa women: 'the framing of the process was similar to that for becoming a nun: that one's parents would not let one go if they knew, but that they would probably ratify it and go along with it after the fact. Whereas running away to join a nunnery was something largely engaged in by women from wealthier families, running away to work in Darjeeling or – later – Kathmandu, was done more by women from poorer (but also middle status) families' (2000: 236).

Fisher notes that 'when mountaineering expeditions inside Nepal began in the early 1950s, Khumbu Sherpas no longer had to go to Darjeeling, for now most of the expeditions were organised in Kathmandu, and porters and 'sherpas' were hired there. Employment with these expeditions, which attempted peaks all over Nepal, reduced the economic pressure to emigrate to Darjeeling and presumably helped staunch the flow of migrants from Khumbu to India. It also eventually forced the recognition that Khumbu Sherpas were divided from their Darjeeling cousins by citizenship: the former were Nepalese, the latter Indian' (Fisher 1990: 63).

As Fisher remarks, 'no one had ever thought this an issue, let alone a problem, until 1953, when both India and Nepal bitterly tried to claim Tenzing Norgay as their own' after the British expedition managed to put two men, Edmund Hillary and Sherpa Tenzing Norgay, on top of the highest mountain in the world. This successful expedition, despite starting out from Kathmandu and approaching Everest from Nepal, employed Sherpas, mainly from Darjeeling.

John Hunt noted, in his account of the ascent of Everest, that 'most of the Sherpas ... had some knowledge of Nepali, which is more widely known, particularly by those who have been associated with the Gurkhas. Those Sherpas living in Darjeeling have a smattering of Hindi' (1953: 62).

Not all of the younger Sherpas who accompanied the expedition did so with the full support of their parents. Hunt recounts how, on the return of the successful Everest expedition to Namche Bazaar, one young Sherpa of 14, who had accompanied it together with his father, had decided to travel on with the party and see the big world outside the Khumbu. But his mother thought otherwise. Arriving on the scene early on the morning of their departure from Namche, she railed at the would-be abductors of her child, and the weeping boy was led unwillingly back home. Another lad, aged 17, the youngest of the team that has ascended to the South Col, persuaded his mother to let him accompany the party as far as Ghat, one day's march down the valley. She agreed. As Hunt remarked, 'needless to say, Ang Tsering is now in Darjeeling with all the other boys' (1953: 224).

Exceptionally, this British expedition employed a number of Sherpanis, or female Sherpas, as porters. This was largely it seems because arrangements for the recruitment of porters was undertaken by the Darjeeling secretary of the Himalayan Club, Mrs Jill Henderson (Hunt 1953: 62). It was still the case, however, that the women were only hired as low level porters and as the non-military equivalent of camp followers. Hunt remarks that 'accompanying the Sherpas were a number of Sherpanis: their wives and sweethearts, who hoped to be engaged as coolies on our journey to their native land of Khumbu. I was delighted to agree with this arrangement, for not only would they add colour and gaiety to our company, but they carry loads as stoutly as their menfolk' (Hunt 1953: 63).

Later, Hunt notes that, among the many minions of Thondup, the chief cook, 'are the Sherpanis, who are busy, some cleaning cooking-pots or mending garments, others combing and plaiting each other's long black tresses' (Hunt 1953: 76-77). So, women on this expedition not only performed the usual female tasks of cooking and doing the laundry but also carried their fair share of loads. They did not, however, take part in the higher level climbing; that was reserved for the men. Indeed, it is difficult to find evidence, even in the 1950s, to find evidence of Sherpa or any other women climbing, although Ortner remarks that 'there is a record of two daughters and a niece of Tenzing Norgay climbing with Claud Kogan on Cho Oyu in 1959' (Ortner 2000: 219).

She notes that women tended to be employed if 'sponsored' by a related man, whether kinsman or husband. *Sardars* – the Sherpa foremen of mountain expeditions – were, and still are, generally reluctant to take an unrelated woman on a climb. This seems to have been the case even when those organising the expedition were women. What was called 'the first women's Himalayan expedition' took place in the spring of 1955, only a few years after the first ascent of Everest. But the Sherpas who supported the foreign women were mainly men. The only female porter was Ang Droma.

The women team leaders were clearly open to the idea of a team of Sherpas comprised of men and women (2000: 79), but seemed to consider that the Sherpa women, though' tough and adventurous', did not climb on snow and ice (2000: 106). Ang Droma, who proved to be an important, influential and imaginative member of the team (2000: 80, 91, 95, 102, 103, 217), is described, arguably patronisingly, by the two female authors of *Tents in the Clouds* (Jackson & Stark 1956, 2000: 43) as 'a sweet little person, about sixteen years old... (who) carried a load almost as big as herself[42] without complaining'. Ang Droma was fine as an ordinary porter and for lighting the cooking fire (2000: 195, 198), even if she sometimes 'went after the *chang* (local drink) with the boys' (2000: 218). She also seems to have been assigned such tasks as washing the foreign women's clothes and lighting a votive fire to curry favour with the spirits of the mountains (2000: 122, 136, 194).

---

42.   Later identified as 'a 50 pound load'.

As soon as the 'real' climbing started, however, she was left behind, even though one of the male Sherpas, Kusung, apologising for his unfitness, commented that in his pre-war days he was as strong as Ang Temba (one of the leading Sherpas) and that his wife, Ang Droma's mother, 'was equally strong' (2000: 157). Even though she was prepared on occasion to lead the other porters, and carried a load 'nearly as big as herself, which did not seem to inconvenience her at all', Ang Droma is still described as 'a comic little figure' (2000: 224). The last we hear of her is during the final stage of the expedition, when she was, apparently, 'so affected by our imminent parting that she took Betty's hand and clung to it all the way to Kathmandu. The two of them walking side by side, tall Betty and tiny Ang Droma, made rather a touching picture' (2000: 246).

It is sad that even the women climbers seem unable to see her simply as another person on the expedition, perfectly capable of sharing in the tasks, and instead is effectively 'belittled'.

❀ ❀ ❀

CHAPTER 30

Internal Migration and Re-Settlement

We have seen that, after both the First and Second World Wars, many ex-Gurkhas, most of whom originated from the hills of Nepal, decided for various reasons to settle in India with their families, thereby contributing to the growth of the Nepali diaspora in India. Generally, in part because of the lack of facilities and in part because of the prevalence of malaria, very few if any decided to settle in the *terai*. Indeed, throughout the 19th century hill people were very wary of spending any time at all in the *terai* (particularly during the summer months, because of the risk of falling ill or dying from malaria.

But in the 1950s, two things unleashed a huge wave of migration from both the hills and from India into the *terai*. Firstly, the government introduced a change in land tenure, with the abolition of the *birta* system of land allocation, in which land was given as a reward for services rendered to the rulers of Nepal, a grant that tax exempt. From the end of the 1950s, all *birta* land was converted to *raikar*, state land that was privately held land which was taxed by the state. Secondly, and arguably even more importantly, the launching of a major campaign by the government supported by the US and the WHO to eradicate malaria from the *terai*, by systematic spraying of DDT and the virtual elimination of infected mosquitoes, brought about a significant change in physical environmental conditions. The privatisation of land across the *terai*, combined with the effective elimination of malaria, within a few years together constituted a veritable revolution in the conditions under which agriculture was to develop over the next decades.

We have seen that migration has been a significant features of the hill economy and society of Nepal for two centuries; but it is only in the 1950s that reasonable reliable statistics on migration became available. The census of 1952-

54 suggest that only 2.6 per cent of the enumerated population had been absent from home for six months or more, and 97 per cent of these were from the hill and mountain areas. Most of these were migrants workers in India. Between 1952 and 1961, there was relatively little population growth in the *terai* – 0.7 per cent per annum; but, between 1961 and 1971, annual average population growth was 3.5 per cent, and during the next decade was 4.2 per cent (National Population Commission 1982, cited in Seddon 1987). This shows the dramatic increase in population in the *terai* from the late 1950s onwards, largely as a result of migration from the hills.

At the end of the 1950s, the population density of the *terai* as a whole was still low relative to the population density in the hills of Nepal to the north and, even more so, in comparison with the population density of areas across the border to the south, in India. The greatest disparity was in the far west. In Kanchanpur in the far western *terai*, for example, population density in 1961 was 31 people per square mile, while in the neighbouring hill district of Dandeldhura, it was 146, nearly five times greater. Forest still covered much of the *terai*, particularly in the far-west. In the west central *terai*, by contrast, Kapilvastu and Rupandehi had been largely cleared for cultivation, but Nawalparasi was still heavily wooded.

In the eastern *terai*, the forest had been substantially reduced by this time, as clearance and settlement proceeded apace; in Saptari and Siraha, in the eastern *terai*, the forest accounted for a little less than 6 per cent of the 'land use'. Overall, while the average growth rate of the population in Nepal as a whole was just over 2 per cent a year between 1961 and 1971, in the western and central *terai* – the fastest growing regions in the country - it was well over 4 per cent a year; in Chitwan, where Guneratne reports that 'most of the valley remained in jungle until the end of the 1950s' (1996: 14), the population grew by grew by 6.8 per cent a year between 1954 and 1961, according to Kansakar (1979: 63). In the eastern *terai*, the rate of annual population growth was significantly slower, at 2.4 per cent, as migration there from the eastern hills had been going on for much longer.

In 1961, the eastern *terai* showed a net gain of just over 68,000 people; the eastern hills showed a net loss of over 69,000; the western and central *terai* showed a net gain of some 5,700 people; the central inner *terai* (ie Chitwan) experienced a net gain of over 25,000 people, the western and central *terai*, some 5,700. The western and central hills experienced a net loss of around 32,600. The four/five districts of the eastern *terai* (Siraha, Saptari, Morang/ Sunsari and

Jhapa) increased their aggregate population from 740,777 to 1,387,551 – not far short of double – between 1952 and 1972 (Seddon 1987: 100, Table 4.3). Ten years later, in 1971, the population density index in the hills was greatest in the eastern hills (6) with the mid-west and far-west next (4 and 3 respectively). In the *terai,* the highest population density was in the west (15), followed by the east (14), central (13), mid west (12 and far west (11) in that order (Gurung 2001: Table 12, p. 36).

By 1961, some 4 per cent of the population of Nepal was recorded as having been away from home for six or more months at the time of the census – that is, were regarded as migrants. Not all of this, however, was the result of migration to the *terai* and to the towns within the country; the proportion of migrants living and working abroad also increased from 2.3 per cent of the total population in 1952-55 to 3.4 per cent of the population in 1961. Migration to India did not decline as a result of mass migration to the *terai;* it actually increased. Nepal was 'on the move'.

But, given the general direction and increasing importance of internal migration, the government of Nepal began during the 1950s to try to control and direct migration and re-settlement in the *terai.* The Rapti Valley Development Project, launched in Chitwan district was one example of an early project for re-settlement. The establishment in 1964 of the Nepal Re-Settlement Company was another response to immigration into the *terai.* The results of these initiatives were limited, and most migrants re-settled 'spontaneously' and were regarded by the government agencies, particularly the employees of the forestry department who saw their primary task to defend the forests against these 'squatters' (*sukumbasi*).

Immigration into the *terai* from the hills and mountains of Nepal did not just increase the population, forest clearance and deforestation, the area under cultivation and agricultural output; it also began to change the ethnic and caste composition of the local population. Not surprisingly, the majority of those deciding to leave their homes and move to another part of the country with very different ecological and economic potential were those relatively disadvantaged in terms of land-ownership and socially discriminated against back in the hills and mountains. The influx of people significantly altered the ethnic and caste composition of the *terai.*

The population of the *terai* before the 1950s comprised largely the Tharus and other ethnic groups, often referred to misleadingly as indigenous 'tribal' or *adhivasi* groups (including Chidimars, Dhimals, Gangais, Jhangars/Uraons, Kisans, Koches, Kushwadias/Pathakattas, Meches, Mundas, Rajbanshis, Santhals, Tajpuriyas and Tharus), as well as the different Hindu caste groups, including *dalits*, all of whom had originally immigrated from India (and who are now generally referred to as Madhesis) and the Muslims, who had also originated in India. Most of the people in the *terai* spoke their own languages, but the majority also spoke Hindi.

Now there was an influx from the hills, bringing hill *dalits* as well as higher caste groups, and representatives of many ethnic groups from the hill and (to a lesser extent) from the mountain areas. The hill people brought with them not only different languages, but also a capacity to speak Nepali and a general inability to speak Hindi. They also brought with them significantly different social and cultural practices. For example, generally speaking, and particularly among the different hill ethnic groups, the immigrants tended to be less dominated by the inherent inequalities of the Hindu caste system than were the people of the *terai*. This had profound consequences, particularly for the position of women and attitudes towards female infants and girls.

Relations between the sexes were more egalitarian, marriage took place later, so that brides tended to be older, particularly among hill ethnic groups[43]. Consequently, fertility rates tended to be lower and families tended to be smaller. Infant and child mortality rates in the hills were also generally lower than in the *terai*, particularly as regards females. Females were generally regarded more highly and discrimination against girls was less. The dowry system, whereby the family of the bride was obliged to provide gifts to the groom's family to 'add value' to the bride, was less pervasive. Divorce was more common. All of these factors were mutually reinforcing.

As the proportion of the population of 'hill origin' increased, so the mixture of social and cultural practices found in the *terai* increased and the practices of those 'hill people' now living in the *terai* both affected and, probably more so, were affected by, the practices of the people of the *terai*. For example, while Nepali became more commonly spoken, immigrants also began to speak Hindi to a greater extent; and while the age at marriage and many other features of 'domestic' arrangements and 'domestic' life remained different as between

---

43. The 1976 Nepal Fertility Survey found that mean age at marriage - to be found overwhelmingly in the hills and mountains – was 17.1, markedly higher than that for Hindu women (15.0) and Muslim women (14.2).

immigrants and locals, the prevalence of the dowry among immigrants increased over time, arguably both reflecting and affecting the position of women and increasing the cost of marriage for the family of the bride.

In general terms, although assimilation was limited, at least until the end of the 1960s, there was significant social and cultural influence both ways. However, the distinction between those who came from the hills (*pahari*) and those who saw themselves as indigenous to the *terai,* even if their ancestors had come from India (*madheshis*) remained strong and was to provide the basis for hostility, tension and even conflict in the coming decades.

The wave of migration into the *terai* in the 1960s did not, for the most part, involve migration for employment, with which we have been mainly concerned in previous chapters; but rather involved the wholesale relocation of families and households – men, women and children – to clear the forest and the scrub and open up fields for settled cultivation. We do not have figures broken down into male and female migrant and settlers, but it is reasonable to suggest that, whereas the majority of migrants would have been men – as we have seen was the case throughout the history of foreign migration from Nepal – when it came to migration for re-settlement, the proportion of females would have been significantly higher, as men were accompanied by their wives and families.

In economic terms, the flow of migrants into the *terai* led to an increase in the proportion of small farmers within the rural population, although the *terai* remained, for the time being at least, the region of Nepal where what many have called 'semi-feudal' landowners remained a major feature of rural economy and society, and 'semi-feudal' relations of production remained widespread. It was not until the land reform law of 1964 that an official ceiling for land ownership was established, and even then the larger landowners were generally able to transfer 'surplus' land to relatives and clients, and so maintain effective control over their estates and their labourers despite the new law.

Not all the immigrants to the *terai,* however, were settlers. Some migrated for employment in agriculture and in other sectors as they developed, particularly in the emerging towns of the *terai.* Indeed, one of the features of the 1950s and 1960s was the growth of the urban areas, as not just single migrant workers but whole families – men, women and children - moved from the rural areas to town. The proportion of the population living in urban areas in Nepal was only around 3 per cent in 1952-54, but the rate of growth was dramatic in the decades that followed. It is significant that, apart from Pokhara and Kathmandu, it was the towns of the *terai* that experienced the most rapid growth in the 1960s. as commerce between India and Nepal increased rapidly and border towns in particular, as well as those between the hills and the *terai* (which constituted another kind of 'border'), expanded as a result.

Five *terai* towns – Nepalgunj in the far western *terai*, Janakpur and Rajbiraj in the central eastern *terai*, and Dharan and Biratnagar in the east - recorded an average of nearly 4 per cent annual growth between 1961 and 1971. Nepalgunj was one of the earliest border towns in the western *terai*. It was established in the late 1850s by Jung Bahadur Rana in order to control trade between the more populated hills and India. In the west central *terai*, Butwal and Bhairahawa were already small commercial centres in the late 19th century. In 1934, the local Bada Hakim, arranged for the allotment of housing sites in Dharan and gradually Marwari and other traders from India, as well as Nepalis from Kathmandu Valley, Palpa, Pokhara, and different parts of the eastern hill region settled in Dharan.

Biratnagar had long been a commercial centre, known as Gograha Bazaar. The ruins of temples, palaces and ponds are scattered in a vast area to the south of the current city, in Vedhyari, Buddhanagar. In 1914, district governor or Bada Hakim laid the foundations of modern Biratnagar by moving the hospital, post office, prison and the customs, land registry, forestry and auditor offices to Gograha Bazaar from Rangeli, at that time the district capital of Morang. The town was named Biratnagar in 1919. Rajbiraj was designed in 1938, and was the first township in Nepal to involve urban planning; it was declared a municipality in 1959.

❀ ❀ ❀

Chapter 31

'Gurkha' Nurses?

The population of Dharan increased considerably as a result of the influx of Nepali returnees from Assam and Burma after the second world war" (Regmi 1979). Many of those returning to Nepal after the wars preferred to settle in the *terai* and in the rapidly growing urban areas of the plains, rather than to return to their hill villages – although many of course preferred to return home. The tendency to migrate to Dharan, located at the junction between the hills and the *terai,* and even settle there was encouraged when, in 1953, the British Gurkha Recruitment camp was established at Dharan, and many families of ex-Gurkhas came to live there.

The British Military Hospital (BMH Nepal) in Dharan was opened in 1960 to care for Gurkhas and their families (cited in the book *Queen Alexandra's Royal Army Nursing Corps*, by Juliet Piggott). In the summer of 2018, there was considerable on-line debate (www.arsse.co.uk/community/threads/gurkha-women.282414) and www.arrse.co.uk/community/threads/women-recruits-in-the-bde-of-gurkhas.27571/) as to whether Nepali women served as nurses at the BMH in Dharan, or indeed in other British Military Hospitals elsewhere, including overseas. Many of the contributors refer to Nepali women indiscriminately as 'Gurkha' women or girls, meaning that they were members of 'Gurkha' families – that is, members of families of men who were serving in the Gurkhas or who were now ex-Gurkhas, having served in the Gurkhas previously.

We know that, in May 1942, the Women's Auxiliary Corps India (WAC (I) was formed. This Corps recruited Indian women. Recruits had to be a minimum age of 18 years and their duties were almost entirely clerical or domestic. In December 1942, the minimum age was reduced to 17 years and, by the end of the war, 11,500 women had enlisted. Volunteers could enlist on local service or general service terms. Those on general service could be sent to serve anywhere in India. Compared to over two million men, the corps of 11,500 women was small, and recruitment was always hampered by caste and communal inhibitions. Indian women at the time did not mix socially or at work with men and a large part of the corps was formed from the mixed-race Anglo–Indian community. It is not clear whether any of the 'Indian women' who served in the WAC (I) were of Nepali origin.

The WAC(I) had an autonomous Air Wing, which served as the Indian counterpart of the WAAF: the women operated switchboards and similar duties at airfields and air headquarters (AHQ). In the earlier part of the war there was also a Naval Wing, but with the very localised environment of naval base and the very distinct ethos of the wartime naval services, British and Indian, this department was formally hived-off, in 1944, to become the Women's Royal Indian Naval Service (WRINS), with its own uniform, similar to WRNS.

As far as I know, only Indian nationals were recruited to any of these services, and there is no evidence of Nepali women, but a majority were Anglo-Indians and some of mixed descent. Noor Inayat Khan, for example, who was of Indian and American descent, was awarded the George Cross for her service in the Special Operations Executive and Kalyani Sen, a second officer and the first Indian service woman who visited the UK, served in the WRINS during World War II.

There was also, incidentally, a woman's regiment under Netaji Subhash Chandra Bose 's Indian National Army, formed in 1942 to fight against the British during World War II, called the Rani of Jhansi Regiment. This was one of the very few all-female combat regiments of the Second World War on any side. Led by Captain Lakshmi Swaminathan (better known as Lakshmi Sahgal), the unit was raised in July 1943 with volunteers from the expatriate Indian population in Southeast Asia. It was named after Lakshmibai, Rani of Jhansi, an Indian queen of the Maratha princely state of Jhansi, now part of Jhansi district in Uttar Pradesh. She was one of the leading figures of the Indian Rebellion of 1857 and became a symbol of resistance to the British Raj for Indian nationalists.

On the division of the Indian Army from the British according to the Tri-Partite Agreement at Indian independence in 1947, the Indian Gorkhas continued to recruit from Nepal, as well as from among the 'Indoms' (those now domiciled in India) who remained behind when the eight new battalions of the British Gurkhas were deployed to Malaya. The Indian Army also continued to recruit women. Under the Army Act of 1950, however, women were ineligible for regular commissions except in 'such corps, departments or branches which the central government may specify by way of notifications.' On 1 November 1958, the Army Medical Corps became the first unit of the Indian Army to grant regular commissions to women. Today, the Indian Army has no problem both recruiting female 'Gurkhas' (Gorkhas) and advertising for them.

There is considerable debate, however, as previously remarked, as to when, if at all, there were ever 'Gurkha women' serving as nurses in the British Army. One of the earliest comments suggests that any women recruited into 'the Gurkhas' would not be able to join the Royal Gurkha Rifles (RGR) but would other units, such as the Queens Gurkha Signals (QGS), Queens Gurkha Engineers (QGE), Queens Own Gurkha Logistic Regiment (QOGLR) & Gurkha Staff and Personnel Service (GSPS). The author states that 'I was under the impression a number of Gurkha daughters already served, albeit in non-Gurkha units'. There is no reference to a nursing unit in the Gurkhas, but one source states that 'I know there have been female QARANC from Gurkha families, since as long ago as the 60s', and shows a photograph of a young woman, identified as 'Rai Krishna, a nurse with the Gurkha Regiment, meeting members of the Gurkha Band in England, May 07, 1968'. (There then follows a long discussion as to whether the Gurkhas had a band).

It is suggested by another source that 'a handful (fewer than 10) young Nepali women were recruited in the 1950s and early 1960s, through the British Gurkha recruiting centre in Dharan, to serve at the BMH in Dharan and elsewhere – at British Military Maternity Hospitals and Army Chest Hospitals in the Far East where Gurkha soldiers were stationed. It is also suggested that 'they would have been trained in UK at the Royal Herbert and those qualifying as SRNs (state registered nurses) would have been commissioned'.

The Herbert Hospital, renamed the Royal Herbert Hospital in 1900, was originally built on the south side of Woolwich Common, on the western slopes of Shooter's Hill, in the Royal Borough of Greenwich in South East London, as a restorative facility for British veterans of the Crimean War. It was the first specially built military hospital in the country and remained a military hospital until 1977. It was also a centre for the training of the Queen Alexandra's Royal Army Nursing Corps (QARANC). One source on-line mentioned that

'I'm told there was a Gurkha female Sgt QARANC carrying out normal duties for the ranks at the Royal Herbert (a long defunct military hospital in Woolwich) in the late '60s and that, as a Sgt, she would already have been at least a State Enrolled Nurse. I've personally met a retired Gurkha QARANC. I would not try telling such women that they weren't real QARANC.

It is suggested by one source that the young Nepali women recruited and trained as nurses in this way were from 'Gurkha' families and were often 'line-girls' educated in British army schools. 'They would be trained in UK and those qualifying as SRNs would be commissioned'. They would have been trained not only at the Royal Herbert, however, but also at other military hospitals, and not only recruited through Dharan from within Nepal, but also through other avenues from 'Gurkha' families living overseas, as 'locally employed personnel' (LEPs). This source asserts that 'Gurkha females were first recruited into QARANC in the late fifties, primarily to serve in BMHs, British Military Maternity Hospitals and Army Chest Hospitals in the Far East where Gurkha soldiers were stationed'.

Another source agrees that 'there were indeed daughters from Gurkha families cap badged and uniformed QA at the time, but they weren't QAs either under UK TACOS or fully deployable, transferable, etc, but were LEPs (Locally Employed Personnel) employed under local terms and conditions of service and only employable locally. It was simply a 'badge of convenience'. While LEPs were treated as QAs locally, and uniformed and trained as such just as others were to RN, RMP, RAEC, RCT, R SIGS, RAVC, RAMC, APTC, etc, they were LEPs as distinct from members of QARANC (or RN, RMP, etc)'.

One source in the on-line discussion (28 August 2018) shows a photocopy of an item in the Kuala Lumpur press (undated) stating that

'two attractive Gurkha women, who are about to create a revolution in Gurkha thinking and way of life, arrived here today by RAF plane from the Cameron Highlands military hospital. They are Miss Bimala Dewan (18) and Miss Radha Rawat (22). They aim to be the first fully qualified Gurkha nursing sisters. They have been selected for three years training in England to become State Registered Nurses – the basic qualification needed by nursing officers of the QARANC. If they pass, they will become the first Gurkha women ever trained as nurses in the history of Nepal and the first Gurkha women officers in the British Army. They will return to Malaya to serve with the Brigade of Gurkhas'.

The Cameron Highlands Military Hospital was one of several military hospitals in the Cameron Highlands in Malaya. One other source suggests that although they were indeed daughters from Gurkha families, cap-badged and uniformed as QAs, they were not strictly Qas, but LEPs employed under local terms and conditions of service and only employable locally. It is remarked that 'the preferential treatment here also becomes quite apparent when we see that these ladies have been granted not only the same as their British counterparts but have been trained at the British Government's expense whereas the female nurses serving the Gurkha families in the Gurkha battalions had to be well trained and experienced at the time of their enlistment'.

One source argues that 'every time the subject of parity for pay pension and other perquisites of the British Gurkhas with that of their British counterparts comes up the British Government sidesteps the issue by pointing towards the Tripartite Agreement. This document states that 'the Government of the United Kingdom have agreed to use the corresponding Indian pay codes and rates of pay as the basis of the scale to be applied to Gurkha officers and soldiers and to give appropriate additional allowance during service abroad'. This is well and true but, why does this same statement not apply to the very few 'hand - picked' (14 of them to be exact) Gurkhas, the so-called Sandhurst Commissioned Gurkhas[44], and the Gurkha female nurses serving in the Queen Alexandra's Royal Army Nursing Corps (QARANC)?'

The same source asks, rhetorically, 'what was the reason behind the enlistment of a handful of Gurkha females (less than 10) in the late fifties and early sixties into the Queen Alexandra's Royal Army Nursing Corps through the auspices of the British Gurkhas Nepal in Dharan? The preferential treatment here also becomes quite apparent when we see that these ladies have been granted not only the same as their British counterparts but have been trained at the British Government's expense whereas the female nurses serving the Gurkha families in the Gurkha battalions had to be well trained and experienced at the time of their enlistment. Why were these ladies allowed to marry other foreign nationals and were not properly accounted for and repatriated to Nepal at the end of their contract as is the case with the rest of the Gurkha soldiers?'

---

44. The first of these so-called Sandhurst Commissioned Gurkhas was Office Cadet Subash Gurung, who was commissioned into the Royal Gurkha Rifles at the Royal Military Academy Sandhurst, on Friday 11 April 2014, the first Gurkha soldier to be commissioned as a Direct Entry officer into the RGR.

Another source remarked that 'the Nepalese women who were taken on to work in BMH Nepal in Dharan in the 60's were Nepalese - they weren't Gurkhas, they weren't in the Brigade, and if they didn't learn at teaching hospitals like the Royal Herbert in Woolwich then where were they supposed to learn?' Another source adds that 'written evidence to the Gurkha Welfare Inquiry, appears to say that Gurkha women serving as nurses were specifically mentioned in the Tripartite Agreement of 1948. Also that a small number of women from Nepal, described as Gurkha although I understand the argument that this label is used incorrectly, were recruited into the QARANC in the 1950s and 1960s and served on normal conditions of service as members of the British Army, unlike the women you were on about who were recruited on special terms as LEP nurses for Gurkha families' (see https://gurkhainquiry.files.wordpress.com/2014/03/exhibit-6-gurkhas-in-the-service-of-the-crown-satyagrah.pdf).

Yet another source commented generally that 'the question of exactly how LEPs fit into the rest of the Army is a complex one, particularly for those who've never been part of /worked with the LEP system, and it varies massively not just from location to location but even from unit to unit within the same location at the same time so it's hardly surprising the press (and the military) so often get it so badly wrong and judge, totally wrongly, by appearances'. This source cites a number of examples:

❖ In Hong Kong the RHKR(V) were nothing to do with the British Army or MoD but were an auxiliary militia, directly employed and paid for by the Hong Kong government, with PSIs who were on Loan Service (seconded, not attached), but they were still on the BFHK ORBAT as part of 38th Brigade.

❖ The HKMSC, also in Hong Kong, were part of the British Army but were LEPs, paid for by the Hong Kong government through the MoD, with different TACOS (no pensions), and although they did the same training as the British Army .... including UK courses from full APTC to QMs, none were allowed to transfer to British Regular Army even if they had full citizenship, although some joined the TA once in the UK. Although home duties only and not permitted to go to the Gulf for GW1, some didn't stay home duties but went to UNFICYP instead during GW1, releasing ambulance drivers from UNFICYP to go to GW1 in their place.

❖ The ASD guard in Hong Kong were Sikh LEPs, cap-badged RAOC, commanded by a commissioned Sikh LEP lieutenant (who was left stateless on handover) whose military training was limited.

❖ The Royal Gibraltar Regiment are an infantry battalion (with a few quirks), but for home duties only, who do all normal UK courses (CIC, RMAS, Brecon, etc), but while not LEPs they are very much LPs despite supposedly being open to any and all British, Commonwealth or Irish recruits.

❖ The FIDF are similar to the RHKR(V) in as much as they are a local auxiliary militia (but trained along broadly RM not Army lines), directly employed and paid for by the Falklands and again not under the MoD - probably just as well since when called out on 1 April 1982 only 23 turned up out of 120 (which otherwise would have led to quite a few charge sheets).

While Singapore limits integration and Nepalis in the Gurkha Contingent Singapore Police Force (GCSP) are not allowed to marry Singaporeans, there have never been any such restrictions on Nepalis in the British Brigade of Gurkhas and they've been free to marry other foreign nationals and many have done (Brits, Hong Kong Chinese, Malays, etc) and, subject to normal immigration regulations, to settle abroad without being 'properly accounted for and repatriated to Nepal at the end of their contract'.

On the other hand, the vast majority of the men in these different units tended to marry women from their country of origin, Nepal, usually from the village or at least the area from which they themselves originated and from the caste or ethnic group to which they themselves belonged. These women would be stationed wherever their husband was serving. But we have no reliable information regarding the employment of these women, as 'Gurkha' nurses or in other capacities, during the period under consideration.

❀ ❀ ❀

Conclusion

Running throughout this book is the story of Nepali women's migration and re-settlement, of their foreign employment, of their struggle to maintain their families and households in the absence of their menfolk, and, above all, of their pervasive involvement over two hundred years with military service in India and overseas. Not all of these women were linked directly to the military; many were farmers and settlers, many others were employed in various capacities in India and beyond.

We have seen that, for the two centuries or so up until the 1960s, women from Nepal (and from other parts of the Himalayas) played a significant role – indeed a variety of roles – in the history of the British Empire, in India and overseas, as well as in the history of Nepal. We still see them indistinctly, however, because even now, the information for a proper appreciation of their contribution is lacking. It is hoped that this incomplete work will stimulate more detailed research, so that a fuller picture may eventually emerge.

We have also included women of other nationalities who served the British in various capacities, mainly as nurses during numerous military campaigns, including those of the two World Wars, in which the British army – and the Indian army, with its Gurkha contingents – fought to defend and preserve the British Empire.

All of these, we would claim, were, in their own different ways, *lahure* women.

✿ ✿ ✿

References and Bibliography

–(1914). *Ratan Singh Gurung ko Outpostko Kathi (The Tale of Ratan Singh Gurung at the Outpost)*. Banaras.

Acharya, Meena & Lyn Bennett. (1981). *The Rural Women of Nepal: an aggregate analysis and summary of eight village studies*. Kathmandu: CEDA.

Acharya, Meena & Lyn Bennett. (1983). *Women and the Subsistence Sector: economic participation in household decision-making in Nepal*. World Bank Staff Working Paper no.526. Washington DC: World Bank.

Adhikari, J. (1996). *The Beginnings of Agrarian Change: a case study in central Nepal*. Kathmandu, T M Publications.

Adhikari, J. (1998). *Decisions for Survival: Farm Management Strategies in the Middle Hills of Nepal*. New Delhi: Adroit Publications.

Adhikari, J. (2001). 'Mobility and agrarian change in central Nepal', *Contributions to Nepalese Studies*. 28(2), 247-267.

Adhikari, J. (2009). *Migration, Security and Livelihoods. A Case of Migration between Nepal and India*. Kathmandu: Nepal Institute of Development Studies.

Adhikari, J. & Bohle, H-G. (1999). *Food Crisis in Nepal: how mountain farmers cope*. New Delhi: Adroit Publications.

Adhikari, J. Seddon, D., Gurung, G., Bhadra, C. & Niraula, B.P. (2006). *Nepali Women and Foreign Labour Migration*. Kathmandu: UNIFEM (now UNWomen) and Nepal Institute of Development Studies.

Adshead, D. R. & J. P. Cross. (1970). *Gurkha: the legendary soldier*. London: Leo Cooper.

Allen, Charles. (2000). *Soldier Sahibs: the Men who Made the North-West Frontier*. ISBN 0-78670-861-1.

Allen, Charles. (2015). *The Prisoner of Kathmandu: Brian Hodgson in Nepal 1820-43*. ISBN 978-1-910376-11-9.

Arora, Vibha (2008). Routing the Commodities of Empire through Sikkim (1817-1906). *Commodities of Empire, Working Paper no. 9*.

Aryal, Manisha. (1991). 'To Marry a Lahuray', *Himal*, 4 (3).

Badenach, W. (1826). *Inquiry into the state of the Indian army, with suggestions for its improvement, and the establishment of a military police for India*. London: John Murray.

Balicki, A. (2008). Lamas, Shamans and Ancestors: village religion in Sikkim. Leiden: Brill.

Barker, Marianne. 1989. Nightingales in the Mud: the Digger sisters of the Great War, 1914-1918. Sydney: Allen & Unwin.

Bassett, Jan. (1997). Guns and Brooches: Australian Army Nursing from the Boer War to the Gulf War. Melbourne: Oxford University Press.

Basu, Shrabani. (2015). *For King and Another Country: Indian Soldiers on the Western Front, 1914-18*. London, Oxford, New York, Delhi, Sydney: Bloomsbury.

Bingley, A. H. & A. Nicholls. (1918). *Caste Handbooks for the Indian Army: Brahmans*. Calcutta: Superintendent Government Printing

Bishop, Edward. (1976). *Better to Die. The Story of the Gurkhas*. London: New English Library.

Bista, Dor Bahadur. n.d. *Padipur: a village in the central terai,* typescript.

Blaikie, P.M., Cameron, J & Seddon, D. (1979). *The Struggle for Basic Needs in Nepal*. Paris: OECD.

Blaikie, P. M., Cameron, J. & Seddon D. (1980, 2001). *Nepal in Crisis: growth and stagnation at the periphery*. Oxford: Clarendon Press; Delhi, Adroit Publishing.

Bolt, David. (1967). *Gurkhas*. London: Weidenfield and Nicolson.

Bredin, A. E. C. (1961). *The Happy Warriors: the Gurkha soldier in the British army*. Gillingham, Dorset: Blackmore.

Brodie, Fawn. (1986). *The Devil Drives: a Life of Sir Richard Burton*. Eland Publishing.

Brook Northey, W. (1937). *The Land of the Gurkhas*. Cambridge: W. Heffer

Brook Northey, W. & C. J. Morris. (1927). *The Gurkhas*. London: J. Lane

Brower, Barbara. (1992). *Sherpas of Khumbu: People, Livestock and Landscape*. Delhi

Bruce, C. G. (1928). Foreword to Northey, W. B. & C. J. Morris, *The Gurkhas: their manners, customs and country*. London: John Lane, the Bodley Head.

Bruce, C. G. (1934). *Himalayan Wanderers*. London: Maclehose.

Buchanan, Francis. (1928). *Account of the District of Purnea in 1809-1810*. New Delhi: Archaeological Library; Patna: Bihar and Orissa Research Society..

Bullock, C. (2009). *Britain's Gurkhas*. Third Millennium Publishing.

Candler, E. (1919). *The Sepoy*. London: John Murray.

Caplan, Lionel. (1970). *Land and Social Change in East Nepal. A Study of Hindu Tribal Relations*. Berkeley, CA, University of California Press.

Caplan, Lionel. (1995). *Warrior Gentlemen: 'Gurkhas' in the Western Imagination*. Providence & Oxford: Berghahn Books

Cardew, F. G. (1891). 'Our recruiting grounds of the future for the Indian army', *The Journal of the United Service Institution of India*, 20 (86): 131-56.

Cavenaugh, O. (1851). *Rough Notes on the State of Nepal, its government, army and resources*. Calcutta: W. Palmer, Military Orphan Press.

Chakravarty, B. C. (1964). *British Relations with the Hill Tribes of Assam since 1858*. Calcutta: Firma K. L. Mukhopadhyay.

Chant, C. (1985). *Gurkha: the illustrated history of an elite fighting force*. Poole: Blandford.

Chapple, J. L. (1980). *Bibliography of Gurkha regiments and related subjects*. Gurkha Museum Publication, no.4.

Chatterjee, S. P. (1997). *Known yet unknown Darjeeling/Siliguri: facts and figures*. Siliguri : Kashi Nath Dey.

Chaudhuri, K. C. (1960). *Anglo-Nepalese Relations: from the earliest times of the British rule in India till the Gurkha war*. Calcutta: Modern Book Agency.

Cochrane, Susan. (1981). *The Determinants of Fertility and Child Survival in the Nepal Terai*. World Bank Population and Human Resources Division, Discussion Paper no. 81-84, Washington DC, World Bank.

Conway, D. & N. Shrestha. (1981). *Causes and Consequences of Rural-Rural Migration in Nepal*. Bloomington, Indiana: Department of Geography.

Corbett, Jim. (1958). *My India*. Oxford: Oxford University Press.

Cross, J. P. (1986). *In Gurkha Company: the British Army Gurkhas, 1948 to the present*. London: Arms and Armour Press.

Dahal, D. R., Rai & A. Manzardo. (1977), *Land and Migration in Far Western Nepal*. Kirtipur: Tribhuvan University, Institute of Nepal and Asian Studies (INAS).

Dalrymple, W. (2002). *White Mughals: Love and Betrayal in Eighteenth Century India*. London.

Dalrymple, W. (2013). *Return of a King: the battle for Afghanistan*. London, New Delhi, New York, Sydney, Bloomsbury.

Davis, K. (1951). *The Population of India and Pakistan*. Princeton: Princeton University Press.

Defoe, Daniel. *The Life and Adventures of Mrs. Christian Davies*.

Defoe, Daniel. (1724). *Roxana; or, The fortunate mistress*.

Defoe, Daniel. (1855). *The life and adventures of Mother Ross*. New York: H. G. Bohn.

Des Chene, Mary. (1986-87). 'Regimental Histories and Army Handbooks: A Bibliography of the Gurkha Regiments'. *SALNAQ - Issue 21 / 22 (Fall 1986 / Spring 1987)* (SALNAQ: South Asia Library Notes & Queries (CONSALD).

Des Chene, M. (1991). *Relics of Empire: a cultural history of the Gurkhas, 1815-1987*. unpubl. PhD, Stanford University.

Des Chene, Mary. (1993). 'Soldiers, Sovereignty and Silences: Gorkhas a Diplomatic Currency', *South Asia Bulletin*, 12 (1-2).

Des Chene, M. (1998). 'Fate, Domestic Authority and Women's Wills, in Skinner, D., Pach, A. & Holland, D. (eds). *Selves in Time and Place: Identities, Experiences and History in Nepal*. Lanham, Rowman & Littlewood, pp. 19-50)

Dozey, E. C. (1922). *Darjeeling Past and Present - A Concise History of Darjeeling District since 1835*. Michigan: University of Michigan Library.

Dunlop, John. (1849). *Mooltan, during and after the siege: being twenty-one drawings, from sketches taken on the spot*. London: Wm. S. Orr & Co.

Dunn, (1959). 'Medical-geographical observations in central Nepal', *Millbank Memorial Fund Quarterly*, xi

Durova, Nadezda. (1836). *The Notes of a Cavalry Maiden* (in Russian).

Durova, Nadezda. (1988). *The Cavalry Maid. The Memoirs of a Woman Soldier.* trans. by John Mersereau Jr. and David Lapeza (Ann Arbor, Michigan, Ardis Publishers.

Durova, Nadezda. (1988). *The Cavalry Maiden. Journals of a Female Russian Officer in the Napoleonic Wars,* trans. by Mary Fleming Zirin, Bloomington: Indiana-Michigan Series in Russian and East European Studies, Indiana University Press.

English, R. (1982). *Gorkhali and Kiranti: political economy in the hills of Nepal,* unpubl. PhD Thesis submitted to the New School for Social Research, New York.

Esdaile, Charles, J. (2014). *Women in the Peninsular War.* Norman: University of Oklahoma Press.

Evans, Rhiannon (ed). (2015). *Joyce's War: The Second World War Journal of a Queen Alexandra Nurse (Voices from History).* Stroud: the History Press.

Farwell, Byron (1963). *Burton: A Biography of Sir Richard Francis Burton.* New York: Penguin Books.

Farwell, B. (1984, 1985). *The Gurkhas.* London: Allen Lane; London: Penguin Books.

Farwell, B. (1989). *Armies of the Raj: from the Mutiny to Independence, 1858-1947.* London: Viking.

Fisher, J. F. (1986). *Trans-Himalayan Traders: economy, society and culture in northwest Nepal.* Berkeley, California: University of California Press.

Fisher, J. F. (1990). *Sherpas: Reflections on Change in Himalayan Nepal.* Berkeley, CA, University of California Press.

Forbes, D. (1964). *Johnny Gurkha.* London: Robert Hale

Fox, R. G. (1985). *Lions of the Punjab: culture in the making.* Berkeley: University of California Press.

Fox, Robin Lane (2004). *Alexander the Great.* London: The Folio Society.

Fürer-Haimendorf, Cristoph. Von (1964). *Sherpas of Nepal.* London: John Murray.

Fürer-Haimendorf, Cristoph. Von (1975). *Himalayan Traders.* London: John Murray.

Gaige, Frederick. (1975). *Regionalism and National Unity in Nepal.* Berkley: University of California Press.

Gait, Edward A. (1906). *A History of Assam.* Calcutta.

Gibbs, H. R. K. (1947). *The Gurkha Soldier.* Calcutta: Thacker, Spink & Co.

Gill, Anton. (1995). *Ruling Passions: sex, race and empire.* London: BBC Books.

Godelier, Maurice. (1978). 'The Concept of the Asiatic Mode of Production and Marxist models of social evolution', in (ed) Seddon, David. *Relations of Production: Marxist approaches to economic anthropology.* London: Frank Cass.

Gough, C. & Innes, A. D. (1986). T*he Sikhs and Sikh Wars: the rise, conquest and annexation of the Punjab State.* Delhi: Gian Publishing House.

Greenhut, J. (1984). 'Sahib and sepoy: an inquiry into the relationship between British officers and native soldiers of the British Indian army', *Military Affairs*, 48: 15-18.

Guha, A. (1967). 'Colonisation of Assam', *The Indian Economic and Social History Review*, iv, pp. 125-40 and 289-318.

Guha, Amalendu. (1977). *Planter-Raj to Swaraj*. Delhi

Gupta, Hari Ram. (1952). *A History of the Sikhs: from Nadir Shah's invasion to the rise of Ranjit Singh, 1739-1799*. Simla: Minerva Book Shop.

Gurung, H. B. (1991). 'The Gurkha Guide', *Himal*, 4 (3): 20)

Gurung, Harka Bahadur. (2001). 'Highlanders on the Move: the migration trend in Nepal', in (eds von der Heide, Susanne & Thomas Hoffmann, *Aspects of Migration and Mobility in Nepal*, Kathmandu: Ratna Pustak Bhandar.

Gurung, Tim. I. (2020) *Ayo Gorkhali: A History of Gurkhas*. Westland Publications Limited.

Hacker, Barton C. (1981). 'Women and Military Institutions in Early Modern Europe: A Reconnaissance', *Signs (University of Chicago Press)*, vol.6, no. 4, Summer: 643-71.

Hamilton (Buchanan), William, Fitzpatrick.(1811, 1971). *An Account of the Kingdom of Nepal and of the Territories Annexed to this Dominion by the House of Gorkha*. Edinburgh: Constable. Reprinted, 1971, New Delhi: Manjushri Publishing House.

Hanna, H. B. Colonel (1899). *The Second Afghan War, its Causes, its Conduct and its Consequences,* vols 1 & 2, Westminster, Archibald Constable & Co., Whitehall Gardens.

Hasrat, Bikram Jit (1970). *History of Nepal: As Told By Its Own and Contemporary Chroniclers*. Hoshiapor, Punjab: the Editor.

Hasrat, Bikram Jit. (1977). *Life and Times of Ranjit Singh: a saga of benevolent despotism*. V. V. Research Institute Book Agency.

Haughten, John. (1878). *Char-Ee-Kar and Service there with the 4th Goorkha Regiment (Shah Shooja's Force) in 1841: an episode of the First Afghan War. War College Series*. ISBN 1296488276 (ISBN13: 9781296488277).

Heathcote, T. A. (1974). *The Indian Army: the garrison of British Imperial India, 1822-1922*. Vancouver: David & Charles.

Hervey, Albert. (1988). *A Soldier of the Company: Life of an Indian Ensign, 1833-43,* abridged by Charles Allen. London: Michael Joseph. AbeBooks.co.uk

Hitchcock, J. T. 'A Nepalese hill village and Indian employment', 6 pp mimeo, supplied by the British Library, Boston Spa, Wetherby, UK.

Hitchcock, J. T. (1963). 'Some effects of recent change in rural Nepal', *Human Organization,* 22 (1), Spring.

Hitchcock, J. T. (1966). *The Magars of Banyan Hill*. New York, Holt, Rinehart & Winston.

Hitchman, Francis. (1887). *Richard F. Burton, K.C.M.G.: His Early, Private and Public Life with an Account of his Travels and Explorations,* Two volumes; London: Sampson and Low.

HMG. (1958). *Census of Population, Nepal*. Kathmandu: His Majesty's Government, Department of Statistics.

Hodgson, B. H. (1833) 'Origin and Classification of the Military Tribes of Nepal', *Journal of the Asiatic Society of Bengal* vol. 17.

Hodgson, Brian, H. (1874). *Essays on the Languages, Literature and Religion of Nepal and Tibet.* London: Trübner & Company.

Hoffman, Thomas. (2001). 'Out-Migration Patterns of Solu Khumbu Distrit; in (eds) von der Heide & Thomas Hoffman, *Aspects of Migration and Mobility in Nepal.* Kathmandu: Ratna Pustak Bhandar.

Holmes, Richard. (2001). *Redcoat: the British soldier in the age of horse and musket.* London: Harper Collins.

Human Rights Watch (1995) *Rape for Profit: Trafficking of Nepali Girls and Women to India's Brothels,* Report vol.12, no. 5 (A), 1995.

Hunt, J. (1953). *The Ascent of Everest.* London: Hodder and Stoughton.

Hunt, J. (1953, 1978). *Life in Meeting.* London: Hodder and Stoughton.

Husain, A. (1970). *British India's Relations with the Kingdom of Nepal, 1857-1947.* London: George, Allen & Unwin.

Hutt, Michael. (1989). 'A Hero or a Traitor? the Gurkha Soldier in Nepali Literature'. *South Asia Research, 9 (1), 21–32.*

Hutt, Michael. (1991). *Himalayan Voices: An Introduction to Modern Nepali Literature.* Berkeley: University of California Press.

Hutt, Michael. (1998). 'Going to Mugalan: Nepali literary representations of migration to India and Bhutan', *South Asia Research,* 18 (2). pp. 195-214.

James, H. (1991). *Tales of the Gurkhas.* Lewes: The Book Guild.

James, H. & Sheil-Small, D. (1965). *The Gurkhas.* London: Macdonald.

James, H. and Shiel-Small, D. (1975) *A Pride of Gurkhas: the 2nd King Edward VII's Own Gurkhas (The Sirmoor Rifles), 1948-1971.* London: Leo Cooper.

Jenkins, L. H. (1923). *General Frederick Young.* London: Routledge & Sons.

Kansakar, V. B. S. (1982). *Emigration, Remittances and Rural Development.* CEDA, Tribhuvan University, Kathmandu.

Kansakar, V. B. S. (1984). 'Indo-Nepal Migration: problems and prospects'. *Contributions to Nepalese Studies,* 11 (2): 80-110.

Kennedy, Dane Keith (1996). *Magic Mountains: Hill Stations and the British Raj.* Berkeley: University of California Press.

Khanduri, Chandra B. (1997). *A Re-Discovered History of Gorkhas.* Delhi: Gyan Sagar Publications.

Khawas, Vimal. (2003). *Urban Management in Darjeeling Himalaya: A Case Study of Darjeeling Municipality.* The Mountain Forum.

Kipling, Rudyard. (1888). The Man Who Would be King, 'in Kipling, Rudyard, *The Phantom Rickshaw and Other Eerie Tales.* Allahabad: Indian Railway Library, A. H. Wheeler & Co.

Kipling, Rudyard. (1895). 'The Man Who Would be King,' in Kipling, Rudyard, *Wee Willie Winkie and Other Child Stories.*

Kirkpatrick, W. (1811). *An Account of the Kingdom of Nepaul.* London: William Miller.

Koirala, B. P. (1938). 'Sipahi', *Katha Kusum.* Darjeeling, Nepali Sahitya Sammelan (also in Hutt, Michael, Hutt. 1991. *Himalayan Voices: An Introduction to Modern Nepali Literature.* Berkeley: University of California Press).

Kolf, D. H. A. (1990). *Naukar, Rajput and Sepoy: the ethno-history of the military labour market in Hindustan, 1450-1850.* Cambridge: Cambridge University Press.

Landor, A. H. S. (1905). *Tibet and Nepal.* London: A. & C. Black Soho Square.

Leonard, R. G. (1965). *Nepal and the Gurkhas.* London: HMSO.

Lunt, J. (ed). (1873, 1970). *From Sepoy to Subedar: being the life and adventures of Subedar Sita Ram, a Native Officer of the Bengal Army written and related by himself.* London: Routledge.

Macfarlane, Alan. (1976). *Resources and Population: a Study of the Gurungs of Nepal.* Cambridge, London, New York, Melbourne: Cambridge University Press.

Mackay, J. N. (1952). *A History of the 4ᵗʰ Prince of Wales' Own Gurkha Rifles, vol. III, 1938-48.* Edinburgh & London: William Blackwood.

Mackay, J. N. (1962). *History of the 7ᵗʰ Duke of Edinburgh's Own Gurkha Rifles.* Edinburgh: Blackwood.

Macmillan, M. (1984). 'Camp followers: a note on wives of the armed forces', in (eds) H. Callan and S. Ardener, *The Incorporated Wife.* London: Croom Helm.

Marks, J. M. (1971). *Ayo Gurkha!* London: Oxford University Press.

Mason, P. (1974). *A Matter of Honour: an account of the Indian army, its officers and men.* London: Jonathan Cape.

Massé, Lt-Col. C. H. (1948). *The Predecessors of the Royal Army Service Corps 1757-1888.* Aldershot: Gale & Polden.

Massé, Lt-Col. C. H. (1948). *History of ASC, vol 1., 1760-1857.* Aldershot: Gale & Polden.

Masters, John. (1956). *Bugles and a Tiger: a personal adventure.* London: Michael Joseph.

Maxwell, R. M. (1986). *Desperate Encounters: stories of the 5ᵗʰ Royal Gurkha Rifles of the Punjab Frontier Force.* Edinburgh: The Pentland Press.

McAlister, R. W. I. (1984). *Bugle and Kukri: the story of the 10ᵗʰ Princess Mary's Own Gurkha Rifles*, vol. 2. Newport, Isle of Wight: The Regimental Trust, 10ᵗʰ PMO GR.

McDougal, C. (1968). *Village and Household Economy in Far Western Nepal.* Kathmandu, Tribhuvan University Press.

McEwen, Yvonne. (2014). *In the Company of Nurses: The History of the British Army Nursing Service in the Great War.* Edinburgh: Edinburgh University Press.

Michael, Bernardo, A. (2013). *Statemaking and Territory in South Asia: lessons from the Anglo-Gurkha War (1814-1816).* Delhi: Anthem Press.

Mikesell, S. L. & J. Shrestha. (1985-86). 'The Gurkhas: a case study of the problem of mercenary recruitment in Barkpak, Nepal', *Strategic Studies*, 6/7: 145-54.

Mishra, C. (1985-86). 'The Gurkhas: its genesis', *Strategic Studies*, 6/7: 155-61.

Mishra, C. (1991). 'Three Gorkhali myths', *Himal*, 4 (3): 17.

Mojumdar, K. (1972). 'Recruitment of the Gukhas in the Indian army, 1814-1877'. *United Service Institution Journal,* 102: 143-57.

Mojumdar, K. (1973). *Anglo-Nepalese Relations in the Nineteenth Century.* Calcutta: Firma K.L. Mukhopadhyay

Morris, C. J. (1933). *The Gurkhas: A Handbook for the Indian Army.* Delhi, Manager of Publications.

Morris, C. J. (1935). Some aspects of social life in Nepal', *Journal of the Royal Central Asian Society,* 22: 425-46.

Mullaly, B. R. (1957). *Bugle and Kukri: the story of the 10ᵗʰ Princess Mary's Own Gurkha Rifles.* Edinburgh: William Blackwood.

Mulmi, Amish Raj. (2017). 'The Nepal-Sikh alliance that could have changed history', *The Wire,* 12 May 2017 (review of L. Stiller, *The Rise of the House of Gorkha,* 1973).

Nakane, Chie (1963). *A Study of Plural Societies in Sikkim: Lepcha, Bhutia and Nepali.* Department of the Army.

Namgyal & Drolma. (1908). *The History of Sikkim,* ms

Napier, Charles, James. (1853). *Defects, Civil and Military, of the Indian Government.*

Napier, William Francis Patrick (1857). *Life & Opinions of General Sir Charles James Napier, Vol I.* London: John Murray.

Neale, J. (2002). *Tigers of the Snow: how one fateful climb made the Sherpas mountaineering legends.* London, Little Brown

Nepal Institute for Development Studies. (2003). *Nepali Women Workers in Foreign Lands: a study conducted for UNIFEM.* Kathmandu: NIDS, July 2003.

Nicholson, J. B. R. (1974). *The Gurkha Rifles.* London: Osprey.

Northey, W. B. (1937). *The Land of the Gurkhas; or, the Himalayan Kingdom of Nepal.* Cambridge: Heffer & Sons.

Northey, W. B. & C. J. Morris. (1928). *The Gurkhas: their manners, customs and country.* London: John Lane, The Bodley Head.

Oldfield, H. A. (1880, 1974). *Sketches from Nepal: historical and descriptive with an essay on Nepalese Buddhism and illustrations of religious monuments and architecture.* London: W. H. Allen; Delhi: Cosmo.

O'Malley, L.S.S. (1999). *Bengal District Gazetteers:* Darjeeling.

Omissi, D. (1991). 'Martial Races: ethnicity and security in colonial India, 1858-1939', *War and Society,* 9: 1-27.

Omissi, D. (1998). *The Sepoy and the Raj: the Indian Army, 1860-1940.* London: Palgrave Macmillan.

Omissi, D. (1999). *Indian Voices of the Great War, Soldiers' Letters, 1914-18.* London: Palgrave Macmillan.

Onta, Pratyoush. (1994). '*Dukha* during the World Wars'. *Himal,* 7 (4).

Onta, Pratyoush (1996). 'Creating a Brave Nepali Nation in British India: the rhetoric of jati improvement, rediscovery of Bhanubhakta and the writing of Bir history', *Studies in Nepali History and Society,* 1, 1 pp. 37-76.

Ortner, S. (1989). *High Religion: a cultural and political history of Sherpa Buddhism.* Princeton: Princeton University Press.

Ortner, S. (2000). *Life and Death on Mount Everest; Sherpas and the Himalayan Mountaineering.* Princeton NJ, Princeton University Press.

Osborne, R. G. (1842, 1952, 2002). *Ranjit Singh: The Lion of the Punjab: Courts and Camps.* Calcutta, 1842, reprint 1952, paperback 2002.

Pahari, Anup. (1991). 'Ties that Bind: Gurkhas in History', *Himal*, 4 (3).

Palit, A. N. (1954). 'With the 5th Gurkhas, 1910-11', *The Gorkha*, pp. 53-58.

Palsokar, R. D. (1991). *History of the 5th Gorkha Rifles (Frontier Force), vol. III, 1858-1991.* The Commandant, 5th GR.

Panaeva, Avdotya. (1899). *Memories.* https://en.wikipedia.org/wiki/Avdotya_Paneva

Pant, M. R. (1978). 'Nepal's defeat in the Nepal-British war', *Regmi Research Series*, 10: 150-9.

Parijat. (1965). *Shirishko Phul.* Biratnagar, Pustak-Samsar, (2nd edn.)

Parijat.(1987). 'Interview', *Vedana, vol. 15 no.3/4.* Kathmandu

Pasha, Basu (1997). *Kirti Laxmi.* Kathmandu: Thaunkanhe Prakashan.

Pearse, H. (1898). 'The Goorkha soldier (as an enemy and as a friend)', *Macmillan's Magazine*, 78: 225-37.

Pemble, J. (1971). *The Invasion of Nepal. John Company at War.* London, Constable & Co. Ltd, Oxford: Clarendon.

Perry, Cindy, L. (1994). *The History of the Expansion of Protestant Christianity among the Nepali Diaspora.* Edinburgh: University of Edinburgh.

Petre, F. L. (1925). *The First King George's Own Gurkha Rifles: the Malaun Regiment (1815-1921).* London: Royal United Services Institution

Piggott, Juliet. (1975). *Queen Alexandra's Royal Army Nursing Corps (Famous Regts. S).* London: Leo Cooper Ltd.

Pignède, B. *Les Gurungs: une population himalayenne du Népal.* Paris

Pignède, B. (2003) *The Gurungs: a Himalayan Population of Nepal.* Kathmandu, Patna Pustak Bhandar (English translation by Alan Macfarlane and Sarah Harrison).

Poynder, F. S. (1937). *The Ninth Gurkha Rifles, 1817-1936.* London: Royal United Services Institution.

Pradhan, Kumar (1984). *A History of Nepali Literature.* New Delhi: Sahitya Akademi.

Pradhan, K. L. (2012). *Thapa Politics in Nepal: With Special Reference to Bhim Sen Thapa, 1806–1839.* New Delhi.

Pradhan, Shiva. (1977). *Giriko Bhavabhu mi 'Yuddhara Yoddha',* Kathmandu: Jyoti Prakashan.

Proudfoot, C. L. (1984). *Flash of the Khukri: history of the 3rd Gorkha Rifles (1947 to 1980).* New Delhi: Vision Books.

Ragsdale, T. A. (1990). 'Gurungs, Goorkhalis, Gurkhas: speculations on a Nepalese ethno-history', *Contributions to Nepalese Studies*, 17: 1-24.

Rana, N. R. L. (1970). *The Anglo-Gorkha War (1814-1816)*. Kathmandu: the Author.

Rathaur, K. R. S. (1987). *The British and the Brave: A History of Gorkha Recruitment in the British Indian Army*. Jaipur and New Delhi, Nirala Publications.

Regmi, M. C. (1971). *A Study of Nepali Economic History (1768-1845)*. New Delhi, Manjushri Publishing House.

Regmi, M.C. (1978). *Thatched Huits and Stucco Palaces: peasants and landlords in 19th century Nepal*. New Delhi.

Regmi, M.C. (1988). *An Economic History of Nepal, 1846-1901*. Varanasi.

Regmi, M. C. (1999). *A Study in Nepali Economic History* (second edition). Delhi: Adroit Publishers.

Risley, H. H. (1894). *The Gazetteer of Sikhim*. Calcutta: The Bengal Secretarial Press.

Roberts Lord. (1897). *Forty-One Years in India: from Subaltern to Commander-in-Chief*, 2 volumes. London: Richard Bentley & Son.

Rothermund, D. (1973). 'Freedom of contract and the problem of land alienation in British India', *Journal of South Asian Studies*, 3 (3): 57-78.

Rundall, F. M. (1889). 'Raising a new Goorkha regiment in India', *Asiatic Quarterly Review*, 7: 46-73.

Russell, A. (2007). 'Writing Travelling Cultures: travel and ethnography amongst the Yakkas of East Nepal', *Ethos*, 72 (3).

Ruthven, Malise. (2014). Review of Justin Marozzi's *Baghdad: city of peace, city of blood*, *London Review of Books* (23 October 2014).

Sagant, Ph. (1978). 'Quand le Gurkha revient de guerre', *Ethnographie*, 120: 155-84.

Sale, Florentia Lady. (1843). *A Journal of the Disasters in Afghanistan, 1841-2*. New York: Harper & Brothers,

Sale, Florentia Lady. (2002). *Lady Sale's Afghanistan: An Indomitable Victorian Lady's Account of the Retreat from Kabul During the First Afghan War*. Amazon.

Sanwal, B. D. (1965). *Nepal and the East India Company*. Bombay: Asia.

Seaton, Thomas. (2011). *From Cadet to Colonel From Cadet to Colonel: The Record of a Life of Active Service, Volume 1*. Nabu Press.

Seddon, David. (1987). *Nepal - a State of Poverty*. New Delhi: Vikas Publishing House.

Seddon, David. (2005). 'Nepal's Dependence on Exporting Labour', *Migration Information Source*, 1 January 2005.

Seddon, David. (2006). 'Women's Migration in the 19th Century' in UNIFEM, *Nepali Women and Foreign Labour Migration*. Kathmandu, UNIFEM & NIDS

Seddon, David. (2006) 'Nepali Women and Migration: Early 20th Century, in UNIFEM, *Nepali Women and Foreign Labour Migration*, Kathmandu, UNIFEM & NIDS.

Seddon, David, Jagannath Adhikari and Ganesh Gurung. (1998). 'Foreign labour migration and the remittance economy of Nepal', in *Himalayan Research Bulletin*, vol. xviii, no.2: 3-10.

Seddon, David, Jagannath Adhikari and Ganesh Gurung. (2000). *Foreign labour migration and the remittance economy of Nepal: A Report to DFID, Kathmandu.* Overseas Development Group, University of East Anglia, Norwich.

Seddon, David, Jagannath Adhikari and Ganesh Gurung (2001). *The New Lahures: foreign employment and the remittance economy of Nepal.* The Nepal Institute of Development Studies, Kathmandu.

Seddon, David, Jagannath Adhikari & Ganesh Gurung. (2021). *The New Lahures: second edition updated.* New Delhi: Adroit Publishers.

Shadwell, L. J. (1898). *Lockhart's Advance through Tirah,* W. Thacker, London.

Shaha, R. (1983/84). 'Historic battles in the Nepal-British war of 1814-16, *Rolamba*, 3 (4): 2-67; 4 (1): 2-5.

Shaha, R. (1986/87). 'The rise and fall of Bhimsen Thapa: the war of 1914-16 with British India and its aftermath', *Rolamba*, 6 (1): 2-7; 7 (2):22-31.

Shakespear, L. W. (1913). The war with Nepal: operations in Sirmoor, 1814-1815', *Journal of the United Services Institute of India,* 42: 369-79.

Shakespear, L. W. & G. R. Stevens. (1912, 1950). *The History of the 2nd King Edward VII's Own Goorkha Rifles (the Sirmoor Rifles).* London: Gale & Polden.

Sharma, G. (1988). *Paths of Glory: exploits of 11 Gurkha Rifles.* Ahmedabad: Allied.

Sharma, Taranath. (1983). *Samasa mayik Sajha Kavita.* Kathmandu: Sajha Prakashan.

Sheil-Smaal, D. (1982). *Green Shadows: a Gurkha story.* London: William Kimber.

Sherchan, Bhupi, 1983: *Ghumne Mechmathi Andho Manchhe.* Kathmandu: Sajha Prakashan (1st edn. 1969).

Sharma, Pandit Hem Raj. (2018). *Pratham Bishwayuddhako Varnan (Description of the First World (Great)War).* Kathmandu: Shree Press.

Sharma, Sanjay & Deepak Thapa, 2013, *Taken for Granted, Nepali Migration to India,* Centre for the Study of Labour and Mobility, Kathmandu.

Shrestha, Nanda R. & Dennis Conway. (2001). 'The Shadow Life of a Migrant's Wife', in (eds) von der Heide, S. & T. Hoffmann, *Aspects of Migration and Mobility in Nepal.* Kathmandu: Rastna Pustak Bhandar,

Shrestha-Schipper, S. (2013). 'Migration from Jumla to the Southern Plain', *European Bulletin of Himalayan Research, 35 & 36.*

Singh, K. (1962). *Ranjit Singh: Maharajah of the Punjab.* London: George Allen & Unwin.

Singh, Patwan. (1999, 2002). *The Sikhs.* London: John Murray (1999); New Delhi: Rupa & Co.(2002).

Sinha, A. C. (2003) 'Indian Northeast Frontier and Nepali Immigrants', in (eds) Sinha A. C. & Subba, *The Nepalis in Northeast India.* Indus Publishing Company.

Sinha, N. K. (1933). *Ranjit Singh.* Calcutta: University of Calcutta.

Smith, E. D. (1973). *Britain's Brigade of Gurkhas.* London: Leo Cooper.

Smith, E. D. (1976). *East of Kathmandu: the story of the 7th Duke of Edinburgh's Own Gurkha Rifles,* vol. II, 1948-1973. London: Leo Cooper.

Stiller, L. F. (1973) *The Rise of the House of Gorkha: a study in the unification of Nepal, 1768-1816.* Kathmandu: Ratna Pustak Bhandar.

Stiller, L. F. (1976). *The Silent Cry: the people of Nepal, 1816-1839.* Kathmandu: Sayayogi.

Stiller, Ludwig. (2017). 'The Nepal-Sikh Alliance that could have changed History', *The Wire,* 12 May 2017.

Strawson, John. (1989). *Gentlemen in Khaki: the British Army, 1890-1990.* London: Secker & Warburg.

Subba, T. (1985). *The Lepchas: From Legends to the Present Day*

Subedi, B. P. (1998). 'Regional patterns of fertility in Nepal', in Thapa, S. *et al. Fertility Transition in Nepal.* Kirtipur: Centre for Nepalese and Asian Studies (CNAS).

Sutton, Brigadier John. (1998). *Wait for the Waggon: the Story of the Royal Corps of Transport and its Predecessors 1794-1993.* Barnsley, S. Yorks.: Leo Cooper.

Thapa, Amar Singh and Bahadur, Sardar (trans.) (1914) *Ratan Singh Gurungko Outpostko Katha.* Banaras: Vishvaraj Harihar Sharma.

Thapa, M. H. (1973). *Khukuri mathi Ek Chauta Badal.* Kathmandu: Yugantara Prakashan.

Thieme, S. (2006). *Social Networks and Migration: Far West Nepalese Labour.* Münster: LIT.

Thieme, S. & U. Müller-Böker. (2009). 'Social networks and migration: women's livelihoods between far west Nepal and Delhi', *European Bulletin of Himalayan Research,* 24 (2): 133-145.

Tyquin, Michael. (1993). *Gallipoli: The Medical War - The Australian Army Medical Services in the Dardanelles Campaign of 1915.* New South Wales University.

Tyquin, Michael. (2016). *Gallipoli: an Australian Medical Perspective.* Big Sky Publishing.

Tyrer, Nicola. (2009). *Sisters In Arms: British Army Nurses Tell Their Story.* London: W&N.

Tuker, F. (1957). *Gorkha: the story of the Gurkhas of Nepal.* London: Constable.

UNIFEM & NIDS. (2006). *Nepali Women and Foreign Labour Migration.* Kathmandu: UNIFEM & Nepal Institute of Development Studies (NIDS).

Uprety, P. R. (1992). *Political Awakening in Nepal: the search for a new identity.* New Delhi, Commonwealth Publishers.

Vansittart, E. V. (1890, 2009). *Notes on Goorkhas: being a short account of their country, history, characteristics, clans, & etc.* Cornell University Library. ISBN 978-1-112-05390-0.

Vanjsittart, E. V. (1894). 'The tribes, clans and castes of Nepal', *Journal of the Asiatic Society of Bengal* 63 (2):213-49.

Vansittart, E. V. (and Herbert H. Risley illustrator). (1895). '*Notes on Nepal*'

Vansittart, E. V. (1890, 1906). *Gurkhas. Handbook for the Indian Army,* Calcutta: Superintendent, Government Printing. Government of India.

Vansittart, E. V. (1915, 1918). *Gurkhas, Handbook for the Indian Army.* Compiled by Lieutenant Colonel Eden Vansittart, revised by Major B.U. Nicolay, Calcutta, Superintendent Government Printing, India (reprint 1918).

Vansittart. E. V. (1991). *Gorkhas: Hand Book for the Indian Army*. India: Asian Educational Services. ISBN 9788120607033 (978-81-206-0703-3)

Vansittart, E. V. (1993). *The Gurkhas*. Anmol Publications Pvt. Ltd. ISBN 9788170417170 (978-81-7041-717-0).

Vansittart, E. V. & John Haughten. (1878, 2010). *With the Gurkhas in Afghanistan: the Defence of Char-Ee-Kar During the First Afghan War, 1841- Char-Ee-Kar and Service There With the 4th Goorkha Regiment and Notes on Goorkhas Including the Goorkha War & Types of Ghoorkha Soldiers* (see Haughten, John).

Von der Heide. (2001). 'Some Aspects of Migration, Mobility and the Democracy Movement among the Thakalis – Effects of Cultural Change and the Danger of Cultural Loss', in (eds) von der Heide, Susanne & Thomas Hoffman (eds). (2001). *Aspects of Migration and Mobility in Nepal*. Kathmandu: Ratna Pustak Bhandar. Leonaur Ltd.

Von der Heide, Susanne & Thomas Hoffman (eds). (2001). *Aspects of Migration and Mobility in Nepal*. Kathmandu: Ratna Pustak Bhandar.

Wheelwright, Julie. (1989, 1990). *Amazons and Military Maids: women who dressed as men in pursuit of life, liberty and happiness*. Pandora/Harper Collins, Rivers Oram Press.

Wheelwright, Julie. (2020). *Sisters in Arms. Female Warriors from Antiquity to the New Millennium*. Oxford: Osprey Publishing.

Whelpton, John. (2005). *A History of Nepal*. Cambridge: Cambridge University Press.

Williamson, Thomas. (1825, 2010). *The East India Vade Mecum; or complete guide to gentlemen intended for the civil, military or, naval service of the East India Company*. British Library, paperback 2010.

Woodyatt, Nigel. G. (1922). *Under Ten Viceroys; the reminiscences of a Gurkha, 1861-1936*. London: H. Jenkins Ltd,

Wright, Daniel. (1877, 2018). *History of Nepal*. London: Heritage Publishers.

Wright, Thomas. (1906). *The Life of Sir Richard Burton*. Vols. 1 and 2. New York: G. P. Putnam's Sons.

Xaxa, Virginius. (1985). 'Colonial capitalism and underdevelopment in North Bengal', *Economic and Political Weekly*, 20 (39): 1659-1665.

Zaman (1973). *Evaluation of Land Reform in Nepal*. Kathmandu: HMG, Ministry of Land Reform.

❀ ❀ ❀

www.ingramcontent.com/pod-product-compliance
Lightning Source LLC
Chambersburg PA
CBHW022032020426
42338CB00032B/1799/J